The Promise of Mediation

· ·

Robert A. Baruch Bush
Joseph P. Folger

The Promise of
Mediation

Responding to Conflict Through
Empowerment and Recognition

Jossey-Bass Publishers
San Francisco

Substantial discounts on bulk quantities of Jossey-Bass books are available to corporations, professional associations, and other organizations. For details and discount information, contact the special sales department at Jossey-Bass Inc., Publishers. (415) 433-1740; Fax (415) 433-0499.

For sales outside the United States, please contact your local Paramount Publishing International Office.

TCF Manufactured in the United States of America on Lyons Falls Pathfinder Tradebook. This paper is acid-free and 100 percent totally chlorine-free.

Library of Congress Cataloging-in-Publication Data

Bush, Robert A. Baruch.
    The promise of mediation: responding to conflict through empowerment and recognition / Robert A. Baruch Bush, Joseph P. Folger.—1st ed.
      p.   cm.—(The Jossey-Bass conflict resolution series)
    Includes bibliographical references and index.
    ISBN 0-7879-0027-3
    1. Mediation.   2. Conflict management.   3. Conflict (Psychology)
4. Social conflict.   5. Social interaction.   6. Interpersonal conflict.   I. Folger, Joseph P., date.   II. Title.
III. Series
HM136. B787   1994   94-27217
303. 6'9—dc20   CIP

FIRST EDITION
HB Printing   10 9 8 7 6 5 4 3 2   *Code 94107*

The Jossey-Bass
Conflict Resolution Series

Consulting Editor
Jeffrey Z. Rubin
Tufts University

To our parents,
who taught us to believe in the ideal of
acting with self-respect and compassion for others,
in all human relations.

....

Contents

* *

Foreword

. . . .

When conflicts arise between individuals or groups, they can be settled or resolved in a limited number of ways. One of these ways is third-party intervention, which in turn can assume a number of forms including arbitration, fact finding, conciliation, and mediation, the subject of this book.

Mediation has received the most attention, by far, among scholars and practitioners working in the field of conflict resolution. Numerous scholarly analyses of mediation theory and research have appeared over the past two decades, including several volumes published by Jossey-Bass. Simultaneously, mediation practice has emerged as the single most powerful tool in the alternative dispute resolution (ADR) movement, which was designed to create alternatives to litigation. Mediation practice has flourished in the United States (and elsewhere, but to a lesser extent) and can be found in contexts ranging from divorce to community conflict to business, labor, and international relations.

At the heart of the mediation movement—as reflected in both theory and practice, basic research and application—is the view that mediation's fundamental objective must be to bring about the resolution of conflict. Above all else, mediation makes it possible for agreements to be reached, and for those agreements to be ones that the disputants find satisfactory. Another important, if secondary, objective of mediation is to improve the relationship between the disputants; if adversaries cannot be transformed into close friends, at least a modicum of relationship enhancement should ensue.

Enter Robert A. Baruch Bush and Joseph P. Folger. Their book, *The Promise of Mediation: Responding to Conflict Through Empowerment and Recognition*, provides a powerful reappraisal of the mediation movement as practiced in the United States and elsewhere, and directly challenges the wisdom of some of our most cherished assumptions about the efficacy and objectives of mediation.

Riding the twin steeds of *empowerment* and *recognition*, Bush and Folger argue that mediation has the potential to do far more than create agreements and improve relationships. It has the potential to transform people's lives, to give them both an increased sense of their own personal efficacy (empowerment) and a greater openness to and acceptance of the person seated on the other side of the table (recognition). Even if no agreement is reached, even if no reconciliation results, mediation should still be regarded as a success if it brings about empowerment and recognition. And if agreement *is* reached as well, so much the better.

Needless to say, this is a unique perspective on the functions of mediation and the role of mediators. In the throes of a conflict resolution culture characterized by the importance of reaching settlement, these two scholars have the temerity to insist that agreement is a side issue in a more important agenda. The fact that Bush and Folger are so frankly ideological and value driven in their analysis will also disturb those readers who wish for a value-neutral appraisal of the mediation industry. But ultimately it doesn't matter at all whether you agree with the authors' perspective. You are certain to find in the pages of this book a refreshingly different perspective on an approach and a set of assumptions that too many of us have come to take for granted.

The Bush and Folger perspective is a powerful one, with lessons for any domain in which mediation occurs. Their lively book contains numerous case studies drawn from their own extensive experience as practicing mediators as well as from published accounts. The settings are domestic, and the authors say little about the place of a transformative approach to mediation in international settings. Still, their formulation is rich enough that one can derive such lessons easily. Isn't it empowerment and recognition that helped make possible the fall 1993 Oslo agreement between Israel and the PLO? And aren't empowerment and recognition requisite processes if such negotiated agreements, once concluded, are to be implemented successfully? Isn't it empowerment and recognition, rather than the details of agreement, that have driven the startling events in South Africa? Isn't that what the South African conflict and its resolution are really about?

The Promise of Mediation is a provocative and important book that illustrates beautifully the objective of the Jossey-Bass Conflict Resolution Series: to bridge theory and practice. So put your feet in the stirrups, grab the reins, and prepare for a journey that you will find adventurous, bumpy, treacherous at times, and ultimately extremely rewarding.

July 1994   Jeffrey Z. Rubin
                                                   Consulting Editor
                              Jossey-Bass Conflict Resolution Series

Preface

• •

This book is about mediation's unique potential for responding to conflict. It is about the opportunities that conflict affords for moral development, and the power of mediation to capture those opportunities by helping people respond with compassionate strength as they address difficult and often painful disputes.

As practitioners and scholars, we have come to believe that mediation's greatest value lies in its potential not only to find solutions to people's problems but to change people themselves for the better, in the very midst of conflict. Time and again, we have seen people change in small but significant ways through their participation in this process. These changes occur because, through mediation, people find ways to avoid succumbing to conflict's most destructive pressures: to act from weakness rather than strength and to dehumanize rather than acknowledge each other. Overcoming these pressures involves making difficult moral choices, and making these choices transforms people— changes them for the better. They discover within themselves capacities for good that they did not know existed. And they learn how to draw on these positive capacities in dealing with life's problems and relating to others.

When people are changed in this way through their participation in mediation, the interactions they have in their families, businesses, neighborhoods, and institutions are in turn changed. As a result, the effects of mediation reach beyond the settlement of particular disputes and have a cumulative impact on the larger social arenas in which daily interactions unfold in our society.

It is the transformative potential of the process that has attracted and sustained our interest in mediation as its use has expanded over the past few decades. And it is the difficulty of achieving this potential that has led us to write this book. For although mediation's unique promise as a response to conflict lies in its transformative potential, that potential has not been widely achieved. Instead, the use of mediation has taken a course that has emphasized other dimensions of the process.

These views are the product of our personal involvement with mediation over many years. This involvement has included practicing mediation, training and supervising mediators, administering and evaluating mediation programs, and studying the mediation process as a whole. These varied experiences gave us the opportunity—and required us—to integrate theory and practice, not only as trainers and supervisors but as reflective practitioners ourselves. As a result, we were steadily forced toward greater clarity about what we consider mediation's most important goal. At the same time, our experience left us with the overall sense that mediation's promise—its transformative potential—remains largely unfulfilled.

In response to these realizations we began asking questions about how mediation is actually practiced in different contexts, what it has and has not accomplished, and why. We sought answers to these questions in the growing body of research on mediation, as well as in our own experience and observations as practitioners, teachers, and scholars. Ultimately, we found that answering these questions required that we look beyond the process itself, to the underlying vision of conflict on which mediation theory and practice are based—the vision of what conflict is and what a constructive response to conflict must entail. We realized that a prevailing view of conflict has shaped mediation practice and limited people's expectations of what the process can and should achieve. We tried to articulate an alternative vision of conflict, based on a framework that values both personal strength and compassion for others, and then we began to explore how this vision could help people understand and enact mediation's transformative potential. Our exploration of these issues led us to write this book.

For those who have themselves sensed the value of this transformative potential, *The Promise of Mediation* offers a clear articulation of what that potential is, why it is important, and how it can be realized in practice. Though not a manual for practice, it presents a basic conceptual and practical vocabulary for understanding mediation's full potential. In addition, this book offers people at all levels in the mediation field—practitioners, administrators, policy makers, researchers—a new and useful perspective to help them take stock of how mediation is currently practiced, assess what it can accomplish, and make choices about how to develop the process in the future. Finally, the concepts presented in this book will be useful to those outside the mediation field, such as managers, counselors, teachers, and others whose work involves recognizing and capturing conflict's inherent opportunities for engendering human growth and development.

Overview of the Contents

In the Introduction we preview where the book as a whole is headed. We suggest that our aim is twofold: to explain and illustrate the potential that mediation has to foster empowerment and recognition—the central goals of transformative practice—

and to show how the fate of the mediation movement is linked, in a larger sense, to an emerging relational vision of human nature and social interaction.

In Chapter One we present four views of the mediation movement. These views are framed as stories that are told by people both to characterize what mediation practice looks like and to prescribe what the mediation movement as a whole should accomplish. As prescriptions, these stories rest on and represent underlying values, and they reveal the expectations that people hold for the mediation movement. Setting these stories side by side suggests that although the transformative vision of practice has been central to one story of the movement, that story has not been the most influential one. Instead, expectations for the movement have been heavily shaped by what we call the Satisfaction Story—an account that emphasizes a problem-solving orientation to conflict and mediation.

Chapter Two offers three short vignettes that illustrate how mediation practice and our expectations for the movement as a whole have been shaped by the Satisfaction Story. These vignettes (and research that suggests they are part of larger trends) indicate that as mediation practice has moved steadily toward the problem-solving orientation, it has lost sight of the transformative potential of the process.

In Chapter Three we offer an assessment of the prevailing, problem-solving approach to mediation, based on a review of existing research. We show how the limitations of current practice emerge from the underlying problem-solving view of conflict in which mediation practice has generally been grounded.

In Chapter Four we describe in detail the transformative vision of conflict and mediation. We explain why the goals of empowerment and recognition are central to the transformative approach, and we clarify what it means to achieve these objectives in practice. We also discuss why practicing mediation from a transformative orientation requires a fundamental change in the way we think about and conduct the mediation process.

In Chapters Five and Six we offer detailed case studies that illustrate what a transformative approach to practice looks like. Our analysis in Chapter Five illustrates how a problem-solving focus led a mediator to overlook the transformative possibilities that arose in a dispute between neighbors. Our analysis in Chapter Six illustrates how a mediator recognized transformative opportunities and worked toward achieving empowerment and recognition in a landlord-tenant dispute.

Chapter Seven summarizes, from a process perspective, what it means to follow the transformative route through a dispute. We offer practical guidelines that mediators can use to recognize opportunities for empowerment and recognition, and we suggest ways that mediators can respond to these opportunities in order to reach transformative objectives.

Chapter Eight discusses the pitfalls that mediators face as they attempt to follow a transformative approach to practice. Our goal here is to alert mediators to the choices that need to be made during a mediation session in order to sustain transformative practice.

In Chapter Nine we suggest how the move toward a transformative approach reflects a much larger shift in thinking about human nature, conflict, and social relations. We show how transformative practice rests on an emerging relational vision of human nature and society, and we contrast this underlying viewpoint with the prevailing individualist vision that underlies a problem-solving orientation to conflict and mediation.

Finally, in Chapter Ten we discuss practical steps that can be taken in training to advance transformative practice, and we address what can be done to overcome a range of obstacles that stand in the way of fulfilling the promise of mediation and making this approach central to the mediation movement.

Acknowledgments

The ideas presented in this book have been developed and sharpened through valuable discussions with many people who care deeply about mediation and other constructive responses to conflict. Our first thanks go to Helen Weingarten, who introduced us to each other on the perceptive hunch that we were somehow ideologically kindred spirits. We are also especially grateful to William Hicks, Linda Putnam, and Jeff Rubin for encouraging us to pursue this project with Jossey-Bass and for providing important insights and commentary along the way; to Cedric Crocker for shepherding us through the completion of the manuscript and Sarah Miller for handling the details of production; and to Mary Beth Flynn for help in preparing the index.

Emily Schmeidler helped launch the project through her contributions in many spirited discussions early on. Since then, many other colleagues have explored ideas with us and offered helpful reactions, especially Chris Carlson, Albie Davis, Marc Galanter, Tricia Jones, Lela Love, Abba Paltiel, Janet Rifkin, Len Riskin, Jonathan Shailor, Norman Stein, Randall Stutman, and Zena Zumeta. We are very grateful to those who read and gave us many thoughtful and constructive comments on preliminary drafts of the manuscript: Margaret Herrman, Deborah Kolb, Craig McEwen, Joseph Stulberg, and Steve Toben. And we want to offer a special note of thanks to Dr. Susan E. Shulamis Bush for her constant encouragement and for the important substantive and editorial insights she contributed at every stage.

We were very fortunate to have had the opportunity to work with many bright and talented students as this book took shape. Their intuitive insights about mediation and conflict have immeasurably strengthened the end result, and their day-to-day interest has been a steady source of inspiration for us both. In particular, we want to thank Karen Wexler for her careful thinking and for her editorial work on the vignettes in Chapter Two.

Several other students did research on specific topics that helped clarify important issues for us: Joe Andruzzi, Anthony DelVecchio, Eric LaRuffa, Lyllian Simins, Robert Stone, Alan Weissman, and Megan Woolley. We also want to recognize and thank the students who have participated in the Hofstra Law School Mediation Clinic over the years, who helped us understand the transformative approach to mediation by subjecting their own work as mediators—and ours—to demanding analysis in case after case: in 1993, Joe Andruzzi, Sharon Colchamiro, Brad Gross, Anthony Senft, Betty Tufariello, and Karen Wexler; in 1991, Christopher Bacotti, Jerry Barbanel, Mike Farley, Amy Gordon, Bruce Greenhaus, Kimberly Spire, and Alan Weissman; in 1990, James Benintendi, Brian Briones, Mandy Cohen, Leslie Evans, Chris Morano, Vinnie Morano, and Laura Murry; in 1987, Joel Ackerman, Judy Blume, James Edwards, Helayne Heller, Jack Mevorach, Cheryl Morrissey, and Sharon Silverman; and in 1986, Jane Cristal, Regina McGuire, John Mitchell, Sherri Rosenberg, Steven Sklar, and Carrie Sutherland. We are also indebted to the graduate students in communication at Temple University—especially Diane Carlin, Kim Eberbach, Mary Beth Flynn, Mariko Kotani, Bob Napper, and Janet Yedes—who have taken a keen interest in the ideological bases of discourse in mediation.

Besides providing us with an abundance of bright and helpful students, both Hofstra Law School and Temple University have supplied valuable material assistance to support the work done for this volume. We are especially grateful to Dean Stuart Rabinowitz of Hofstra Law School and Dean Robert Smith of the School of Communications and Theater at Temple for their appreciation and support of our work.

We owe special thanks to Xenia Freeman, Jim Goulding, Jorge Mendizabal, and Chris Whipple for giving us the opportunity to work with our Mediation Clinic students at the Queens Mediation Center in New York. Thanks also to

Suzanne Chemtob, Bill Pollack, Milt Snitzer, and Jay Stein-gold—volunteer mediators at the Queens Center whose supervisory work with our clinic students provided valuable insights. We are also indebted to several mediation program administrators, including Terry Amsler, Jim Goulding, Judy Kruger, and Les Lopes for the comments they provided about the effects of institutional context on mediation practice.

Special additional thanks are due to Lela Love, who helped make "virtual officespace" a reality for us. Finally, we want to thank Donna Posillico for her meticulous work in preparing more drafts of this manuscript than any of us thought were possible and in managing the flow of material between authors, editors, and publisher with a smooth and professional hand.

July 1994   Robert A. Baruch Bush
                                                      Brooklyn, New York

                                                      Joseph P. Folger
                                                      Philadelphia, Pennsylvania

The Authors

. . . .

Robert A. Baruch Bush is the Rains Distinguished Professor of Alternative Dispute Resolution Law at Hofstra University School of Law, Hempstead, New York. At Hofstra, he co-founded and continues to direct a clinical course in mediation for law students, one of the first such programs in the nation; he also teaches other courses on alternative dispute resolution. He has worked as a consultant on dispute resolution for several public agencies, including court and school systems in New York, California, and Florida.

Bush has practiced mediation in various contexts since founding one of the first community mediation programs on the West Coast, under the auspices of the American Arbitration Association, in San Francisco in 1976. He has also developed and conducted many skills training programs in mediation and dispute resolution, for both private and public agencies.

Bush has conducted research on ethical dilemmas in mediation, funded in part by the National Institute for Dispute Resolution. He has written extensively on mediation and alternative dispute resolution, for journals including *Wisconsin Law Review*, *Florida Law Review*, *Journal of Contemporary Legal Issues*, *Denver Law Review*, *Missouri Dispute Resolution Journal*, and *Negotiation Journal*. Three of his articles, including a monograph called *The Dilemmas of Mediation Practice: A Study of Ethical Dilemmas and Policy Implications*, have won awards for dispute resolution scholarship from the Center for Public Resources.

Joseph P. Folger is a professor of communication and associate dean for research and graduate study at the School of Communications and Theater, Temple University. He is a former member of the Center for Conflict Resolution, Madison, Wisconsin, and has served on the boards of the Ann Arbor Mediation Center and the Center for Mediation in Higher Education. He was program chair for the 1993 National Conference on Peacemaking and Conflict Resolution and is currently vice chair of the conference's board.

Folger has conducted training in mediation, negotiation, and conflict resolution skills in both the private and public sectors and has been an instructor at the Hofstra University Law School mediation clinic. In addition, Folger has helped launch several mediation initiatives, including the Comprehensive Justice Center in Burlington County, New Jersey.

Folger received one of the first research grants from the National Institute for Dispute Resolution, which funded a national study of student grievance procedures in colleges and universities. His work on conflict and mediation has been published in *Mediation Quarterly*, *Negotiation Journal*, *Educational Record*, and *Community Mediation: A Handbook for Practitioners and Researchers*. He is coeditor, with T. S. Jones, of *New Directions in Mediation: Communication Research and Perspectives* (1994). The second edition of his award-winning book (coauthored with M. S. Poole and R. K. Stutman) *Working Through Conflict: Strategies for Relationships, Groups and Organizations* was published in 1993.

Introduction

. . . .

The Future of Mediation:
What's at Stake and Why It Matters

Roughly twenty-five years ago, in a variety of places around the
United States, many groups and individuals became interested in a
process of dispute resolution called *mediation*. While mediation had
long been used in labor disputes, the new surge of interest extended
to many other contexts, including community, family, and interpersonal conflict. The development of mediation in these new areas
is referred to in this book as the *contemporary mediation movement*
or, simply, the *mediation movement*.

Mediation has grown remarkably over the past two and a half
decades. Prior to 1965, the use of mediation outside the labor relations arena was practically unheard of. Then, in the late 1960s,
attention was focused on mediation from two very different directions: civic leaders and justice system officials saw in mediation a
potential for responding to urban conflict and its flash points; and
community organizations and legal reformers saw in mediation a
potential for building community resources alongside the formal justice system. Though the motives and approaches were quite different, the combined effect was to make the idea of mediation of
"neighborhood" or community disputes, if not a household word, a
widely accepted and legitimate concept.

In practical terms, this meant the expansion of the community
mediation field from a few isolated programs in 1970 to nearly two
hundred by the early 1980s and to more than double that number

today (Johnson, 1993). Moreover, as a result of its acceptance in this field, mediation was tried (and usually accepted) in an increasingly broad range of nonlabor disputes: divorce, environmental, housing, institutional (including prisons, schools, and hospitals), small-claims, personal injury and insurance, and general business disputes; and claims involving government agencies (Singer, 1990). In the last five years or so, this trend has accelerated. Private businesses and even lawyers are finding mediation more and more attractive, spurring the start-up and expansion of for-profit mediation services.

Across the mediation movement, mediation is generally understood (based on its previous use in the labor field) as an informal process in which a neutral third party with no power to impose a resolution helps the disputing parties try to reach a mutually acceptable settlement. This common formulation captures some of the major features of the process, especially its informality and consensuality. It also reflects the view that the most significant effect of the process is the production of a voluntary settlement of the dispute.

Beyond the level described by such conventional definitions, however, the mediation process contains within it a unique potential for transforming people—engendering moral growth—by helping them wrestle with difficult circumstances and bridge human differences, in the very midst of conflict. This transformative potential stems from mediation's capacity to generate two important effects, empowerment and recognition. In simplest terms, *empowerment* means the restoration to individuals of a sense of their own value and strength and their own capacity to handle life's problems. *Recognition* means the evocation in individuals of acknowledgment and empathy for the situation and problems of others. When both of these processes are held central in the practice of mediation, parties are helped to use conflicts as opportunities for moral growth, and the transformative potential of mediation is realized.

At the outset of the contemporary mediation movement, few fully grasped either the special capacity of mediation for fostering empowerment and recognition or the immense importance of these two transformative phenomena. Nevertheless, many had strong intuitions on both counts. Therefore, even though the emphasis was on mediation's capacity to help resolve disputes and effectuate settlements, there was an awareness that mediation had other important though less tangible impacts. It was as though a researcher had discovered a substance, very useful for one purpose, that she realized was capable of other valuable effects; but she had not yet determined what those other effects were or how they could be generated.

Gradually, practitioners and scholars have gained a clearer picture of the effects of mediation apart from settlement per se. Increasingly, attention is being paid to the special capacities of the process to generate empowerment and recognition. Some have even come to realize that working for empowerment and recognition usually results in reaching settlement as well, while focusing on settlement usually results in ignoring empowerment and recognition. So, while these different dimensions of mediation are not necessarily mutually exclusive or inconsistent, the relative emphasis given to them makes a crucial difference.

Slowly, many in the mediation movement have begun to grasp how important empowerment and recognition are, and why. The broader significance of these phenomena is becoming clearer as dispute resolution scholars see that mediation's transformative dimensions are connected to an emerging, higher vision of self and society, one based on moral development and interpersonal relations rather than on satisfaction and individual autonomy. Scholars and thinkers in many fields have begun to articulate and advocate a major shift in moral and political vision—a paradigm shift—from an individualistic to a relational conception. They argue that, although the individualist ethic of modern Western culture was a great advance over the preceding caste-oriented feudal order, it is now possible and necessary to go still further and to achieve a full integration of individual freedom and social conscience, in a relational social order enacted through new forms of social processes and institutions.

Mediation, with its capacity for engendering moral growth through empowerment and recognition, represents an opportunity to express this new relational vision in concrete form. Indeed, this potential is what drew many to it in the first place. Mediation was appealing not because resolution or settlement was good in itself and conflict evil, but because of the way in which mediation allowed disputing parties to understand themselves and relate to one another *through and within conflict*. In short, many have come to feel that empowerment and recognition—the transformative dimensions of mediation—matter as much or more than settlement, and they matter not only in themselves but as expressions of a much broader shift to a new moral and social vision. As such, their importance is primary and immense.

So, like the researcher who finally grasped the fuller workings and importance of her mysterious discovery, some in the mediation field have, after two decades, begun to gain a fuller appreciation for the workings and importance of mediation as a transformative process. At the same time, however, the practice of mediation has moved steadily away from placing these transformative dimensions at the heart of the process. Although mediation has a unique *potential* for achieving empowerment and recognition, mediation practice has not realized that potential. Substantial evidence today suggests that mediation practice still focuses largely on settlement, perhaps even more so than in the early years of the movement. It rarely generates empowerment and recognition, and even then it generally does so serendipitously rather than as a result of mediators' conscious efforts. The transformative potential of mediation, and how to realize it through empowerment and recognition, receives far too little attention today in mediation theory, policy, and practice. Precisely how and why this situation exists, and what can be done about it, are the main subjects of this book.

But in a larger sense, this is not simply a book about mediation. This is a book about a process that has the potential to express concretely a new and higher vision of human life, and therefore it is also about the difficulties of pursuing that vision in practical reality. The future of mediation is a matter of general and serious concern, because it implicates the future of an emerging relational vision of society as a whole. If the vision cannot be expressed in a concrete context such as mediation, it remains mere theory. Just as that vision contemplates an integration of individual freedom and social conscience, mediation offers a potential means to integrate the concern for right and justice and the concern for caring and interconnection. In short, mediation presents a powerful opportunity to express and realize a higher vision of human life. To help capture this opportunity and to bring that vision into reality are the larger purposes of this book.

Those in the mediation movement who believe that this higher vision of human interaction can be realized in mediation have seen powerful glimpses of it in practice. From time to time, cases unfold in ways that seem to go beyond what typically happens in mediation. What is often most striking about such cases is how insignificant the final settlement seems in view of the transformative accomplishments of the intervention itself. The ground the parties create for interacting with each other makes the itemized terms of an agreement seem insignificant, almost superfluous. Indeed, by the end of these cases, asking the parties to commit to specific points in an agreement seems almost unnecessary, because the parties themselves are changed in ways that eclipse any particular problem or dispute.

One of the cases recently mediated at a court-annexed community mediation program in Queens, New York, illustrates in a general way what transformative mediation looks like. The case, a dispute involving an assault charge, shows in concrete terms what gets accomplished in mediation when at least some transformative opportunities for empowerment and recognition are realized.

The Sensitive Bully

Regis, a large, stern-looking middle-aged black man, had filed an assault charge against Charles, a young black man of medium height and slight build. Regis came to the mediation with his thirteen-year-old son, Jerome; Charles came alone. After the mediator provided an opening statement about the purpose and ground rules of mediation, he asked Regis to explain why he was there. In a loud, agitated voice and rambling style, Regis said he was fed up with what had been dished out to his son. He said that this guy (pointing across the table to Charles) chased and attacked Jerome and Jerome's friends several times over the past few months. The last time he attacked Jerome, Regis said he had enough. He went after this guy and "pinned him to the street." He said he didn't want to punch him out, just let him know that this would not happen again. As Regis said this, he pulled a silver badge out of his shirt pocket, raised his voice, and said threateningly that he was a correctional officer at Rykers Island Penitentiary and that he "wanted this guy locked up."

The mediator intervened at this point and asked Regis how well he knew Charles. Regis said he did not know him at all. All he knew was that this guy didn't live in the neighborhood. He thought he walked through the area on his way to work and that was when he would harass Jerome and his friends. The mediator then asked whether he knew why Charles might have come after his son. Regis said that Jerome was a minor so any reason would be out of the question. If Charles had an issue with Regis's son, he should have brought it to Regis, not attack a thirteen-year-old. The mediator raised a few other questions to clarify what happened since the altercations, then asked whether Regis wanted to say anything else. Regis said he wanted this guy locked up so he would leave his son alone.

The mediator then asked Regis's son to describe how he saw the dispute. Jerome seemed somewhat withdrawn and reluctant to speak. He said that his "father told everything there was to say." He was asked whether he wanted to add anything to his father's statements. He said no.

Then the mediator turned to Charles and asked him to describe how he saw things. Answering with an undefensive, lump-in-the-throat tone, he started by saying, "Maybe I made a mistake, maybe it wasn't right. I'm not even sure it was always him [looking at Jerome]. But he was always in the group. That I do know." He said that all he wanted to do was to be able to walk through the area as he always had to catch the bus on his way to work or to visit his girl-friend, Claudia. The mediator asked whether Claudia lived in the neighborhood. He said she did. He said that nearly every time he walked through the block or approached his friend's house, Jerome and his friends were there "saying words" to him. He used this expression several times, without being more specific. He said he tried to ignore the kids but finally went up to them and said, "Look, I don't know you—I don't even know your names. Why are you bugging me? I'm not starting with any of you. I just want to walk though the neighborhood." Charles then said Regis attacked him and warned him to leave his son alone. Still speaking somewhat pensively, Charles said he did not want to have anything to do with this guy's family and that he would be willing to walk a different way to get to the bus stop or Claudia's.

At this point Regis interrupted Charles. He started to say that Charles could continue to walk through the neighborhood. He didn't have to walk a different way. The mediator interrupted Regis and asked him to write down what he wanted to say and save it until after Charles finished.

Charles repeated that he didn't need to walk close to Jerome's house anymore but he was worried that if "something else came up, something I didn't have anything to do with, I don't want to be blamed for it." The mediator asked for several clarifications about whether any other factors contributed to the incidents with Jerome and his father. Charles indicated that there was nothing else between them—he did not know Jerome or his father at all. Finally, the mediator asked whether Charles wanted to say anything else at this point. He asked specifically whether Charles wanted to say more about the "words" from Jerome and his friends that had bothered him so much. Charles said no. It was obviously a sensitive subject.

After offering a brief summary of both men's accounts, the mediator turned back to Regis and asked him what he had wanted to say while Charles was speaking. Regis looked toward his son and said, somewhat sternly, "I know kids can be cruel. I told Jerome and his friends not to be cruel, not to throw rocks when we all live in glass houses. I told him that little things like that can lead to larger things like this." He then changed the focus of his comments, turned directly toward the mediator, and said, "You know, he [pointing across the table to Charles] has a bad limp. And I told Jerome not to be cruel."

During the silence that followed Regis's revealing comments, the mediator noticed that Charles had an elevated heel on one of the boots he was wearing; clearly, this condition was the subject of the "words" he had referred to. The mediator asked Charles if he knew that Regis had talked to Jerome and his friends about not being cruel. Charles said he didn't know what Regis had said to them. But he was clearly affected by what Regis had just said.

The mediator then focused on what both parties wanted to see happen. Both men offered their sense of what might prevent future problems. There was a discussion of ways in which Charles could get to Claudia's house and catch the bus without walking near Jerome's block. This was followed by a discussion of ways to deal with Jerome's friends and their attitudes and actions toward Charles. Various options were raised and considered. When the parties had focused on certain steps as the ones they felt would resolve the situation, the mediator asked them to help draw up what they wanted to include in a final settlement. In the end, the agreement included (1) a statement that Charles would not attack Jerome and his friends, (2) a statement that Jerome would not name-call and would ask his friends not to name-call, (3) a description of the route Charles would walk through the neighborhood when he caught the bus and visited Claudia, and (4) a commitment that the parties would exchange addresses so that if any issues came up or if Charles was thought to be involved in any incidents with Jerome or his friends, the two men could contact each other directly to discuss the matter.

· · · · · · · ·

The terms the parties agreed to in this case alleviated a serious and potentially volatile dispute between two relative strangers. The agreement addressed Regis's concerns about protecting his son's safety, and it met Charles's need to walk, unharassed, through the neighborhood. In this sense, the case is a classic instance of successful mediation: it produced a settlement that reflected workable solutions to a problem that had escalated severely.

But in another sense, the agreement reached was a very minor part of what this mediation accomplished. In fact, when the parties agreed on a settlement at the end of the session, it was almost an anticlimax. And the subsequent agreement-writing endeavor seemed somewhat contrived. It was as if these men were being asked to demonstrate that the subtle exchange that had just occurred between them could fit into a settlement framework. It felt as if the terms they were being encouraged to articulate—where Charles would and would not walk, what Jerome would not say to Charles and what he would say to his friends—did not greatly matter, because something had taken place that made any specific agreement unnecessary. It seemed clear that Charles would not attack Jerome, even if he walked through Jerome's neighborhood and was taunted about the limp the way he had been in the past. Given this sense, drafting an agreement about Charles's route through the neighborhood appeared almost superfluous, as if fulfilling some preordained ritual of agreement writing rather than documenting what the parties had actually accomplished.

What happened during the session was much more powerful than the terms of the agreement the parties ultimately signed. These two men came to see each other differently, by recognizing that they were alike—that they both wanted and deserved each other's acknowledgment as fellow human beings. In stating that he may have made a mistake in attacking the abusive teens, Charles acknowledged the father's outrage at the threat to his son's well-being. Even Charles's undefensive demeanor suggested that he was in touch with the father's concern about his son. In stating that Jerome and his friends were cruel, Regis acknowledged the emotional pain someone with a severe limp could feel at such ridicule. When Regis revealed that he had told his son "we all live in glass houses," Regis acknowledged that he, too, may have wounds that could easily be opened by careless words or teenage pranks. He acknowledged that he shared, with Charles, in the vulnerabilities of being human.

It was this exchange of acknowledgments that made it very unlikely that Charles would attack, even if insults were hurled in the future. Being in earshot of such ridicule simply didn't matter half as much now that Charles knew, firsthand, that someone understood the pain such insults could inflict. He had something to draw from—a source of strength—that would mute the hurt, even if Regis could not change his son or his son could not change his friends. The connection Charles made with another human being, in this mediation, would help buffer him from thoughtless cruelties.

Both men also found, through their interactions with each other during the mediation session, capacities within themselves to address a problem in ways they may never have learned in the streets of Queens, or in the court in which the original assault charge was filed. They had examined their own feelings, considered the consequences of moving toward or against each other, and relied on their own (sometimes intuitive) insights about human strengths and frailties in deciding what to say to each other and in making commitments to each other. They both knew, at some level, that during the hour and a half session *they* had made choices—about revealing parts of themselves, about acknowledging concerns for each other—that had powerful, reparative effects. They were aware, at some level, that they themselves had made decisions and commitments that redirected an escalation that easily might have ended up in Queens' homicide files. As a result of this experience of their own power to redirect events, they left the session with a greater awareness of their own potential resources—resources they could draw from when confronted with other escalating circumstances.

Seeing the Crossroads

From time to time, mediators experience sessions much like this one. Not surprisingly, they tend to chalk these cases up to luck, to view them as instances of mediation's elusive potential. They usually conclude that the parties had a good day or were just "ready to settle." Although many disputes do take serendipitous turns, especially under the watchful eyes of a third party, these turns may only be serendipitous because we have come to expect (and emphasize) something quite different. Practitioners may be chalking potentially instructive cases up to luck because they do not have the frameworks to do otherwise—to think of and understand these cases on their own terms and to intervene consciously in ways that foster such outcomes.

What the Sensitive Bully case (and others like it) suggests is that an approach to practice is possible that realizes the transformative potential of the mediation process. But taking this approach means turning off a road that the mediation movement has been following for some time. It means seeing that a crossroads lies ahead and that staying on mediation's current course may mean missing a promising route. Our goal is to offer a clear road map of the choices, a map that describes where mediation is and where it might (or might not) head.

The crossroads we see facing the mediation movement is reflected in the difference between two approaches to mediation that are described and contrasted in this book. Each has roots reaching back to the beginnings of the mediation movement; each is connected to a different dimension that has always been seen as one of the potentials of the mediation process. The first approach, a *problem-solving approach*, emphasizes mediation's capacity for finding solutions and generating mutually acceptable settlements. Mediators make moves that influence and direct parties—toward settlements in general, and even toward specific terms of settlement. As the mediation movement has developed, the problem-solving potential of mediation has been emphasized more and more, so that this kind of directive, settlement-oriented mediation has become the dominant form of practice today.

The second approach, a *transformative approach* to mediation, emphasizes mediation's capacity for fostering empowerment and recognition, as illustrated in the most general way by the Sensitive Bully dispute. Transformative mediators concentrate on empowering parties to define issues and decide settlement terms for themselves and on helping parties to better understand one another's perspectives. The effect of this approach is to avoid the directiveness associated with problem-solving mediation. Equally important, transformative mediation helps parties recognize and exploit the opportunities for moral growth inherently presented by conflict. It aims at changing the parties themselves for the better, as human beings. In the course of doing so, it often results in parties finding genuine solutions to their real problems. However, as the movement has grown and developed, the transformative potential of mediation has received less and less emphasis in practice.

We believe that the transformative approach should become the primary approach to practice in all the contexts in which mediation is used, reversing the direction in which the mediation movement has been heading. Our goal is to explain why this shift in practice should occur, showing both the limitations of the problem-solving approach and the strengths of the transformative approach. We delineate the transformative approach to mediation, contrasting it with other approaches, giving concrete case illustrations, and suggesting how it can be implemented in the present institutional context of the mediation movement.

Part One

. . . .

Mediation at the Crossroads

1

The Mediation Movement:
Four Diverging Views

While the growth of mediation in the past two decades is remarkable, what is even more striking is the extraordinary divergence of opinion about how to understand that growth and how to characterize the mediation movement itself. This divergence is so marked that there is no one accepted account of how the mediation movement evolved or what it represents. Instead, the literature of the field reveals several very different accounts or "stories" of the movement, told by different authors and stressing different dimensions of the mediation process and its societal impacts. Thus, the movement is portrayed by some as a tool to reduce court congestion and provide "higher-quality" justice in individual cases, by others as a vehicle for organizing people and communities to obtain fairer treatment, and by still others as a covert means of social control and oppression. And some, including ourselves, picture the movement as a way to foster a qualitative transformation of human interaction. Indeed, these are the four main accounts of the mediation movement that run through the literature on mediation. We call them, respectively, the *Satisfaction Story* of the movement, the *Social Justice Story*, the *Oppression Story*, and the *Transformation Story*.

The fact that there are four distinct and divergent stories of the movement suggests two important points. On one level, it suggests that the mediation movement is not monolithic but pluralistic— that there are in fact different approaches to mediation practice, with varied impacts. The stories represent these different approaches. On a deeper level, the existence of divergent stories suggests that, while everyone sees the mediation movement as a means for achieving important societal goals, people differ over what goal is most important. The stories thus also represent and support different goals, each of which is seen by some people as the most important one for the movement to fulfill.

Recounting the different stories of the movement is therefore a good way both to illustrate the diversity of mediation practice and also to identify the value choices implicit in varying approaches to practice. The following summary of the four stories presents each one as it might be told by its authors and adherents.

The Satisfaction Story

According to this story: "The mediation process is a powerful tool for satisfying the genuine human needs of parties to individual disputes. Because of its flexibility, informality, and consensuality, mediation can open up the full dimensions of the problem facing the parties. Not limited by legal categories or rules, it can help reframe a contentious dispute as a mutual problem. Also, because of mediators' skills in dealing with power imbalances, mediation can reduce strategic maneuvering and overreaching. As a result of these different features, mediation can facilitate collaborative, integrative problem solving rather than adversarial, distributive bargaining. It can thereby produce creative, 'win-win' outcomes that reach beyond formal rights to solve problems and satisfy parties' genuine needs in a particular situation. The mediation movement has employed these capabilities of the process to produce superior quality solutions to disputes of all kinds, in terms of satisfaction of parties' self-defined needs, for *all* sides.

"Furthermore, in comparison to more formal or adversary processes, mediation's informality and mutuality can reduce both the economic and emotional costs of dispute settlement. The use of mediation has thus produced great *private* savings for disputants, in economic and psychic terms. Also, by providing mediation in many cases that would otherwise have gone to court, the mediation movement has also saved *public* expense. It has freed up the courts for other disputants who need them, easing the problem of delayed access to justice. In sum, the movement has led to more efficient use of limited private *and* public dispute resolution resources, which in turn means greater overall satisfaction for individual 'consumers' of the justice system.

"This holds true for all the various contexts in which mediation has been used. Child custody mediation, for example, has produced better-quality results for both children and parents than litigated rulings. Small-claims mediation has resulted in higher party satisfaction with both process and outcome, and higher rates of compliance than litigation. Environmental and public policy mediation have produced creative and highly praised resolutions, while avoiding the years of delay and enormous expense that court action would have entailed. Moreover, mediation in these areas has reduced court caseloads and backlogs, facilitating speedier disposition of those cases that cannot be resolved without trial in court. In these and other kinds of disputes, mediation has produced more satisfaction for disputing parties than could have been provided otherwise."

• • • • • • •

The Satisfaction Story is widely told by a number of authors. Many are themselves mediators, either publicly employed or private practitioners or "entrepreneurs." Some are academics. Some who are both practitioners and teachers have been very influential in supporting this story of the movement (for instance, Fisher and Ury, 1981; Fisher and Brown, 1989; Susskind and Cruikshank, 1987). Also quite influential are the many judges and other justice system officials who tell this story, including former Chief Justice Warren Burger (1982) and many other judicial leaders (see Galanter, 1985).

The next two interpretations of the mediation movement, the Social Justice Story and the Transformation Story, differ somewhat from the Satisfaction Story. The Satisfaction Story claims to depict what has generally occurred in the use of mediation thus far, while the other two describe something that has admittedly occurred only in part thus far. In effect, these are "minor" stories of the movement, but each is still seen by its adherents as representing the movement's most important potential.

The Social Justice Story

According to this story: "Mediation offers an effective means of organizing individuals around common interests and thereby building stronger community ties and structures. This is important because unaffiliated individuals are especially subject to exploitation in this society and because more effective community organization can limit such exploitation and create more social justice. Mediation can support community organization in several ways. Because of its capacity for reframing issues and focusing on common interests, mediation can help individuals who think they are adversaries perceive a larger context in which they face a common enemy. As a result, mediation can strengthen the weak by helping establish alliances among them.

"In addition, by its capacity to help parties solve problems for themselves, mediation reduces dependency on distant agencies and encourages self-help, including the formation of effective 'grass-roots' community structures. Finally, mediation treats legal rules as only one of a variety of bases by which to frame issues and evaluate possible solutions to disputes. Therefore, mediation can give groups more leverage to argue for their interests than they might have in formal legal processes. The mediation movement has used these capacities of the process, to some extent at least, to facilitate the organization of relatively powerless individuals into communities of interest. As a result, those common interests have been pursued more successfully, helping ensure greater social justice, and the individuals involved have gained a new sense of participation in civic life.

"This picture applies to many, if not all, of the contexts in which mediation is used. Interpersonal neighborhood mediation has encouraged co-tenants or block residents, for example, to realize their common adversaries, such as landlords and city agencies, and to take joint action to pursue their common interests. Environmental mediation has facilitated the assertion of novel (and not strictly legal) claims by groups that have succeeded in redressing imbalances of power favoring land developers. Even mediation of consumer disputes has helped strengthen consumers' confidence in their ability to get complaints addressed, which has led to other forms of consumer self-help and increased consumer power. In short, mediation has helped organize individuals and strengthen communities of interest in many different contexts—and could be used more widely for this purpose."

• • • • • • •

The Social Justice Story of the mediation movement has been told for a long time, though by a relatively small number of authors, usually people with ties to the tradition of grass-roots community organizing. Examples include Paul Wahrhaftig (1982), an early figure in community mediation, and Ray Shonholtz (1987), founder of the Community Boards Program, long known for its organizing orientation. More recently, Carl Moore (1994) and Margaret Herrman (1993) have echoed this account. While the numbers of its adherents are few, this story has been told consistently from the earliest stages of the movement.

The third story, the Transformation Story, focuses on some of the same features of the mediation process as the first two. However, it characterizes them, and especially their consequences, in distinct and quite different terms than the other stories.

The Transformation Story

According to this story: "The unique promise of mediation lies in its capacity to transform the character of both individual disputants and society as a whole. Because of its informality and consensuality, mediation can allow parties to define problems and goals in their own terms, thus validating the importance of those problems and goals in the parties' lives. Further, mediation can support the parties' exercise of self-determination in deciding how, or even whether, to settle a dispute, and it can help the parties mobilize their own resources to address problems and achieve their goals. The mediation movement has (at least to some extent) employed these capabilities of the process to help disputing parties strengthen their own capacity to handle adverse circumstances of all kinds, not only in the immediate case but in future situations. Participants in mediation have gained a greater sense of self-respect, self-reliance, and self-confidence. This has been called the *empowerment* dimension of the mediation process.

"In addition, the private, nonjudgmental character of mediation can provide disputants a nonthreatening opportunity to explain and humanize themselves to one another. In this setting, and with mediators who are skilled at enhancing interpersonal communication, parties often discover that they can feel and express some degree of understanding and concern for one another despite their disagreement. The movement has (again, to some extent) used this dimension of the process to help individuals strengthen their inherent capacity for relating with concern to the problems of others. Mediation has thus engendered, even between parties who start out as fierce adversaries, acknowledgment and concern for each other as fellow human beings. This has been called the *recognition* dimension of the mediation process.

"While empowerment and recognition have been given only partial attention in the mediation movement thus far, a consistent and wider emphasis on these dimensions would contribute powerfully— incrementally and over time—to the transformation of individuals from fearful, defensive, and self-centered beings into confident, empathetic, and considerate beings, and to the transformation of society from a shaky truce between enemies into a strong network of allies.

"This picture captures the potential of all branches of the mediation movement, not just certain areas in which human relationships are considered important (implying that elsewhere they are not). Consumer mediation can strengthen and evoke mutual recognition between merchants and consumers, transforming both the individuals involved and the character of commercial transactions and institutions. Divorce mediation can strengthen and evoke recognition between men and women (even if as childless ex-spouses they will have no further contact), changing both the people involved and the character of male-female interaction generally. Personal injury mediation can strengthen and evoke recognition between individuals who work for loss-coverage institutions and individual accident victims, transforming both the persons involved and the character of compensation processes and institutions in our society. In every area, mediation could, with sufficient energy and commitment, help transform both individuals and society."

· · · · · · ·

The Transformation Story of the mediation movement is not widely told in the published literature of the field. The few who expound it include practitioners such as Albie Davis (1989) and academics such as Leonard Riskin and Carrie Menkel-Meadow (in some of their work, see Riskin, 1982, 1984; Menkel-Meadow, 1991; see also Dukes, 1993), as well as the authors of this volume (see Folger and Bush, 1994, and Bush, 1989). Nevertheless, beyond the world of the printed word, this story is given voice in informal discussions among both academics and mediation practitioners. It is, as it were, the underground story of the movement, often the motivating force behind practitioners' involvement. Perhaps it goes unstated because it is not easy to articulate, or perhaps people are hesitant to articulate (or enact) it for fear of seeming too idealistic and impractical. Yet whenever the story *is* told, it generates a remarkably enthusiastic response, which suggests that it has much more currency than its published expressions would indicate.

Here, then, are three very different accounts of the mediation movement. Each of them expresses two different kinds of messages about the movement. On one level, each story is a description, purporting to recount what the mediation movement has actually done and what its actual character is today (in whole or in part). On another level, each story is a prescription, suggesting what the movement *should* do to fulfill what the story's authors see as the most important societal goal or value that mediation can help achieve.

The final story of the movement differs from all the others. The first three all see positive effects or potentials in the movement, although each sees them differently. The fourth, by contrast, sees only negative effects or potentials. It presents not a prescription for the movement but a warning against it. We call it the Oppression Story.

The Oppression Story

According to this story: "Even if the movement began with the best of intentions, mediation has turned out to be a dangerous instrument for increasing the power of the strong to take advantage of the weak. Because of the informality and consensuality of the process, and hence the absence of both procedural and substantive rules, mediation can magnify power imbalances and open the door to coercion and manipulation by the stronger party. Meanwhile, the posture of 'neutrality' excuses the mediator from preventing this. Therefore, in comparison to formal legal processes, mediation has often produced outcomes that are unjust, that is, disproportionately and unjustifiably favorable to stronger parties. Moreover, because of its privacy and informality, mediation gives mediators broad strategic power to control the discussion, giving free rein to mediators' biases. These biases can affect the framing and selection of issues, consideration and ranking of settlement options, and many other elements that influence outcomes. Again, as a result, mediation has often produced unjust outcomes.

"Finally, since mediation handles disputes without reference to other, similar cases and without reference to the public interest, it results in the 'dis-aggregation' and privatization of class and public interest problems. That is, the mediation movement has helped the strong to 'divide and conquer.' Weaker parties are unable to make common cause and the public interest is ignored and undermined. In sum, the overall effect of the movement has been to neutralize social justice gains achieved by the civil rights, women's, and consumer's movements, among others, and to help reestablish the privileged position of the stronger classes and perpetuate their oppression of the weaker.

"This oppressive picture is found in all the movement's manifestations. Divorce mediation removes safeguards and exposes women to coercive and manipulative 'bargaining' that results in unjust property and custody agreements. Landlord-tenant mediation allows landlords to escape their obligations to provide minimally decent housing, which results in substandard living conditions and unjust removals for tenants. Employment discrimination mediation manipulates victims into accepting buy-offs and permits structural racism and sexism to continue unabated in businesses and institutions. Even in commercial disputes between businesses, mediation allows the parties to strike deals behind closed doors that disadvantage consumers and others in ways that will never even come to light. In every area, the mediation movement has been used to consolidate the power of the strong and increase the exploitation and oppression of the weak."

· · · · · · ·

The Oppression Story is clearly a different *kind* of story than the other three. Rather than offering a description of and prescription *for* the mediation movement, it sounds a warning *against* it. This story is almost as widely told as the Satisfaction Story, but by very different authors. They include numerous critics of the mediation movement, such as early and influential figures Richard Abel (1982) and Christine Harrington (1985). Minority critics of the movement, like Richard Delgado (1985), and feminist critics, like Martha Fineman (1988), also tell the Oppression Story. In general, many—although not all—writers and thinkers concerned with equality tend to interpret the mediation movement through the Oppression Story and to see it as a serious threat to disadvantaged groups (see Fiss, 1984, and Nader, 1979).

Now that all the stories have been presented, a clarification of one crucial term is in order. Some authors have used the term "transformation" to mean the *restructuring of social institutions* in a way that redistributes power and eliminates class privilege (see Harrington and Merry, 1988, and Dukes, 1993). It should be clear that as we use the term here—in the Transformation Story and throughout the book—transformation does *not* mean institutional restructuring but rather a change or refinement in the *consciousness and character of individual human beings.* Transformation, in the sense used here, necessarily connotes *individual moral development*, although this kind of change will very likely lead to changes in social institutions as well. On the other hand, when the term is used to mean institutional restructuring, it does not carry any necessary implication of individual moral growth, but rather connotes a reallocation of material benefits and burdens among individuals and groups. We see this aim as encompassed within the concept of social justice or fairness, and in the framework presented here this kind of societal restructuring is the concern of the Social Justice and Oppression Stories, not the Transformation Story.

Implications of the Stories: What Is and What Should Be

Although all four accounts of the mediation movement are in circulation, they are rarely laid out side by side as presented here. A few observers have noted the existence of multiple accounts of the movement, although they have not identified the whole range described above (for instance, Harrington and Merry, 1988). Far more commonly, however, only one of the four stories is told, by a given author or speaker who believes it to be the "true" story of the movement. One account describes mediation as creative problem solving, which produces settlements that satisfy disputing parties on all sides of conflicts. Another sees mediation as helping to organize and build coalitions among individuals, so as to generate greater bargaining power for the "have-nots." A third pictures mediation as working to engender moral growth in disputing parties, thus producing stronger and more compassionate human beings out of the crucible of human conflict. The fourth sees mediation as applying pressure and manipulation in ways that cause greater unfairness to the already disadvantaged.

Placing all four stories side by side reveals some important points. First, it supports the view that the mediation movement is diverse and pluralistic. Not all mediators follow the practices described by any one story of the movement. Rather, there are different approaches to mediation practice, with different and varied impacts, and the different stories depict these different approaches. Therefore, at a factual level, none of the stories is "the true story" of the movement; rather, each is probably a valid account of the practices of some number of mediators working in the field today.

At the same time, setting out all the stories together, and then looking at what we know about current mediation practice in general, makes it clear that the stories are not *all equally* reflective of the actual state of the movement today. For example, a growing body of research tells us that, despite diversity among mediators, a dominant pattern of practice has emerged, and this dominant approach to mediation practice focuses on solving problems and getting settlements (see Folger and Bush, 1994). It gives little attention to coalition building or to transforming disputants through empowerment and recognition. In short, the different stories of the

movement are not equally accurate as "reports" of the overall state
of mediation practice and its impacts at present.

While views differ, people in the mediation field itself generally
see the Satisfaction Story as the most convincing report of the current state of the movement. Supportive outsiders share this view,
although critics tend to see the Oppression Story as more reflective
of the movement's current reality. And almost everyone would agree
that neither the Social Justice nor the Transformation Story reflects
the "what is" of the mediation movement today, except in some
small corners of the field.

As noted earlier, however, a second insight that emerges from
recounting the four stories is that there are different views of what
societal goal the mediation movement should seek to achieve. In
this light, each of the four stories presents a different view of not
only *what is* but *what should be* the character of the mediation
movement. Regardless of which story we accept as a report of the
movement's present character, setting a direction for the future
depends on which story we believe in as a prescription for what the
movement should be. If the Satisfaction Story reflects the bulk of
what is actually going on today and the Transformation Story
reflects only a minor element in the movement, the question
remains: does this correspond to our view of how things *should* be?
The answer depends on how we feel about each story's premises
regarding what ought to be considered the most important goal of
the mediation movement as a whole.

Those premises should be evident from the stories themselves.
The Satisfaction Story's premise is that the most important goal is
maximizing the satisfaction of individuals' needs or, conversely, minimizing suffering—producing the greatest possible satisfaction for
the individuals on both (or all) sides of a conflict. This story stresses
mediation's capacity to reframe conflicts as mutual problems and to
find optimal solutions to those problems, because this is how the
ultimate goal is met—all parties' needs get satisfied.

Both the Social Justice and Oppression Stories are driven by
another premise: the most important goal is promoting equality

between individuals or, conversely, reducing inequality. These two stories take opposite views of the mediation movement from one another, but only because they make different assessments of mediation's impact on this single goal. The Social Justice Story stresses mediation's capacity to organize individuals around common interests and concludes that the resulting coalitions further the ultimate goal of attaining equality. The Oppression Story stresses mediation's capacity to manipulate and exert pressure covertly and warns that such manipulation and pressure will work against the disadvantaged and risk making inequality worse.

Finally, the Transformation Story's premise is that the most important goal is engendering moral growth and transforming human character, toward both greater strength and greater compassion. This story stresses mediation's capacity for fostering empowerment and recognition, because when these occur in conflict, it signifies that the ultimate goal of moral development has been attained to some degree by one or both parties.

Whatever our view of where the mediation movement stands today, our view of what its future direction *should* be depends on which of the premises regarding ultimate goals we find most convincing. Let us assume that the present reality of mediation practice, and its impacts, is accurately described by the Satisfaction Story. If so, and if we agree with the premise that satisfaction should be considered the most important goal, continuing in the present direction makes good sense. If instead we adopt the premise that equality is the most important goal, we might argue for less attention in mediation practice to settlement or problem solving and more to coalition building and safeguarding weaker parties *against* pressured settlement. In either case, we would not care much whether mediation was producing "transformative occurrences," like those noted in the Sensitive Bully case, and probably would not even be aware of them when they occurred. Only the premise that transformation is the most important goal would lead us to argue for less attention to settlement *and* protection and more focus on transformative opportunities and ways to capture them.

Implicit in this discussion is the assumption that, in mediation as in any other social process, it is difficult if not impossible to fully achieve all the different goals together. In practice, achieving one inevitably means neglecting the others to some degree, whether because of direct conflicts between the steps necessary to achieve them or simply because of limited resources. Therefore, setting the movement's future direction requires, at the least, a view of which of the different goals underlying the different stories should be assigned the highest priority. Just as the stories cannot be "combined" into a single description of the movement, they cannot be combined into a single prescription either. Rather, the stories present us with choices regarding what the prescription for the movement's future should be.

Of all the different stories, the Transformation Story has received the least attention in discussions within the mediation field. Nevertheless, we believe that it offers the best prescription for the future of the mediation movement. That account, and its premise that moral growth and transformation should be considered the most important goal, constitutes a basis for guiding the mediation movement that we believe is sounder, more coherent, and more justifiable than that offered by any of the other stories and their premises. As we strive to articulate a transformative approach to mediation throughout the remainder of the book, we will also present our reasons for advocating this approach. For now, however, an initial statement can give some idea of why we think this story best describes the unique promise of mediation and, indeed, why it deserves to be adopted as the guiding vision of the movement.

The Value of Transformation: An Initial Statement

The strongest reason for believing that the Transformation Story should guide the mediation movement is the story's underlying premise: that the goal of transformation—that is, engendering moral growth toward both strength and compassion—should take precedence over the other goals mediation can be used to attain, even though those other goals are themselves important. It makes sense to see transformation as the most important goal of mediation, both because of the nature of the goal itself and because of mediation's special capacity to achieve it.

The goal of transformation has a unique character compared to the goals underlying the other stories of the movement. Contrast the nature of this goal with that of the goals of satisfaction and fairness. Satisfying peoples' unmet needs—or, conversely, alleviating suffering—is surely an important goal. Preventing unfairness, which usually also means reducing suffering, is similarly important. However, both of these aims involve changing people's *situations* for the better. Transformation is a different *kind* of goal. It involves changing not just situations but people themselves, and thus the society as a whole. It aims at creating "a better world," not just in the sense of a more smoothly or fairly working version of what now exists but in the sense of a different kind of world altogether. The goal is a world in which people are not just better off but better: more human and more humane. Achieving this goal means transforming people from dependent beings concerned only with themselves (weak and selfish people) into secure and self-reliant beings willing to be concerned with and responsive to others (strong and caring people). The occurrence of this transformation brings out the intrinsic good, the highest level, within human beings. And with changed, better human beings, society as a whole becomes a changed, better place.

Embedded here are really two points regarding the unique nature of the goal of transformation. First, though satisfying needs and reducing unfairness can make people temporarily better off, only a changed world of changed people can ever really hope to achieve this. In a world in which people remain the same, solved problems are quickly replaced by new ones; justice done is quickly undone. Therefore, people are made better off in one instance only to be made worse off in the one that follows, because nothing has changed fundamentally in the way people tend to act toward each other. But when people themselves change for the better, so that respect and consideration come naturally, it is possible to imagine fuller and fairer satisfaction of needs as a permanent condition. In short, when we have a better world—in the sense of a changed world—then and only then will we have a world in which everyone is really better off. In this respect, the goal of transformation is unique because it carries the other goals along in its train.

Second, the goal of transformation embodies the premise that it is not only being better off that matters but being better. Human beings are more than receptacles for satisfaction; we are possessors of moral consciousness. We have within us the potential for positive and negative, good and evil, higher and lower, human and inhuman, and the ability to know the difference. What ultimately makes our existence meaningful is not satisfying our appetites but developing and actualizing our highest potentials. Put differently, the highest human need is to be fully developed, fully human. A smoothly working world of satisfaction and equity leaves this need untouched. Only a changed world, of changed individuals, fulfills it. In this respect, the goal of transformation is unique because it involves a supreme value that the other goals do not encompass.

Not only is the goal of transformation uniquely important, it is also a goal that the mediation process is uniquely capable of achieving. This is an additional reason to see transformation as the primary goal of mediation. Other dispute resolution processes, like adjudication or arbitration, can probably do as good a job as mediation, or even better, in satisfying needs and ensuring fairness. But, by the very nature of their operation, those other processes are far less capable than mediation (if at all) of fostering in disputing parties greater strength and compassion, and thus of achieving moral growth and transformation. Mediation's capacity for doing so, by generating empowerment and recognition, is unique among third-party processes (Bush, 1989). Adjudication and arbitration both disempower disputants in differing degrees, by taking control of outcome out of the parties' hands and by necessitating reliance on professional representatives. As for fostering recognition, at best these processes ignore it; at worst, they destroy even the possibility of recognition, by allowing or encouraging varying degrees of adversariness. In short, even if the goals of satisfaction and fairness are important, there are other and perhaps better means to achieve them; but if the goal of transformation is important, only one dispute resolution process is likely to achieve it: mediation. It therefore makes sense to see transformation as the most important goal of mediation, since this valued goal is one that mediation alone can achieve.

Many people in the field share this view of mediation's ultimate purpose, though they may not label it as a transformative view. This was exemplified by a conversation we recently had at a workshop with a colleague, a veteran mediator and program administrator. "What is so impressive about mediation," she said, "is that it assumes people are competent—that they have the capacity to handle their own problems." And, we added, it also assumes they have the capacity to give consideration to others. People can work things out for themselves, and they can extend themselves to each other. They also have the desire at some level to do both of these. All of which is to say that people have the capacity and the desire to be morally mature. "And even though they may not do these things automatically," our colleague pointed out, "if you create the right environment and give them some support, which is what mediation can uniquely do, people often will rise to the occasion and fulfill all these potentials. And when this happens, the individuals involved are changed for the better, and ultimately that changes the whole social environment."

Whether or not the label was used, the point is clear: transformation matters, and mediation is unique among third-party processes in its capacity to be transformative. It is this transformative power that makes mediation so important and worthwhile, not simply its usefulness in satisfying needs. This is the message the Transformation Story conveys: not that satisfaction and fairness are unimportant but that transformation of human moral awareness and conduct is even more important. And mediation has a unique capacity for achieving this goal, for engendering transformation.

Despite our view that the Transformation Story is the best prescription for the future of the mediation movement, we acknowledge that it is far from describing the present reality. The current state of the movement is much more consistent with the picture presented by the Satisfaction Story than the one presented by the Transformation Story. Mediation practice has moved steadily in the direction of emphasizing its problem-solving potential and deemphasizing its transformative potential, with the result that the Satisfaction Story's picture has come to dominate the field. The next chapter sets forth some of the evidence for believing that this is the case.

2

· ·

Losing Sight of the
Goal of Transformation:
The Focus on Satisfaction and Settlement

There is considerable evidence that the Satisfaction Story captures the way most people in the field think about and practice mediation today. In recent years, mediation has increasingly been viewed and utilized as a valued technology for problem solving and satisfaction of parties' needs, across all the various contexts in which the process is employed. Moreover, the Satisfaction Story's view of mediation's objectives and values are evident at both the micro- and macrolevels of practice. It shapes the moves mediators are willing to make during individual sessions, the policies institutions are willing to adopt for their programs, and the expectations people have come to see as realistic and appropriate for the societal impact of the mediation movement as a whole.

To provide a vivid sense of the way in which mediation has been shaped at all these levels by the Satisfaction Story, this chapter describes three recent incidents and shows how each is connected to a larger trend documented in current research. These incidents typify the ways in which mediation practice has steadily moved in the direction of emphasizing the problem-solving and settlement-producing dimensions of the process. Conversely, they illustrate how this trend has simultaneously meant deemphasizing mediation's transformative dimensions. The overall result is that, as the Satisfaction Story has gained sway as the guiding vision of the movement, other visions such as that of the Transformation Story have been attended to less and less.

Individual Practice: The Conference Role-Play

At a recent conference of dispute resolution professionals, one session focused on neutrality issues in divorce mediation. After some brief introductory remarks to the fifty practitioners in attendance, the presenters (two men and a woman, all experienced mediators) began the panel discussion by role-playing a hypothetical mediation session.

The case involved a middle-class couple who had been married for twenty years and had two teenage boys. Both spouses held well-paying, professional jobs. The couple owned a house and had about $40,000 in savings. The wife had made a decision to leave the relationship, and the husband had come to accept the divorce as inevitable. The wife clearly was somewhat uncomfortable with insisting on the breakup, but she was also quite anxious to move on with her life. Most of the financial and custody options were discussed at a prior session. The husband and wife had been asked to consider these options (seeking outside counsel if necessary) and to come to the next session prepared to make decisions about terms for the agreement.

As the role-play started, the mediator asked the couple what their thoughts were about property and custody. The wife spoke first. She said that it was important that her husband have custody of the two sons, given their age and close relationships with their father. She said she wanted to be able to spend time with the boys, perhaps one weekend each month and at major holidays. She made it clear, however, that ultimately the time spent with the boys would be determined by them. She would see them when they wanted to see her. She said she wanted the boys to be able to stay in the house with their father. As a result, she wanted a lump sum of $30,000, with no further claim to the house or joint assets. The husband agreed to the terms the wife proposed.

The mediator asked both spouses several questions about the proposed arrangements. He asked the wife whether she had consulted her attorney about the arrangements. She had. He also asked her why she felt comfortable with leaving all the house equity to the husband. She said that she thought it was fair because of the father's future responsibilities for the boys. What was most important to her, she said, was that she was "getting out." The mediator then asked her to clarify why she was willing to leave visitation with her sons fairly open. The wife said that the boys were much closer to their father, and she did not want to jeopardize their relationships. She said she had caused considerable tension by deciding to leave the marriage and did not want to add further strain. When the husband was asked about the wife's proposal, he said that he and his wife had talked things out and agreed that these terms were best for all. In concluding the session, the mediator asked again whether they both felt they had thought through this agreement and were comfortable with it. Each spouse said this was what they wanted. The mediator ended the session by indicating that he would write up the agreement.

This role-play took about fifteen minutes. Immediately afterward, the presenters asked the audience what they thought. Everyone who spoke criticized the mediator's intervention. The responses ranged from mild irritation to outright hostility. One person contended, "This was not neutrality—it was not mediation at all!" The objections centered on what was seen as the mediator's hands-off style. People thought that the wife was giving up too much, probably because she was "running" and felt guilty about leaving the family. The solution being reached was a poor one, and the mediator was remiss for sitting by and letting it happen.

Without reacting to the audience's objections, the presenters asked whether someone wanted to take the mediator role and replay the same session. Two women from the audience offered to co-mediate. The presenters once again took the husband and wife roles. In the replay, the new mediators asked the wife what she wanted in the agreement. The wife provided the same overview of her terms for custody and property. The mediators then posed a series of challenges to the wife. They questioned why she did not want a greater share of the financial assets, especially since she was giving the house to her husband. They also asked why she was treating visitation so "loosely"—how she could be comfortable seeing her boys only when the boys wanted to see her. When the mother began to explain her position, one of the mediators bluntly asked, "What is your conception of motherhood?" The session then trailed off with the mediator indicating that no agreement had been reached. When asked, the audience was complimentary of the second mediators' reenactment of the case.

. . . .

The audience's reactions in this conference session suggest that many mediators work from the premise that their job, and the goal of the process, is to help find optimal solutions to disputants' problems. The practitioners watching this role-play strongly rejected what they saw as the overly laissez-faire approach of the first mediator. Given the wife's position, they felt that the first mediator had not done enough to protect the wife (and perhaps the children) from choosing a poor solution. They were much more comfortable with the second approach, which was more directive in the way it challenged the wife's views. These mediators felt that challenging the wife and persuading her to revise her stance would lead to a better settlement for all concerned—one that was more workable, stable, and equitable. Even if this did not occur, the mediators' intervention would at least forestall the adoption of a poor solution. The directive approach was seen as useful because it could catch possible missteps in the settlement process. In employing this approach, the second mediators were helping the parties to avoid posturing, overreacting, and other pitfalls that could easily prevent them from having a clear sense of their own real needs. They were pursuing not simply settlement but good-quality settlement. The approach to mediation practice reflected in the replay of the case, and endorsed by the audience, was one focused on finding solid solutions to parties' problems—the Satisfaction Story's picture of how mediation does and should work.

Growing evidence suggests that the response at this conference session was characteristic of a large majority of mediators' views and practices. The moves mediators make are strongly driven by the desire to achieve strong, good-quality settlements. One important consequence of this is that many mediators are willing to be quite directive—that is, to exert strong influence over the substantive outcome of a case. Sometimes this means directing parties toward a settlement; sometimes, as in the conference role-play, it means directing them away from certain terms of settlement. Either way, directiveness, for the sake of ensuring good-quality settlements, has become a common and accepted part of mediation practice.

Consider the results of one study. Folger and Bernard (1985) asked a sample of 150 practicing divorce mediators from the Academy of Family Mediators to respond to a series of short case scenarios. Each scenario tested mediators' attitudes about accepting or rejecting terms that parties jointly propose for settlement. The cases were drawn from discussions with mediators who described settlement issues that actually arose in their practice. The responses to these cases suggested that mediators are willing, in a wide range of situations, to reject terms of settlement that parties themselves propose and find acceptable. Moreover, the main reason they are willing to challenge the parties' choices is that these choices would not lead to what the mediators consider optimal solutions.

For instance, one of the scenarios presented to mediators in the survey dealt with a proposed property arrangement and the rights of a dependent spouse:

> A couple who had been married for fifteen years decided to divorce, and they wanted to employ mediation. They had two children ages fourteen and twelve. They owned a home, some stocks and had a joint savings account. They also held joint ownership in a small business that was the major source of

their income. The wife was responsible for the finances and planning of the business. The husband was employed there in a service capacity. The husband had never completed high school and was, for all practical purposes, functionally illiterate. He was also a shy man who said he had great difficulty finding work on his own. He was not confident of his ability to manage money.

The couple proposed a settlement for custody and property. The wife wanted sole custody of the children with liberal visitation for the husband, who agreed. The couple also agreed that the wife should be given eighty percent of the property and managerial control over the business. The husband would be allowed to continue working there. The husband accepted this arrangement because it meant that he could keep his job and continue a friendly relationship with his wife. He said these conditions were very important to him. You are asked to recommend this agreement to the courts. What will you do [pp. 11–12]?

A large majority of mediators (96 of the 150 respondents) said they would reject the proposed terms of settlement in this case. Most indicated that they would refuse or further challenge the settlement terms because one or both of the spouses were not making a "reasoned choice" or were not being treated "justly." In explaining why they saw the parties' choices as not being "reasoned" or "just," mediators often did so by reference to their own views of what an optimal solution would (or would not) be. For example, in response to an open-ended question about their willingness to reject the parties' proposal in this case, mediators offered the following rationales:

These two people are getting divorced, not married. The husband's thoughts are naive with regard to his priorities for settlement.

This is not a divorcing process. His remaining an employee is contingent upon a number of conditions and may be in jeopardy regarding his job and his feelings of inadequacy.

The disturbing elements here include some potential for a lingering psychological marriage as the husband combines or re-establishes what would previously have been a one-down marital position.

These rationales closely reflect the type of thinking expressed in the conference session. They suggest that mediators are willing to take strong measures to influence the outcome of a case, based on their own sense of what would be a good solution, and they are willing to do so even if it means challenging and redirecting the parties' own views. Other research points to the same willingness to shape and direct parties' thinking in order to move them toward outcomes that meet the mediators' sense of what will best solve the problem and meet the parties' needs (Greatbatch and Dingwall, 1989; Felstiner and Williams, 1978; Lam, Rifkin, and Townley, 1989; Shailor, 1994).

In sum, both anecdotal and research evidence suggest that most mediators are taking an approach to practice that focuses on finding good solutions to problems that frustrate the fulfillment of parties' needs. Sometimes, this approach is supported as being necessary to protect parties from unfairness, or from their own bad judgment. In the final analysis, however, the underlying concern is for the satisfaction of parties' needs. The premise of the approach is that the mediator's job, and the goal of the process, is to help find optimal solutions to disputants' problems and thus satisfy needs on all sides. Of course, this is the premise of the Satisfaction Story itself. Thus, at the most microlevel of mediators' moves in individual cases, there is substantial evidence that the Satisfaction Story has steadily gained sway over mediation practice and now accurately represents its general state.

The role-play incident and the research also suggest a second point. As individual mediators' practices have come to reflect the Satisfaction Story, emphasizing the problem-solving objectives and dimensions of the process, they have simultaneously given less and less attention to mediation's transformative objectives and dimensions. The members of the role-play audience, in their rejection of the first enactment of the case and their endorsement of the second, not only demonstrated their approval for a directive approach to practice, aimed at ensuring optimal satisfaction, they also showed their relative unconcern for fostering empowerment by supporting party decision making and control over outcome. The audience considered the first mediator's moves as insufficiently concerned with the quality of the solution, although those moves were well suited to preserving party self-determination. They treated the second mediators' moves as well suited to achieving a quality solution, although those moves evinced little concern for party control. In both reactions, the audience's concern for problem solving and satisfaction was accompanied by a converse lack of concern for empowerment and transformation. Similarly, the research evidence, in the Folger and Bernard study and others, shows a positive alignment of most mediators with an approach to practice that emphasizes finding quality solutions. And although some mediators align themselves with an approach that stresses empowerment, the research shows that the majority is largely unconcerned with this matter.

The overall point is that the evidence leads to two simultaneous conclusions: individual practice has moved steadily in the direction of an approach aligned with the Satisfaction Story, and the flip side of this trend has been a move away from the approach to practice envisioned by the Transformation Story. Though both stories have roots in the movement's earliest days, mediation practice today has generally taken on the Satisfaction Story's image, and as it has done so the image painted by the Transformation Story has faded.

Institutional Policies: The Planning Meeting

The director of a major urban community mediation center, funded
by a statewide dispute resolution agency, was recently asked to
attend a planning meeting with the state agency head. The agenda
for the meeting was to discuss a proposal to require all state-funded
community mediation centers to utilize a mediation-arbitration
(med-arb) process rather than straight mediation. Med-arb is a process in which the third party starts out trying to mediate the dispute; but if no agreement can be reached, the neutral "switches
hats" and makes a binding decision as an arbitrator. The proposal
to make med-arb the standard process had been incorporated in an
official report on mediation programs in the state, after one of the
other state-funded dispute resolution centers had used the process
and evaluated it positively.

The director's center had always used a pure mediation process
from its inception fifteen years earlier. In hearing about the proposed
change to med-arb, the director felt that the process was inappropriate for a community dispute resolution center. He felt that the
process might be too coercive. Although med-arb might be welcomed by some other directors in the state, he strongly believed that
it should not be mandated for all community mediation centers. He
decided to argue this point at the upcoming meeting.

In attendance at the meeting were the state program head, one
of his regional administrators, a lawyer from a bar-sponsored small-
claims arbitration program, and the director of the center that used
med-arb in all its cases. The meeting opened with the regional
administrator summarizing the background of the report that rec-
ommended standard use of med-arb. The recommendation was
based on two major points: the use of med-arb guaranteed final disposition of cases, even when no agreement was reached; and med-
arb facilitated court enforcement where necessary, because all
resolutions became "arbitrators' awards."

The center director whose program used med-arb spoke force-fully for its universal adoption. His main point was that using med-arb did not eliminate the use of mediation at his center. Instead, it made mediation more effective. The vast majority of his cases, he said, reached agreement in the mediation phase. The real value of med-arb was that it made mediation more successful. Agreements were more likely because the parties realized that if they did not reach agreement, the decision would be taken out of their hands, and the med-arbiter might make a decision they would not like. This gave mediators a powerful persuasive tool. They could remind parties of their power as potential arbiters when the parties were reluctant to move from a position. The director noted that, as a result, more cases could be settled using med-arb than straight medi-ation, even without actually resorting to the arbitration phase. Therefore, since it was still mediation (but a more effective form), it made sense to use it as widely as possible. When the director fin-ished, the regional administrator added that this effectiveness argu-ment had actually been the major factor behind the report's recommendation to use med-arb in all programs.

The director whose center used only mediation spoke next. Not wanting to criticize the other center director or offend the state pro-gram people, he limited his statements to one basic point: If it ain't broke, don't fix it. He said his program had worked well with straight mediation for fifteen years; his people were used to it; and without doubting the success of med-arb, he did not think all cen-ters should be forced into one mold.

After several other concerns about implementation were raised, the state program head began discussing how a switch to med-arb might be accomplished. He addressed how technical problems of training, recruitment, and evaluation might be handled. The notion that med-arb was a better, more effective form of mediation—because it produced higher settlement rates—seemed to hold sway, and it seemed that planning for the switch-over would go forward. Although the "mediation-only" center director had not changed his feelings, he decided not to raise further questions at this meeting. To date, the plan to use med-arb has not been implemented statewide. Meanwhile, the director of this center has continued to use a straight mediation process in his program.

．．．．．．．．

The interest in med-arb expressed at this planning meeting was one outgrowth of a general interest in more effective settlement techniques. This larger concern is very typical among program administrators and policy makers in the mediation field today. The real issue driving the meeting, and the evaluation study that prompted it, was a concern for how to make the state's mediation programs more effective in generating settlements in cases submitted to mediation.

Seen in this light, the views expressed at the planning meeting suggest that, like individual mediators, most administrators operate on the premise that the goal of the mediation process is to produce satisfaction by solving disputants' problems and generating mutually acceptable settlements. Therefore, administrators are interested in process variations, techniques, and training that increase effectiveness in reaching settlements, because these all support mediators in their work toward the goals of satisfaction and settlement. Med-arb was appealing to the participants at this meeting because it held out the promise of helping individual mediators to achieve good settlements. The director who had used med-arb in his program argued that more cases are voluntarily settled in the mediation phase of the process because mediators have more clout. As he put it, using med-arb simply makes *mediation* more effective. Med-arbiters can encourage disputants to address issues and reach settlements by reminding them that the third party will have final say if mediation fails. Having this ultimate power gives mediators an extra tool to help parties overcome bargaining pitfalls like posturing, overreaching, and overreacting. It gives them more ability to steer parties away from poorly reasoned choices and toward terms that offer solid and workable solutions to the problems presented.

In short, the administrators at this meeting saw med-arb as one technique—one among many, but arguably quite a good one—that could help their mediators in doing exactly what the practitioners in the conference role-play session considered important: achieving good-quality settlements. The administrators' implicit logic was that giving their mediators more effective techniques would result in more and better settlements, and reaching such settlements would produce more satisfaction of parties' needs. The expression in this meeting of support for med-arb as a settlement-promoting technique was a clear reflection of the Satisfaction Story's picture of what mediation can and should be: an effective technology for solving problems and producing satisfaction.

A glance at recent research on mediation suggests that the meeting, like the role-play session, presents a microcosm of attitudes within the mediation movement—in this case, at the administrative and policy-making level. The positive views of med-arb expressed by most of those at the meeting are typical of mediation administrators' favorable attitudes about the value of satisfaction and settlement, which underlie and produce their interest in settlement-promoting techniques like med-arb.

Although research studies do not directly measure administrators' attitudes, they carry clear implications about those attitudes. For example, most major evaluative studies of mediation—not only internal program evaluations, but also academic studies—concentrate on three measures of performance: rates of settlement, levels of party satisfaction, and quality of substantive outcome, as indicated by different factors (see Pearson and Thoennes, 1984; Tyler, 1987; Hermann and others, 1993). The use of these criteria speaks for itself: the goals of the Satisfaction Story are used as the primary measures of mediation's success. Moreover, the fact that researchers take this view of mediation's goals, in assessing its impacts, suggests that this view is widely held by people who plan and run mediation programs, whose claims and premises the researchers are testing. Thus the consistent focus of evaluative research implies that administrators commonly see mediation's goals as helping parties reach settlements that satisfy their needs, and that they look for ways to help mediators achieve these goals.

Another group of studies strengthens this implication about administrative attitudes. These are research studies on the effectiveness of different mediator strategies or behaviors. In one of the first major collections of research on mediation, Kressel and Pruitt's *Mediation Research* (1989), roughly a dozen studies examined the effectiveness of particular mediator techniques in increasing the likelihood of settlement. One of these studies in particular (Pruitt and others, 1989) looked at whether med-arb itself worked as an effective technique for promoting settlement. The consistent focus of these effectiveness studies suggests again that, at the level of program policy and administration, there is a strong interest in identifying and implementing techniques that can help individual mediators achieve settlements and generate party satisfaction, which are seen as the main goals of the process. As with the practices of individual mediators, the evidence thus suggests that the attitudes of institutional administrators have become strongly aligned with the Satisfaction Story's picture of mediation and its goals.

At the same time, the evidence suggests a converse development—a deemphasis at the administrative level on mediation's transformative objectives. The discussion of med-arb at the administrators' planning meeting demonstrated a strong interest in settlement and satisfaction. At the same time, it evidenced no real concern for fostering empowerment by preserving party self-determination. The med-arb center director's comments focused squarely on the usefulness—for achieving the goal of settlement—of the med-arbiter's "clout," the power to decide the case if the parties cannot settle. No one voiced the concern that, since med-arb gives mediators more power to pressure parties and encourages them to use this power to reach settlements, it may weaken or restrict party self-determination. The administrators' strong interest in how med-arb would help achieve settlements and satisfaction was paralleled by an apparent lack of interest in how med-arb might negatively affect empowerment and transformation. (The one exception was the "mediation-only" center director, who felt such concerns and later decided to follow up on them by contacting outside consultants, to advise him on how to broaden his program's focus to include objectives other than settlement. Nevertheless, his was clearly a minority position—so much so that he felt he could not express it openly at the meeting.)

The broader picture suggested by the research literature is similar, if we point not only to what *is* studied but to what is *not*. With rare exception, evaluative research looks *only* at settlement and satisfaction; almost no studies attempt to assess mediation's transformative impacts or measure effects such as empowerment or recognition (see, however, Deutsch, 1993; Pearson and Thoennes, 1984). Even more clearly, research on mediator behavior focuses exclusively on effective *settlement* techniques; no major study has examined what mediator behaviors are effective in fostering empowerment and recognition. Over a decade ago, Sally Merry (1982) noted that there was a tendency to view mediation's impacts in terms of settlement production alone and neglect other possible measures. This tendency has grown even stronger in the ensuing years.

In sum, as with individual practice, the evidence regarding views of mediation at the institutional level suggests both that the Satisfaction Story has gained sway over the field and that, as it has done so, the voice of the Transformation Story has been more and more muted.

Aggregate Impact: The Response to the King Case

In the summer of 1992, people across the United States were hit by the shock waves of the Rodney King police brutality case: the brutal beating by the police; the graphic video of the beating; the jury verdict exonerating the police officers; the subsequent violence that erupted in the streets; the suggestion of racial bias at each stage. The King case and the events surrounding it carried deeply disturbing messages about our society's failure to produce within us any real regard for law and justice or for each other as fellow citizens and human beings.

Representatives of the minority community in Los Angeles claimed that the beating of Rodney King was no isolated incident. Many said it was the tip of the iceberg of police abuse that goes relatively unchecked in cities across the country. Furthermore, they explained, the problem was not just police abuse but unfair treatment of all kinds. The verdict in favor of the police officers was viewed as an even worse example of this unfairness. It suggested that minorities had nowhere to turn for redress and justice, not even to the courts.

In the rioting that followed the verdict, it appeared that the participants felt alienated not only from the government and its institutions but from their own community as well. After the riots, the question was often asked: Why would people destroy their own community? The most telling response: People did not feel that it was their community, even though they lived there. They did not feel any real control over or stake in the community, and they felt powerless to change things in a constructive way. As one woman put it to a reporter, "They say we don't have any power. Well, we showed them who has the power. We closed down the whole city."

The events also reflected the deep divisions among individuals and different groups in the community. One journalist, an African American, suggested that when the white jurors looked at Rodney King, they did not see a human being at all; all they could see was "a large, brutish black man . . . a menace . . . ready to wreak mayhem on an innocent Los Angeles" (Pearson, 1992, p. 27). The author noted that he sees white people looking at him on the street in the very same way and ended by wondering whether blacks and whites will ever learn to see beyond their frightful stereotypes.

Others spoke about how cultural blinders led different groups to mistrust each other. One news channel filmed a discussion between a Korean family and two African American young men. The youths said they disliked Koreans because Koreans had a "cold," "no smile" attitude that showed disrespect for African Americans. The Koreans explained that their culture teaches them "lack of smiling," not to be unfriendly but because smiling is seen as "unworkmanlike."

Perhaps most disturbing of all was the déjà vu quality of the events in Los Angeles. The disorder was almost a replay of the events that occurred in Watts, Detroit, and other cities across the country almost twenty-five years earlier. The entire episode reflected a level of misery, frustration, and division—of person against person, group against group, citizen against government—that seemed to have changed little in two decades.

In the aftermath of the disorder, numerous commentaries raised questions about underlying causes and about what could have prevented the events from unfolding as they did. Much of the discussion focused on how the conditions that produced the explosion might have been avoided, if better efforts had been made to deal with urban problems over the years: better police training and supervision, better government policies on urban housing and employment, more economic development efforts, and so on. Many areas were mentioned in this connection, by commentators in different fields. People in those fields were asking themselves, "What could we have done differently that might have helped avoid this tragedy, and what should we try to do differently from now on?"

Within the dispute resolution field, however, there was no noticeable public attention to the same kind of question: could better efforts at dispute resolution and mediation have helped reduce the sense of alienation and division that pervaded the South Central Los Angeles community and probably fueled the riots? People in the field certainly discussed the events among themselves as individuals, and many may have talked about this question. Nevertheless, the subject did not become the focus of conference or workshop sessions, nor did commentaries or editorials on it appear in the major journals and publications of the field. On the other hand, the field continued to overflow with discussion, in both conferences and written publications, of the actual and potential utilization of mediation and ADR in divorce cases, commercial disputes, patent and high-tech cases, and many other contexts.

· · · · · · ·

The response within the mediation field to the King case and its aftermath reflects, at the broadest level, current attitudes about what can and should be expected from the mediation movement as a whole. The absence of visible public comment on the events in Los Angeles, within the mediation field, was itself an implicit expression of those attitudes. It suggested that there was indeed nothing to be said, because nothing could have been done within the mediation movement to produce a positive impact on the conditions that produced the disorder. The implicit statement was that, whatever can be done by other social institutions, the use of mediation cannot fairly be expected to have the aggregate impact of reducing the conditions of despair and alienation in urban centers to any significant degree. To think that it might have such an effect would be unrealistic. It would be asking for something that the movement could never deliver.

At the same time, the subjects that have attracted attention in the literature of the field, both before and since the King case, suggest what people *do* see as realistic expectations for the mediation movement in the aggregate. As the use of mediation has spread to an ever-increasing range of disputes, attention has focused more and more on its usefulness in dealing with cases expeditiously and, at the same time, producing solutions that satisfy the needs of disputing parties (see Singer, 1990; Susskind and Cruikshank, 1987). The literature of the field is filled with reports and analyses of mediation's successes in these terms, together with recommendations on how to make greater use of mediation to gain these benefits. Across a wide range of contexts—including family, business, public policy, and environmental conflict—supporters of mediation have reported how problems have been solved, situations improved, and stalemates prevented as a result of mediation's ability to address disputes expeditiously through an informal and consensual process. Studies on mediation, documenting high settlement rates and satisfaction levels, have been offered to support these claims.

Taken together, these sources present a consistent view of what can and should be seen as the aggregate impact of mediation's use: large numbers of individual disputes have been settled, with problems solved, parties satisfied, and undue time and expense avoided. The focus of attention on these kinds of impacts—and the discounting of others—as the realistically attainable and important benefits of the mediation movement strongly reflects the Satisfaction Story's view of what mediation can and should be expected to do: it can serve as a powerful technology for solving problems and satisfying needs. Thus, just as it has gained sway over individual practice and institutional policy, the Satisfaction Story's picture has become the accepted view of mediation's aggregate impact, shaping expectations of what that impact is (and is not) likely to be.

The response to the King case suggests a second general point, about attitudes in the field regarding what can be expected of the mediation movement and how those attitudes have changed in the past two decades. The first community mediation programs, which marked the birth of the contemporary mediation movement, were themselves established as a response to the urban disorders of the late 1960s. Many felt then that mediation *could* reach the underlying levels of intergroup and interpersonal conflict and thus have a positive impact on conditions in urban centers. The reasoning behind this expectation was based on a certain view of the mediation process and its capacities. Part of the reasoning was that mediation can give people a sense of their power to solve problems for themselves, even with limited resources, and a sense of control over their lives—it can empower people. Another aspect of the reasoning was that mediation can "humanize" people to each other, helping them to look beyond their assumptions and see each other as real persons with real human concerns and needs, even in the midst of disagreement—it can evoke recognition. In sum, it was felt that even small measures of empowerment and recognition, over thousands of cases and over decades, could mount up and have some significant cumulative impact on the sense of disempowerment and mutual alienation that would otherwise continue to dominate urban America. These expectations were not seen as naive and unrealistic, although everyone realized that they would not be easy to fulfill. In fact, they represented a major theme in the attitudes of those in the field at that time (see Danzig and Lowy, 1975; Shonholtz, 1984; Stulberg, 1975).

Against this background, the response to the King case suggests how attitudes about the movement's aggregate impacts have changed in the past two decades. At its start in the late 1960s, the mediation movement was indeed considered capable of helping to change the conditions that fueled the disorders of that decade, even if only gradually. Today, it seems that few think of the mediation movement as even *relevant* to the problems of disempowerment, division, and alienation that lie at the heart of societal tragedies like the events in Los Angeles. What the historical background makes clear is that this change in expectations represents not only a shift *toward* the Satisfaction Story's picture of the movement but also a shift *away* from the Transformation Story's picture.

As just explained, the expectations people held for the movement at the start were based in large part on the assumption that mediation practice would emphasize the transformative dimensions of the process—empowerment and recognition. In effect, then, the early expectations of the movement were shaped to a great extent by the Transformation Story. The gradual abandonment of those expectations as unrealistic has thus meant a move away from the story itself as a guiding vision for the movement.

In sum, with attitudes about mediation's aggregate impact, as with individual practice and institutional policy, the growth of the Satisfaction Story's influence has been accompanied by a weakening of the Transformation Story's influence. At all levels, the Satisfaction Story holds sway over the movement today, and the Transformation Story exercises only minor influence.

Gains and Losses

The steady direction the mediation movement has taken, toward the picture of the Satisfaction Story and away from that of the Transformation Story, can be viewed in different lights. For example, one view of the change that took place in attitudes about mediation's impacts is that the movement simply "grew up," leaving behind naive expectations for more realistic ones as it did so. As one critical observer of the mediation field told an audience of practitioners at a recent conference, "The important thing for you to realize is that you are not a 'social movement' after all. You are a group of people with some useful skills, for which there is an interested market of potential users. My advice is, go ahead and figure out how to market your services more effectively, and forget about changing society."

In effect, the speaker's comment suggests that the Satisfaction Story's picture of mediation offers something of limited but nevertheless real value, while the Transformation Story's picture offers something that looks very grand but is ultimately illusory and unattainable. If this implicit assessment is valid, then the move that has occurred, toward the vision of the Satisfaction Story and away from that of the Transformation Story, has meant gaining something of value while losing nothing of any real importance. This would mean that the present direction of the mediation movement is a wise one. The key question is whether this assessment of the two stories is as sound as it seems. Our view is that it is not.

Indeed, our assessment of the two stories is the reverse of that suggested by the conference speaker quoted here. The value offered by the Satisfaction Story is not as real as widely believed, and the value offered by the Transformation story is more realistically attainable than commonly thought. Therefore, contrary to the prevailing view, the strong likelihood is that continuing the present direction of the mediation movement will mean gaining something of questionable value while losing something of great importance. The remaining chapters explain in depth *why* we believe that this is the case and *what* can be done about it. The next chapter examines why the Satisfaction Story has gained such sway and looks more closely at its limitations and the gap between what it promises and what it delivers.

3

Solving Problems:
The Limits of
Current Mediation Practice

The steady growth in the popularity and influence of the Satisfaction Story, overshadowing other stories of the mediation movement, has not been a chance development. It has occurred because this story resonates with deep-seated attitudes held by many in the field about conflict in general. In effect, people were predisposed by these attitudes to accept the Satisfaction Story, and this gave it great influence over developments in the field.

Satisfaction and Problem Solving

The way most people have looked at mediation over the past twenty-five years stems largely from the way they look at conflict in general. Like all the stories in Chapter One, the Satisfaction Story, as an account of the character of the mediation movement, rests on and expresses a set of premises about the nature of conflict in general. To be more specific, this story's account of the movement is consistent with and reinforced by a broader, coherent, and well-articulated framework known as the problem-solving orientation to conflict. Indeed, the appeal and influence of the Satisfaction Story is largely due to its connection to the problem-solving orientation. The problem-solving framework is the Satisfaction Story's inner logic.

An *orientation to conflict* is a worldview of conflict. It tells us how to think about conflict by shaping two fundamental sets of expectations (Littlejohn, Shailor, and Pearce, 1994). First, it offers a sense of what conflict *is*. It tells us how we should explain conflict to ourselves, how it can be identified, thought of, and discussed. Second, an orientation to conflict suggests a view of what the ideal *response* to conflict should be. It prescribes what people in conflict should do to reach successful results—results that the orientation itself defines and prizes.

In the problem-solving orientation, conflict is seen as the manifestation of a problem in needs satisfaction. That is, when a conflict exists, a problem exists, and a problem exists because of a real or apparent incompatibility of parties' needs or interests. The incompatibility appears to make satisfaction of parties' needs impossible, at least temporarily. In short, the dissatisfaction typically associated with conflict stems from the existence of an unsolved problem—a problem of how to satisfy simultaneously what appear to be incompatible needs.

This view that conflict emerges from unmet and incompatible needs leads to a corresponding view, that the ideal response to conflict is taking collaborative steps to solve identified problems. Addressing conflicts means finding solutions that meet the needs of all involved parties to the greatest possible degree, and thus maximizing joint satisfaction. Parties' moves are consistent with problem-solving objectives when they clarify needs or when they suggest and evaluate solutions that address a problem. Optimal solutions are ones that creatively meet the diverse needs of all parties. Less optimal solutions are ones that parties embrace when they are willing to ignore or drop some needs in order to construct an acceptable, albeit imperfect, solution.

The framework problem solving establishes for understanding conflict, both what it is and how one should respond to it, was succinctly summarized by management theorists several years ago:

> The capacity of a group to develop new, innovative solutions
> to difficult problems is especially important in resolving

conflicts constructively. Where disagreements or conflicts
exist, there typically is no readily available solution seen by all
parties as acceptable. A new, innovative, integrative solution
which will meet the needs and desires of *all* interested parties
must be found [Likert and Likert, 1976, p. 133].

Over the last three decades, problem solving has become theorists'
household view of the way successful conflict unfolds. It is woven
through discussions of conflict in law (Fisher and Ury, 1981;
Menkel-Meadow, 1984; Riskin, 1991, 1993), psychology (Likert and
Likert, 1976; Maier, 1967; Maier and Solem, 1962; Pruitt, 1983;
Pruitt and Rubin, 1986), organizational management (Schmidt and
Tannenbaum, 1960; Blake and Mouton, 1964; Kepner and Tregoe,
1965; McKersie, 1964; Filley, 1975; Ruble and Thomas, 1976; Pruitt
and Lewis, 1977), and communication (Borisoff and Victor, 1989;
Putnam and Poole, 1987; Folger, Poole, and Stutman, 1993).

Why has this view of conflict gained such wide acceptance?
There are several reasons. First, it was advanced partly in response
to a different orientation to conflict that many felt was too destructive and costly—the distributive orientation. That orientation views
the sorting out of competing claims for resources as the central activity of conflict resolution. In the distributive view, conflict is defined
as an adversarial, winner-take-all contest among competing
claimants for resources. The ideal response to conflict is the assign-
ment of contested resources to the party with the superior claim,
according to principles of rights and fairness. This orientation underlies the formal legal dispute resolution system, as well as the arbitration process and even adversarial approaches to negotiation
(although power rather than principle may determine claims in all
three, to varying degrees). Problem solving offers an alternative to
the distributive outlook, an alternative based on a less adversarial
and more expansive view of both resource use and self-interest. It
suggests that parties can get more of what they want if they treat
conflicts as problems that can be defined mutually and addressed in

ways that seek comprehensive solutions. Resources can be expanded, value can be created rather than claimed, and addressing others' needs is the best way to address one's own (Lax and Sibenius, 1987; Menkel-Meadow, 1984). It was in part this contrast with what it replaced that made problem solving almost a cause célèbre and rooted it firmly in accounts of ideal conflict resolution.

Apart from avoiding the limitations of the distributive orientation, problem solving offers real strengths that in themselves are broadly appealing. These strengths are part of the everyday parlance of problem solving today: parties can clarify and pursue their own interests as they consider others' interests; they can enhance both the process and outcome of dispute resolution by emphasizing openness, collaboration, and creativity; and they can avoid the pitfalls of power imbalances, escalation, and destructive avoidance of issues. These are real advantages that practitioners and theorists extol.

Problem solving was also welcomed and furthered by social scientists who found in it a trainable and measurable approach to conflict intervention. The problem-solving view was a boon to applied research in conflict resolution. Researchers demonstrated how problem-solving efforts could be enhanced by drawing from work on creativity and heuristics. Specifically, they drew attention to techniques to expand, redefine, and reframe problems and possible solutions. They also generated numerous paper-and-pencil inventories that tapped parties' ability to think and act in problem-solving terms. All this work in the social sciences served as useful technology for the problem-solving orientation and further enhanced its perceived credibility, utility, and appeal.

Even this brief sketch of problem solving clarifies that it is a coherent, well-articulated, and persuasive view of conflict. It is a gestalt that encases many people's thinking about ideal conflict resolution. For some, it is so inculcated that defining conflicts as problems seems almost tautological. It seems impossible to view conflicts as something other than problems or sets of incompatible interests. This is especially true for people who work with consensual and informal dispute resolution processes like negotiation and mediation rather than binding and formal processes like adjudication in court.

It should be clear that it is the deep-rootedness of the problem-solving view of conflict that explains the great popularity and influence of the Satisfaction Story. The underlying problem-solving orientation reinforced the Satisfaction Story and predisposed people to accept its account of the mediation movement. Both the way problem solving defines conflict and the response it prescribes are totally consistent with and supportive of the Satisfaction Story and its view of mediation's potential. Indeed, the central claim of the Satisfaction Story is that, in practice, mediators help solve problems: mediation is assisted problem solving. In effect, the Satisfaction Story is a direct expression of the problem-solving orientation, an account of how problem solving is enacted when mediators intervene in conflict and attempt to assist disputing parties.

Problem Solving in Mediation Practice

The problem-solving orientation predisposes people to accept the Satisfaction Story's account of what mediation should be expected to accomplish. At the same time, it leads people to adopt an approach to the actual practice of mediation, which the Satisfaction Story describes and endorses. Underlying everything—the approach to practice, the view of mediation's objectives, and the account that describes both—is the problem-solving orientation to conflict. This strong connection between the problem-solving orientation and the practice of mediation is demonstrated by a growing body of research. This research shows that problem solving is deeply ingrained in current mediation practice, just as the Satisfaction Story suggests.

Some of the strongest evidence of this comes from research on radical differences in mediator styles (Silbey and Merry, 1986; Donohue, 1991; Kressel and others, 1994). Although the styles identified in these research studies *are* considerably different, they nevertheless all remain within a problem-solving orientation to conflict. In fact, examining these "differences" reveals a surprising sameness that shows just how pervasively the problem-solving orientation influences mediation practice.

Susan Silbey and Sally Merry's (1986) classic study of mediator style differences is a case in point. Based on their close observation and analysis of forty mediators, they suggest that two consistent styles or "settlement strategies" were employed: a bargaining style and a therapeutic style.

Silbey and Merry characterize these two styles of mediation as follows:

> In the bargaining mode, mediators claim authority as professionals with expertise in process, law, and the court system, which is described as costly, slow and inaccessible. The purpose of mediation is to reach settlement. The bargaining style tends toward more structured process and toward more overt control of the proceedings. In the bargaining style, mediators use more private caucuses with disputants, direct discussion more and encourage less direct disputant communication than in the therapeutic style. . . . The job of the mediator is to look for bottom lines, to narrow the issues, to promote exchanges and to sidestep intractable differences of interest. . . .
>
> By contrast, the therapeutic style of mediation is a form of communication in which the parties are encouraged to engage in a full expression of their feelings and attitudes. Here, mediators claim authority based on expertise in managing interpersonal relationships and describe the purpose of mediation as an effort to help people reach mutual understanding through collective agreements. Like the bargaining style, the therapeutic mode also takes a negative view of the legal system; but, instead of emphasizing institutional values and inadequacies, the therapeutic style emphasizes emotional concerns, faulting the legal system for worsening interpersonal relation-

ships. In this mode, agreement writing becomes a collective activity, with mediators generally maximizing direct contact between the parties wherever it may lead. . . . [Mediators] rely more heavily upon expanding the discussion, exploring past relations and going into issues not raised by the immediate situation, complaint or charge [pp. 19–20].

These two styles of mediation are quite different in some respects. But Silbey and Merry's discussion and case illustrations demonstrate (although this is not their purpose) that *both styles* are ultimately driven by a problem-solving approach to mediation. The bargaining style describes the most direct route mediators can take through a problem-solving process. Bargaining mediators address interests that are most readily viewed as problems; they narrow concerns, keep tight control over interaction, and move steadily toward solutions that are mutually acceptable. "Bottom line" thinking is valuable because it focuses on solutions that work. Free-form interaction or discussion of emotions is dangerous because it can easily swerve off the problem-solving course. The bargaining style of mediation is consummate problem solving.

Therapeutic mediators, on the other hand, expand issues, allow for more unstructured interaction, and encourage parties to express their feelings. However, these steps are taken as a way of finding workable solutions that can be the basis for settlements. In other words, the therapeutic approach is also primarily directed toward solving problems, but it does so by enhancing communication among the parties and searching for shared interests—approaches considered far too time-consuming and dangerous by bargaining mediators. For the therapeutic mediator, this more circuitous route is attractive at times because it offers a more realistic and comprehensive approach to addressing issues. It can do more to deal with the complexity of problems because it acknowledges their sub-terrain—the history that led to current circumstances and the emotional reactions that issues carry. Ultimately, however, the therapeutic style is just as concerned with producing solutions to problems as the bargaining approach. Even if a broader conception of what problems are gets set in place in the therapeutic approach, solving problems is still at the heart of the process.

This point is clearly illustrated in the case study Silbey and Merry (1986) use as an example of therapeutic mediation. In this case, the mediator first expands a narrow dispute over a financial debt between a divorcing couple into "far broader and emotional areas." But then, even though "the parties resisted slightly," the mediator returns "at the end to the narrower problem of negotiating the money" (p. 25). Solving the immediate problem—what to do about the debt—is ultimately treated as being more important than anything else. And ultimately the mediator presses the wife to agree to a settlement she clearly is not committed to. Even though deeper issues are explored, the mediation turns on whether the money problem gets addressed and the parties move toward solving it. Behind this mediator's strategy, Silbey and Merry note, is "the theory that the expression of feelings is *a necessary precondition to reaching a resolution* [italics ours]." Expanding issues and exploring emotions serve the same ends that the bargaining approach seeks. The therapeutic style remains at base a problem-solving endeavor.

What the Silbey and Merry study suggests is that even the polar ends of current mediation practice reflect the same overall problem-solving orientation to conflict. This is in part because the therapeutic style is itself influenced by problem-solving objectives and in part because when both occur, problem solving wins out. In a way, of course, seeing the *similarity* between two things that are different requires a contrast with something else, something that makes difference look like similarity. The contrast shows that the two different things are just ends of the same pole. The therapeutic style starts to move in a different direction from problem solving. But it has no place to go, because it has not been linked to an alternative view of what conflict is and what the ideal response to it should be. As a result, even when mediation practice starts heading in an alternative direction, it soon gets overrun by problem solving.

Examining other studies of differences in practice leads to similar conclusions. Even styles of mediation that appear quite different on the surface are still driven by the same underlying orientation to conflict, an orientation that leads disputants and third parties alike to view their task and direct their efforts toward identifying problems and constructing solutions. Almost all descriptive characterizations of practice found in the literature fall within the general problem-solving orientation (Kolb, 1983; Kressel and Pruitt, 1989; Alfini, 1991; Riskin, 1993). In the world of practice today, mediation is generally problem-solving mediation.

The Patterns of Problem-Solving Practice

The mediation styles just discussed begin to capture what mediation currently looks like in practice, at least in broad terms. There is, however, another side to problem-solving mediation—a side that is well documented but far less recognized. Certain types of mediator behaviors are induced by the problem-solving orientation and are a logical extension of it; however, these behaviors raise concerns because they considerably alter the process and goals of mediation as envisioned by the Satisfaction Story. In effect, they call into question whether the Satisfaction Story—and problem-solving mediation—can ever deliver what it promises.

These problematic features all stem from the role mediators play as intervenors within a problem-solving process. For this reason, they have not surfaced in other formal or informal problem-solving contexts in which parties negotiate issues on their own. In other words, it is not problem solving per se that leads to the difficulties but the third party's involvement in the problem-solving process. What mediators actually do suggests that, when they operate under the mandate to define and solve problems, mediators cannot help but influence the process and outcomes in ways that tend, paradoxically, to defeat the spirit and purpose of problem solving altogether.

Three overall patterns of mediator conduct characterize problem-solving mediation. First, early in the process, mediators tend to decide what the case as a whole is about, labeling the dispute in a way that seems recognizable and manageable. Second, mediators often influence settlement terms in surprisingly directive ways. Third, mediators tend to drop issues that cannot readily be handled within a problem-solving approach. These three patterns, taken as whole, threaten the very objectives problem-solving values. Ironically, they may be inevitable as long as mediation is based on the problem-solving orientation.

Global Assessments of Parties' Circumstances

As disputants tell their opening stories—the history of events that led to the present circumstances—mediators tend to search for and define problems that need to be solved or addressed. Mediators fold historical background, chronologies of events, and expressions of frustration or anger into more global and tangible problems. Shapiro, Drieghe, and Brett (1985) find, for example, that early in labor grievance mediations, mediators ask themselves what kind of case or problem is in front of them, so that they can begin formulating possible solutions. Mediators tend to consult a "repertory of case patterns they know" in order to make a "quick cognitive evaluation of the potential outcome of a case" (p. 112). Similarly, Carnevale and his colleagues (1989) suggest that, early in the process, mediators assess whether there is sufficient common ground between parties to develop a mutually acceptable solution.

Our own informal observations at several mediation centers support what this research suggests: problem solving forms a lens through which mediators view parties' contributions from the outset of the process. This lens quickly focuses mediators on "diagnosing" the problem, identifying a set of specific issues from the comments presented in opening stories. It discourages mediators from focusing on individual comments or move-by-move interaction as it unfolds. Instead, it leads them to unearth underlying interests and needs, thereby identifying and shaping the "problem" that these needs create. Like an artist who steps back to peruse a large canvas after every few brush strokes, mediators repeatedly step back from the parties' comments to identify the problem that disputants' statements reveal. Moreover, in doing so, they often diagnose cases by "type," based on their past experience. As one mediator proudly told us, "Most of the cases I deal with are boilerplate conflicts. You can tell, from the start, what they are about and what they are going to come down to." This tendency to rely on a "boilerplate" approach also derives directly from the problem-solving orientation.

Influence over Settlement Terms

A spate of recent research documents that mediators use a range of strategies—specific moves made during the process—to shape arguments, frame proposals, and influence outcomes (Folger and Bernard, 1985; Lam, Rifkin, and Townley, 1989; Greatbatch and Dingwall, 1989; Donohue, 1991; Shailor, 1994; Felstiner and Williams, 1978). Using these strategies, mediators direct their moves primarily toward the creation and acceptance of settlement terms that solve problems. Moreover, much like the mediators' challenge to the wife in the divorce mediation role-play discussed in Chapter Two, these strategies are often used to challenge the parties' own preferences for settlement or their own willingness to reach agreements.

Researchers identify a number of specific moves or strategies that mediators use to influence settlement terms while working toward the acceptable goal of solving problems. Greatbatch and Dingwall (1989), for example, provide a case illustration of how a mediator in a divorce case directs the interaction toward one particular outcome. Specifically, the mediator kept the focus of discussion on one solution—the suggestion that the wife remain in their primary home and the husband move to a second property they owned jointly. The mediator did not pursue discussion of other options such as the possibility of selling both houses and dividing the money.

The mediator kept control over what got discussed through what Greatbatch and Dingwall call "selective facilitation." In pursuing discussion of some issues and not others, the mediator selectively facilitates the discussion of only certain options. If one or both of the parties sense that favored treatment is being given to one option, they may protest. However, selective facilitation is often quite subtle. It can easily go unseen or unacknowledged. The mediator can easily be viewed as simply guiding the process—keeping the session moving toward a useful or acceptable solution. Greatbatch and Dingwall (1989) suggest that when selective facilitation occurs it indicates that "the mediator is working with notions of what kind of settlement would be desirable (a favored outcome) and what kind of settlement would be undesirable (a disfavored outcome) and seeks to guide the interaction accordingly" (p. 618). In the divorce case they describe, there is little doubt that the mediator has a favored outcome—she goes so far as to state explicitly her opposition to the alternative during the session.

Numerous other studies, as noted earlier, identify mediators' moves aimed at shaping solutions or convincing the parties of the strengths or advisability of one solution over others. Mediators have been found to reframe issues, reformulate parties' concerns, or use directive questioning to shape arguments or justify overt opposition to parties' desired solutions. All of this evidence makes essentially the same point: for a wide range of reasons, mediators often shape settlement terms as much as or more than the disputants themselves.

Dropping Concerns That Cannot Be Treated as Problems

Most conflicts involve multiple issues or layers of concerns, any of which could be viewed as part of the problem that needs to be addressed. Typically, as a conflict unfolds, some of the layers get addressed while others are avoided entirely or dropped along the way. When no third party is involved in a conflict, the parties themselves decide which of these layers they need to address. The entry of a third party complicates things because it creates the potential for the third party to influence what issues get addressed.

In mediation, there is a documented tendency for the third party to drop certain types of issues and thus influence the way problems typically get defined. Like the pattern of mediator behaviors just discussed, this pattern also involves mediator influence over the final settlement, but it is influence over the way problems get defined in the first place. It is influence that occurs before parties even begin to consider which substantive options should be chosen as the basis for settlement.

Donohue's (1991) research on divorce mediation, for example, suggests that mediators influence which problems get addressed during mediation. He analyzed the interaction in twenty mediations that were conducted at the Los Angeles County Family Mediation and Conciliation Court. The goal was to compare mediations that reached agreement with those that did not. He reports that in agreement sessions, mediators focused on substantive issues that could readily be addressed as tangible problems with concrete solutions. In agreement sessions, "Mediators talked about interests because the couples were ready to hear one another's interests. The mediators translated these interests into specific proposals and they were readily accepted by the couples" (p. 160). In sessions in which no agreements were reached, couples frequently raised relational issues such as trust and self-worth. These concerns tended to stymie mediators' efforts, prompting responses that seemed almost inappropriate for the issues the parties raised: "The no-agreement disputants talked about relational problems while their mediators pursued factual issues" (p. 164). Donohue reports that in mediations in which agreements were not reached, the sessions lasted, on the average, half as long. This result occurred because relational issues arose in these sessions and mediators swerved from these obstacles in the road, avoiding background events and relationship history that might thwart efforts to construct acceptable settlements. The mediators essentially terminated the session when parties emphasized concerns that did not head easily toward concrete settlement terms involving money, property, or custody arrangements.

The tendency to drop issues that cannot be treated as tangible problems is noted in other analyses of mediation practice and is consistent with our own observations of mediators in community, landlord-tenant, divorce, and juvenile mediation programs (Silbey and Merry, 1986; Lam, Rifkin, and Townley, 1989). It is a tendency that is entirely consistent with a problem-solving orientation to conflict. Some issues disputants raise are readily addressable as problems; they lend themselves to definable parameters and concrete arrangements or exchanges that can be formulated as solutions and settlement terms. Relational or identity issues, however, are more difficult to address in problem-solution formats. As Sillars and Weisberg (1987) have noted, "in important relational conflicts, the source of the conflict is diffuse and selectively perceived. Attempts to communicate are therefore frustrated by a failure to agree on a definition of the conflict" (p. 151).

If conflicts are viewed and approached from a problem-solving stance, the very basis for communicating at all is undermined when relational or identity issues arise. Mediators may try to recast these more elusive issues into problems that have tangible solutions. But, if disputants resist or recasting appears impossible, mediators may see no alternative but to drop the issue or end the mediation entirely. Mediators' inclination to avoid or drop these dimensions of parties' problems is a sensible and expected response from a problem-solving point of view.

The Limitations of Problem-Solving Mediation

All three patterns of mediator conduct point toward two general conclusions. First, mediators' tendencies to form global assessments, shape settlement terms, and drop intangible issues all confirm that much of what mediators actually do in practice follows directly from the problem-solving orientation to conflict. Making global assessments of parties' circumstances ensures that the process will not get lost in the twists and turns of the moment. It ensures that all interaction within the session becomes, instead, the basis for defining and solving problems. Similarly, shaping settlement terms and dropping intangible issues help to ensure that optimal solutions are eventually found and accepted. In short, mediation as generally practiced today is problem-solving mediation, or assisted problem solving, in which the mediator's role is to help find solutions to parties' problems.

The three patterns of mediator behavior point to a second and perhaps more important conclusion about current practice. All of these behaviors indicate that mediators *influence* conflicts as they unfold during mediation. Global assessments influence what the parties come to think the dispute is about; they mark what is relevant or appropriate to talk about. When mediators drop issues, they go even further in influencing what will remain on the table for discussion. In effect, they "tell" parties what is important about their conflicts, or at least what is relevant to the mediation process. And, in shaping settlement terms, mediators influence what parties finally agree to, what they see as solutions to their problems. Taken as a whole, these behaviors suggest that when mediators focus on the objective of solving problems, they generally use a strong, directive hand in trying to do just that.

In other words, problem-solving mediation tends to become directive mediation. At its most obvious, this directiveness translates into a kind of four-step version of practice, in which the mediator "hears the case," diagnoses the problem, formulates what he or she sees as a good solution, and tries to persuade the parties to accept this solution (or some version or modification of it). Even when it is less obvious, however, the tendency to be directive is still common in current practice.

The trouble with this type of mediator influence or directiveness is that it changes the fundamental character of problem solving.

Specifically, the emphasis problem-solving places on satisfaction of the parties' needs gets lost. When parties problem-solve without the assistance of a mediator, they alone define their needs and make choices about what solutions will be acceptable. Problems get defined and redefined as parties change or prioritize needs. And parties convince each other whether a solution will be found and what it will be. Indeed, this type of persuasive interaction is part and parcel of what it means to do problem solving. However, these choices remain solely in the hands of the parties themselves. It is the parties' conflict to direct and solve as they wish. As next-door neighbors overhearing a conflict through open windows, we may shake our heads and think that someone is foolish for saying certain needs are important or accepting certain solutions as workable. But as eavesdroppers, we have no impact on what will be said next, who will change whose mind, or how problems eventually get defined or solved.

Mediators, however, are not neighbors who overhear conflicts. Mediators enter conflicts. They become participants in the unfolding interaction and have an influence on the way it develops. And, as the three patterns of problem-solving mediation practice show, the type of influence embodied in those patterns shifts the focus away from mutual satisfaction of needs *as the parties define them*. The effect of this shift in focus is to undermine the problem-solving enterprise at its very core.

It is important to recognize that the source of mediators' tendency to be directive is the problem-solving orientation itself, not the personal inclinations of individual practitioners. When mediators act as problem solvers, their interests are thrown into the problem-solving pot with the parties'. Mediators have an interest in solving *some* problem in the sessions they conduct, because their work is guided by a view of conflict that defines this outcome as the desired end and thus as the mediator's goal. And mediators have an interest in solving problems in ways that are consistent with their own judgment, because they have inclinations about what solutions will work best, and solving a problem normally means finding a good-quality solution. In other words, mediators feel compelled, because of the problem-solving orientation itself, both to solve problems and to solve them well. As one mediator recently asked, "Why shouldn't I advise the parties what to do if I know what is going to work best in their situation? The whole reason I'm here is to help them find a solution to their problem!"

The point is that mediators' interests, as shaped both by the problem-solver role and by their own values, become forces at play in mediated conflicts. However, as these third-party interests enter a conflict, the problem-solving focus shifts away from a sole concern with disputants' needs to a joint focus on disputants' and third-party interests. Problem-solving mediation becomes problem solving with more than the parties' needs at stake. As a form of conflict resolution, it is not after "win-win" solutions but "win-win-win" solutions.

Given the preceding points, it is somewhat surprising that mediator influence or directiveness is not commonly viewed as problematic by those who tell the Satisfaction Story. There are two main reasons why it is not. First, it is partly because mediator influence is not obvious; in fact, it is easily masked. Problems get solved through the process, even if they are defined as much by the mediator's as the parties' interests. Indeed, in this respect, mediator influence is helpful; it produces the appearance that the process is delivering what it promises to deliver: mutual satisfaction of the parties' needs. As Silbey and Merry (1986) have put it, "The mediator's exercise of power goes largely unnoticed by the bargainer. It appears instead as a simple extension of an accepted logic and practice" (p. 27). In our terms, the "exercise of power" is the influence that mediators are known to have over problems and solutions and the "accepted logic and practice" is the problem-solving view of conflict itself.

Second, to the extent that the Satisfaction Story does acknowledge mediator influence, this influence is viewed in much the same way as the influence parties have over each other when they are negotiating on their own. Parties can accept or resist mediator influence just as they might accept or resist each other's influence. The underlying premise here is that when mediators' influence has an impact, it is because the parties have come to *accept* the mediator's views as their own. In the end, the issues parties address and the solutions they accept *are* the parties' after all, even if the mediator influenced them during the process. In this view, the mediator's influence is seen as either beneficial or innocuous.

However, the Satisfaction Story's view of mediator influence—as innocuous at worst and helpful at best—has been criticized on several counts. To begin with, mediators can influence the outcome of a mediation while not actually convincing parties or achieving party satisfaction. Disputants can "accept" mediator influence nominally and can move in directions that the mediator initiates, but remain unconvinced and unsatisfied by the steps they themselves have taken. This was very much the case in the mediation session we described earlier illustrating Silbey and Merry's therapeutic style of mediation. The wife in the case agreed to a settlement despite her own better judgment because the mediator pushed in this direction and because she felt the agreement would soon be overturned in court anyway. Time pressure, impatience, indifference, and other such factors often combine with mediator pressure to produce such "illusory" settlements. In these instances, the mediator's influence leads to agreements, but the needs of one or both parties are left fundamentally unaddressed. Only the *appearance* of mutual satisfaction of parties' needs is achieved.

Furthermore, it is dangerous to view mediator influence as innocuous because mediators carry biases with them and tend to express these biases in their mediations. This view is taken by those who tell the Oppression Story, as described in Chapter One. They claim that mediators' moves—their management of the interaction, arguments, and suggestions—typically favor the stronger parties' interests in a conflict. This is sometimes because mediators bring their own oppressive biases to the issues that arise in mediation and sometimes because they stay within an oppressive frame that the parties themselves bring to the table. In either case, the results are the same. Weaker parties are more vulnerable and thus more likely to be influenced in ways that do not serve their interests. Women end up with weak custody agreements, tenants with poor conditions, consumers with deceptive advertising and faulty products. In this view, mediator influence is pernicious because it perpetuates the evils of inequality and oppression (Nader, 1979; Fineman, 1988; Bryan, 1992).

We do not share the ultimate conclusion of the Oppression Story, that mediation is of little value unless it can address deeply rooted social injustices and inequalities. However, we *are* concerned about what problem-solving mediation actually provides. Given the kinds of directive mediator practices that have been documented in research, it seems unlikely that the most common result of "successful" problem-solving mediation is satisfaction of parties' needs. Rather, it is probably a settlement that, even if optimal in the mediator's view (and even if it contributes to high settlement rates), leaves both parties unsatisfied or satisfies one at the expense of the other.

Some observers have begun to suggest that the greatest cause for concern in the mediation field today is not the directiveness of the problem-solving approach but the advent of an "adversarial" form of mediation that greatly narrows and adversarializes the process, an approach often associated with mediators who are former judges (see Riskin, 1993; Alfini, 1991; McEwen, 1991). It is too soon to tell whether this is in fact a distinct approach or simply an extreme version of problem-solving mediation in which mediator directiveness is even more pronounced. In any event, this development does not lessen, and may even heighten, the seriousness of the situation described in this chapter—that the problem-solving approach, which currently dominates practice, has very real defects that need to be addressed. The possibility that another, even more problematic development may be emerging should not reduce attention to the documented limitations of problem-solving mediation itself.

Of course, there are some mediators who do not follow the general patterns of the problem-solving approach in their practices and who consciously strive to avoid the directiveness typical of that approach. They are more careful about limiting their role to helping parties clarify issues and options, and avoiding any kind of influence over parties' decisions. Indeed, some of the same research studies that document the prevalence of the directive, problem-solving approach suggest that a minority of mediators differ from this approach and instead follow the principle of party self-determination more scrupulously (Folger and Bernard, 1985). As a result, if their cases reach settlements, the product is more likely to be what the Satisfaction Story promises: joint satisfaction of parties' real needs. Nevertheless, the available research on current practice indicates that this kind of practice is the exception, not the rule.

• • • • • • •

In sum, the evidence suggests both that current practice generally follows the problem-solving approach and that problem-solving mediation does not do a good job of solving problems at all. The type of mediation pictured by the Satisfaction Story, in actual practice, simply does not have this impact. Indeed, if the incidents and trends described in Chapter Two are examined more critically, they can easily suggest the impacts described and warned against by the Oppression Story: As in the role-play incident, mediators tend to steer parties in certain directions, because of their need to achieve settlement and their own values and biases, resulting in dissatisfaction or unfairness to parties. As in the meeting incident, administrators often look for ways to give mediators more power to pressure parties into settlements on terms seen as acceptable by the mediator. The aggregate result, as in the account of the King case, is not more satisfaction and justice but less. Recent research tends to support this view of current practice and its impacts. As noted earlier, studies of actual mediator practices have documented that practice is widely characterized by mediator behaviors that focus almost entirely on reaching settlement, often on terms strongly influenced, if not imposed, by the mediators themselves. These studies suggest that while mediation reaches settlements, the settlements may not actually provide optimal solutions and satisfaction (Tomasic, 1982). Research on outcomes of mediation—though often made difficult by the lack of a baseline for comparison—suggests that current practice may permit and even facilitate outcomes that are unfair to disputants from certain groups, including consumers (Nader, 1980), women (Fineman, 1988; Grillo, 1991), and minorities (Hermann and others, 1993).

These disturbing consequences of mediator influence in problem-solving mediation cannot be explained as the product of deficiencies on the part of individual practitioners. *The problem is not with individual mediators but with the approach as a whole.* The effects described are the unintended but, ironically, inevitable consequence of basing third-party intervention on a problem-solving orientation to conflict. In that orientation, mediators are problem solvers. But in practice, "problem-solving mediation" turns out to be a contradiction in terms. When mediators act as problem solvers, they are powerfully drawn to steer parties both toward settlement per se and toward specific terms of settlement. Yet, when this happens, the parties' problems and needs often get displaced or obscured. Settlement, in this context, does not necessarily mean mutual satisfaction; it often means dissatisfaction or even oppression. Those who tell the Satisfaction Story need to recognize and acknowledge the ways in which mediator influence ironically reshapes the problem-solving process and, as a result, undermines the values of the Satisfaction Story itself.

Dealing with the Inevitability of Mediator Influence

Acknowledging the role that mediator influence plays in current practice means coming to grips with it. But this is no simple matter. For many it has meant looking for ways to remove or limit mediator influence—to define and enact a neutral role for the problem-solving mediator. But the paradoxical nature of this quest soon becomes apparent. In effect, mediators are told to solve problems but to refrain from the very kinds of moves that are necessary to do so. Or, they are told to control process but not influence content, though the distinction easily blurs in actual practice. In short, problem-solving mediation from a neutral stance is increasingly recognized as practically impossible to do, under any meaningful definition of neutrality (Cobb, 1991; Rifkin, Millen, and Cobb, 1991). Instead, problem-solving mediation seems necessarily to mean directive mediation with all the attendant problems discussed earlier.

Given this dilemma, a second response to mediator influence has been to reject the process entirely. Because of its lack of formality and structure, critics suggest that mediation cannot adequately regulate third-party influence and even tends to encourage abuse. Without rules of law guiding mediators' response to parties' issues, mediators can alter the very terms of disputes that the parties themselves have framed. Without formal rules of evidence and procedure, less skillful or powerful parties are likely to be placed at a serious disadvantage during the process. And, without public scrutiny of or accountability for what goes on in the privacy of mediation sessions, there is no way to monitor or limit third-party abuses. As a result, mediation affords no recourse for dealing with inevitable mediator influence. It needs to be rejected outright or sharply curtailed (Fineman, 1988; Delgado and others, 1985).

If these were the only possible responses to the documented forms of influence that occur in current practice, the future of mediation might not look promising. However, our interest in and hope for the movement rests on an alternative response. While some form of mediator influence is inevitable, the *specific* forms of influence that are currently documented in research are not. It is clear that conflicts do not remain unchanged during the course of intervention. There is no such a thing as the "parties' conflict" when third parties are involved. Conflicts are inevitably changed as they are processed, and mediators are an inevitable part of that change. Of necessity mediators contribute to the shaping of a conflict as long as they are interacting with the parties (Mather and Yngvesson, 1980–81; Sarat, 1988; Cobb, 1991; Folger, Poole, and Stutman, 1993; Greatbatch and Dingwall, 1994; Shailor, 1994). To deny this is to deny all that we know about the way face-to-face communication of any sort unfolds.

But the sort of influence mediators currently tend to exercise—shaping both the definition of problems and the choices parties make about how to solve them—is not the only influence imaginable. It just seems that way when we stand under the canopy of the problem-solving orientation. The kind of mediator directiveness prevalent in current practice is what we can expect to see as long as problem solving guides our sense of what conflict is and how we should respond to it. As long as problem solving guides mediation, even those whose prescription is based on the Satisfaction Story will be disappointed by the gap between what the movement promises and what it delivers.

Whatever our prescription for the mediation movement, the problematic aspects of current practice and our inability to address them from within the problem-solving vision signal a need to re-examine the validity of this underlying orientation to conflict as a whole. If our current vision tells us that mediator influence is inevitable and incurably problematic, we can either give up on mediation or look beyond the vision itself. It is not just the value of transformation but the problems with doing problem solving in mediation that point us in the direction of a new vision of conflict and a correspondingly different approach to mediation. That approach may already be at least partly implicit in the practices of the minority of mediators who do not follow a problem-solving approach today. It is time to bring it forward and consider its value explicitly.

Part Two

· ·

The Transformative Approach
to Mediation

4

Changing People, Not Just Situations:
A Transformative View of
Conflict and Mediation

To construct a different approach to mediation practice, we have to begin with the underlying basis on which practice rests and reexamine our views of both what conflict is and what the ideal response to conflict should be. Rethinking the problem-solving orientation starts by questioning the premise that conflicts need to be viewed as problems in the first place. A different premise would suggest that disputes can be viewed *not* as problems at all but as opportunities for moral growth and transformation. This different view is the *transformative orientation* to conflict.

In this transformative orientation, a conflict is first and foremost a potential occasion for growth in two critical and interrelated dimensions of human morality. The first dimension involves strengthening the self. This occurs through realizing and strengthening one's inherent human capacity for dealing with difficulties of all kinds by engaging in conscious and deliberate reflection, choice, and action. The second dimension involves reaching beyond the self to relate to others. This occurs through realizing and strengthening one's inherent human capacity for experiencing and expressing concern and consideration for others, especially others whose situation is "different" from one's own. Moral thinkers like Carol Gilligan (1982, 1988), among others, suggest that full moral development involves an *integration* of individual autonomy and concern for others, of strength and compassion. Therefore, bringing out both of these inherent capacities *together* is the essence of human moral maturity. In the transformative view, conflicts are seen as opportunities for developing and exercising both of these capacities, and thus moving toward full moral development.

A conflict confronts each party with a challenge, a difficulty or adversity to be grappled with. This challenge presents parties with the opportunity to clarify for themselves their needs and values, what causes them dissatisfaction and satisfaction. It also gives them the chance to discover and strengthen their own resources for addressing both substantive concerns and relational issues. In short, conflict affords people the opportunity to develop and exercise both self-determination and self-reliance. Moreover, the emergence of conflict confronts each party with a differently situated other who holds a contrary viewpoint. This encounter presents each party with an opportunity for acknowledging the perspectives of others. It gives the individual the chance to feel and express some degree of understanding and concern for another, despite diversity and disagreement. Conflict thus gives people the occasion to develop and exercise respect and consideration for others. In sum, conflicts embody valuable opportunities for both dimensions of moral growth, perhaps to a greater degree than most other human experiences. This may be why the Chinese have a tradition of using identical characters to depict crisis and opportunity.

In the transformative orientation, the ideal response to a conflict is not to solve "the problem." Instead, it is *to help transform* the individuals involved, in both dimensions of moral growth. Responding to conflicts productively means utilizing the opportunities they present to change and transform the parties as human beings. It means encouraging and helping the parties to use the conflict to realize and actualize their inherent capacities both for strength of self and for relating to others. It means bringing out the intrinsic goodness that lies within the parties as human beings. If this is done, then the response to conflict itself helps transform individuals from fearful, defensive, or self-centered beings into confident, responsive, and caring ones, ultimately transforming society as well. This, of course, is the vision of the Transformation Story of the mediation movement.

Just as the underlying problem-solving orientation explains why most mediators have accepted the Satisfaction Story, the underlying transformative orientation explains why others have continued to regard the Transformation Story as a sounder guiding vision for the movement. Even if this orientation has not been so clearly articulated as the other, it has long affected and guided mediators at an intuitive level. This explains why many mediators are so powerfully affected by the "serendipitous" moments of transformation that sometimes occur in mediation. As in the account of the Sensitive Bully case, it is striking when parties sometimes seem to reach, at least momentarily, an almost exalted state of both dignity and decency, as each gathers strength and then reaches out to the other. At such moments it seems that "the light goes on," that an illumination of human goodness seems to eclipse in importance everything else that happens. The clear articulation of the transformative orientation confirms that these occurrences are indeed of transcendent importance, that our intuitive response to them is appropriate. But it goes further and suggests that these kinds of occurrences do not have to be, and should not be, serendipitous. They should be the very aim of the enterprise, and practice should be designed and conducted to bring them about.

On a deeper level, the view that fostering moral growth should be a primary goal of social processes like mediation rests on a belief, grounded in what can be called a Relational vision of human life, that compassionate strength (moral maturity) embodies an intrinsic goodness inherent in human beings. Bringing out that goodness is itself a supremely important human enterprise, because it is the surest if not the only way to produce a truly decent society and because it embodies and expresses the highest and best within us as human beings. These views are explained at length in Chapter Nine. For now, the point is that in the alternative viewpoint based on these premises, conflicts are seen as rich opportunities for growth, and mediation represents a way to take full advantage of these opportunities.

Transformative Mediation's Objectives: Empowerment and Recognition

Success has different meanings in the problem-solving and transformative approaches to mediation. In problem-solving mediation, success is achieved when an agreement is reached that solves the problem and satisfies all sides. At the simplest level, problem-solving mediation defines the objective as improving the parties' *situation* from what it was before. The transformative approach instead defines the objective as improving *the parties themselves* from what they were before. In transformative mediation, success is achieved when the parties as persons are changed for the better, to some degree, by what has occurred in the mediation process. More specifically, transformative mediation is successful when the parties experience growth in both dimensions of moral development mentioned earlier—developing both the capacity for strength of self and the capacity for relating to others. These are the objectives of *empowerment* and *recognition*.

In a transformative approach, empowerment and recognition are the two most important effects that mediation can produce, and achieving them is its most important objective. However, these terms need careful definition, both conceptually and practically. It is fairly easy to understand the statement that "an agreement was reached that solved the problem and satisfied all sides," at least conceptually speaking. But what does it mean to say that empowerment and recognition were achieved in mediation, even conceptually? In the most general terms, empowerment is achieved when disputing parties experience a strengthened awareness of their own self-worth and their own ability to deal with whatever difficulties they face, regardless of external constraints. Recognition is achieved when, given some degree of empowerment, disputing parties experience an expanded willingness to acknowledge and be responsive to other parties' situations and common human qualities.

These are general definitions of transformative mediation's objectives. But it is important to be as concrete as possible so as to demonstrate that empowerment and recognition are not mere abstract concepts but very real effects that can be recognized when they occur within and beyond mediation.

Empowerment

Involvement in conflict affects everyone in similar ways. Disputing parties are typically unsettled, confused, fearful, disorganized, and unsure of what to do. As a result, they feel vulnerable and out of control. This is as true for "powerful" executives and officials as it is for consumers, family members, or schoolchildren. From this starting point of relative weakness, parties are empowered in mediation when they grow calmer, clearer, more confident, more organized, and more decisive—and thereby establish or regain a sense of strength and take control of their situation.

It is possible to define this objective very concretely by pointing to the kinds of things which, when they occur within mediation, show that it has been achieved. Here is a description of some of the specific kinds of occurrences that constitute empowerment within the mediation process:

- A party is empowered in mediation when

   She reaches a clearer realization, compared to before, of what matters to her and why, together with a realization that what matters to her is indeed important.

   She realizes more clearly what her goals and interests are in the situation at hand, why she holds those goals, and that her goals are important and deserving of consideration.

   (Empowerment as to goals)

•A party is empowered in mediation when

> She becomes aware of the range of options available to
> secure her goals in whole or part, and of her control over
> those options.

> She realizes that choices exist about what to do in the sit-
> uation and that she has some control over those choices.

> She realizes that she can choose whether or not to stay in
> or leave the mediation, accept or reject legal or other
> advice, accept or reject a possible solution, and so forth.

> She realizes that regardless of external constraints, there
> are always some choices open to her and the control over
> those choices is hers alone.

> (Empowerment as to options)

•A party is empowered in mediation when

> She increases or adds to her own skills in conflict resolution.

> She learns how better to listen, communicate, organize
> and analyze issues, present arguments, brainstorm and
> evaluate alternative solutions, and so forth, and then
> strengthens those skills by using them practically in the
> mediation.

> (Empowerment as to skills)

•A party is empowered in mediation when

> She gains new awareness of resources already in her
> possession (or readily available to her) to achieve her
> goals and objectives.

> She realizes more clearly than before that: she holds some-
> thing that is of value to the other party; she has an
> ability to communicate or persuade effectively; her
> resources can be rearranged to make them reach farther;
> her resources are sufficient to implement a solution not

previously considered; she can add to her resources by tapping into an additional source of support she had not previously considered.

(Empowerment as to resources)

• A party is empowered in mediation when

She reflects, deliberates, and makes conscious decisions for herself about what she wants to do—including decisions about what to do in the mediation discussions themselves, and decisions about whether and how to settle the matter or what other steps to take.

She assesses fully the strengths and weaknesses of her arguments (and the other party's), and the advantages and disadvantages of possible solutions and of nonsettlement options, and makes decisions in light of her assessments.

(Empowerment as to decision making)

When these kinds of things occur within mediation, the party experiences a greater sense of self-worth, security, self-determination, and autonomy. Even if the external constraints of the party's circumstances still impose certain limits on her, within those limits she has exercised greater control over her own situation, and the self is strengthened as a result. When the mediator helps to bring about any of these kinds of things in the mediation session, the objective of empowerment has been achieved to some degree.

Given this meaning of empowerment, it should be clear that *empowerment is independent of any particular outcome of the mediation.* If a party has taken the opportunity to collect herself, examine options, deliberate, and decide on a course of action, empowerment has occurred, regardless of the outcome. Whether the outcome is a settlement that the mediator finds "fair and optimal" or unfair or even stupid, or a decision not to settle at all, the objective of empowerment has been met. The party has gained increased strength of self from the process of self-awareness and self-determination enacted in the mediation session.

And if a mediator is tempted to think, "Perhaps steering the party to what I know is a better outcome is really more empowering," the definition of empowerment per se reminds the mediator that even a "poor outcome" produced by the party's own process of reflection and choice strengthens the self more than a "good outcome" induced by the mediator's directiveness or imposition. Indeed, even if it were certain that mediators can reliably identify good solutions, giving the parties a good solution produces satisfaction rather than empowerment. And satisfaction alone does not engender strength of self, unless accompanied by the process of empowerment. Solving problems *for* parties is not transformative mediation, because it fails to empower and perhaps even disempowers the parties. It is the concrete steps toward strengthening the self within the session that constitute empowerment, not the nature of the outcome or solution.

As already noted, empowerment refers to effects that occur not only within but beyond the mediation session. What are the longer-term effects encompassed within the meaning of empowerment? They are "spillover" effects produced by the mediation experience that give parties greater strength of self on an ongoing basis. For example, drawing from their experience in transformative mediation itself, parties may carry over into other situations more ability to be clear about their own goals and objectives; more confidence that their interests matter and deserve consideration; more awareness that they have options and choices about how to achieve those goals; enhanced conflict resolution skills, including greater ability to identify the resources they possess to achieve their goals, within external constraints; and greater ability to make deliberate and conscious decisions about the choices they identify.

In follow-up research conducted on students in a conflict resolution program that has a transformative approach, the results indicated that the participants showed increased confidence, awareness, skills, and decisiveness in school, home, and peer group situations afterward (Deutsch, 1993). Empowerment, as an objective and an effect of mediation, can extend beyond the immediate case to the parties' ongoing activities.

Recognition

In the heat of conflict, disputing parties typically feel threatened, attacked, and victimized by the conduct and claims of the other party. As a result, they are focused on self-protection; they are defensive, suspicious, and hostile to the other party, and almost incapable of looking beyond their own needs. From this starting point of relative self-absorption, parties achieve recognition in mediation when they voluntarily choose to become more open, attentive, sympathetic, and responsive to the situation of the other party, thereby expanding their perspective to include an appreciation for another's situation.

Again, it is possible to define this objective quite concretely by pointing to the kinds of things which, when they occur within mediation, show that it has been achieved. Here is a description of some of the specific kinds of occurrences that constitute recognition within the mediation process:

- A party gives recognition in mediation when

    He experiences the realization that, beyond possessing the strength to deal with his own situation, he possesses the capacity to reflect about, consider, and acknowledge in some way the situation of the other party, not just as a strategy for helping himself but out of genuine appreciation of the other's human predicament.

    He realizes that he feels secure enough to stop thinking exclusively about his own situation and to focus to some degree on what the other party is going through.

    (Consideration of giving recognition)

• A party gives recognition in mediation when

> He realizes that, beyond possessing the *capacity* to consider and acknowledge the other's situation, he has the actual *desire* to do so.
>
> He realizes that he wants to focus his attention on what the other is experiencing and to find some way of acknowledging that experience by his conduct in the session.
>
> (Desire for giving recognition)

• A party gives recognition in mediation when

> He actually allows himself to see the other party, and her conduct, in a different and more favorable light than before.
>
> He consciously engages in reinterpreting the past conduct and behavior of the other party and tries to see it in a new and more sympathetic way.
>
> He consciously lets go of his own viewpoint and tries to see things from the other party's perspective.
>
> He sees, for example, that what he had taken as an intentional insult was the unpremeditated product of understandable frustration or merely a different mode of communication.
>
> He sees, for example, that what seemed to be opportunistic or exploitative behavior directed against him was instead the product of the other party's understandable attempt to deal with real and severe pressures placed on her by her own constrained circumstances and so forth.
>
> At such moments, "the penny drops," or "the light bulb goes on," as it dawns on him that he does not have to view the other so harshly and negatively as he had been doing, and he consciously moves to a new and more sympathetic view.
>
> (Giving recognition in thought)

• A party gives recognition in mediation when:

> He openly acknowledges his changed understanding of the other and/or decides to communicate it to her.
>
> He admits to the mediator, even privately, how he now sees what happened differently and acknowledges how it casts the other party in a different and more favorable light; or he says this to the mediator in the other's presence or to the other party directly.
>
> He accompanies a statement of new understanding with an apology of some kind.
>
> He apologizes for having "thought the worst" about the other party in the past and/or for "retaliatory" conduct of his own that was based on his harsh interpretation of the other's behavior toward him.
>
> (Giving recognition in words)

• A party gives recognition in mediation when

> He decides, in light of his changed understanding of the other's past conduct and her situation, to make some concrete accommodation to her in terms of how the disputed issues are handled. He decides, if a first offer of accommodation is not sufficient to produce a mutually satisfactory solution, to make some further accommodation.
>
> If his own circumstances are so constrained that an accommodation sufficient to settle the matter cannot be found, he expresses genuine regret that this is so.
>
> (Giving recognition in actions)

When these kinds of things occur within mediation, the party realizes and enacts his capacity to acknowledge, consider, and be concerned about others. Though he is in the midst of difficulties of his own, he has chosen not to focus exclusively on his own needs and concerns but to strive consciously to understand the perspective and take account of the concerns of the other party. As a result, he reaches beyond himself to relate to another person's common humanity in a concrete way. When the mediator helps to bring any of these kinds of things about in the mediation, the objective of recognition has been achieved to some degree.

Given these examples of the concrete definition of recognition, it should be clear that recognition does not mean the experience of validation or satisfaction that a party gets from *receiving* recognition. (In fact, that experience of validation may be an aspect of empowerment, for the party receiving recognition.) Rather, recognition, as an objective of transformative mediation, is the experience of moving beyond a focus on self that a party experiences from *giving* recognition to another. The objective is met when a party *gives* recognition to the other in some fashion. Recognition can occur, can be given, in many different *degrees*. Of course, an actual offer of accommodation (especially one that satisfies the other's needs) is a powerful expression of giving recognition. Nevertheless, lesser measures—even a party's mere act of thinking about the idea of considering what the other is going through, and certainly moments when reinterpretations occur, regardless of whether this gets communicated to the other—also count as recognition.

Such "slight" steps constitute recognition because in each of them, there is some move by the party away from an exclusive focus on self and toward a consideration for the other as well. Every such move is an actualization to some degree of the capacity for relating to others. Indeed, depending on the situation and the severity of the conflict, a very slight move of this sort can mean a great deal in terms of the kind of moral growth underlying the objective of recognition in the transformative approach. Of course, there is such a thing as "lip service," the mere feigning of recognition without any real content; but in most cases it is not hard to distinguish between this and genuine recognition.

Recognition often comes and goes, waxes and wanes, during a mediation session. A party will take several steps that give recognition, including expressions of new understanding and even an offer of accommodation. But then, if the case falters, if the offer does not lead to a settlement, the "light" of recognition may go off and the party may revert to her former harsh, negative views of the other. In fact, this happens fairly often. But in these instances, the effect of recognition, the activation of the capacity for relating to others, still occurred and changed the party to some degree. That change may be greater when the recognition continues and increases throughout the session, but even small changes count as meeting the objective.

Realizing that slight and even transitory steps can still constitute recognition is important for another reason. Recognition is not recognition at all unless it is freely given. It is the *decision* of the party to expand his focus from self alone to include the other that represents the moral growth expressed in giving recognition. If that decision is itself the result of pressure, cajoling, or moralizing, it represents nothing but self-preservation. Forced recognition is a contradiction in terms. A mediator who thinks that only large degrees of recognition count will be sorely tempted to force things. Yet, when force is applied, recognition vanishes. The key is for the mediator to understand that the objective is met by achieving *whatever degree of recognition the parties are genuinely willing to give.*

Another way of saying this, which begins to explain the relationship between the two objectives of transformative mediation, is that recognition must be based on empowerment. That is, a party must feel and experience their freedom to make decisions in different directions. Then the party can choose to take (or not take) the step of giving recognition. Until the point is reached where parties are consciously choosing their steps, recognition is unlikely to occur or to be genuine or meaningful.

As with empowerment, recognition refers to effects that occur not only within but beyond the mediation session. In this case, it refers to spillover effects produced by the mediation session that expand parties' ability and willingness, on an ongoing basis, to relate to others with more understanding and consideration. For example, drawing from their experience in transformative mediation itself, parties may carry over into other situations more ability and willingness to relate to others less defensively, more respectfully and more empathetically; to be less judgmental of others; to give others the benefit of the doubt; to find elements of common experience and common concern with others; to be more tolerant of others with diverse experience and concerns. As an objective and an effect of mediation, recognition can extend beyond the immediate case to the ongoing lives of the parties.

A New Definition of "Success"

We have taken care to explain and illustrate empowerment and recognition at length because these concepts lie at the heart of the transformative approach to mediation. However, they are not novel concepts in mediation theory. These concepts have been identified and discussed by writers on mediation including such well-known figures in the field as Fuller (1971), Stulberg (1981), Riskin (1984), Davis (1985, 1989) Folberg and Taylor (1984), and McEwen and Maiman (1984). Each of these authors has identified one or the other of these two objectives as a primary goal of mediation. The transformative approach to mediation we envision is building on a very solid tradition within the field that long ago identified these concepts as central to the mediation enterprise.

With regard to the definitions and illustrations of empowerment and recognition, two general points should be noted. First, empowerment is an objective that can be achieved in *all* cases; recognition, on the other hand, can only be attained when parties willingly give it—either in response to a mediator's efforts or spontaneously. Second, despite what was just said, recognition, because its meaning includes even small steps, is achievable much more often than normally assumed. It is possible, in *all* cases, for mediators at least to focus parties on the possibility or opportunity of giving recognition.

Therefore, we propose a more concrete definition of successful mediation, in terms of the objectives of transformative mediation. A mediation is successful (1) if the parties have been made aware of the opportunities presented during the mediation for both empowerment and recognition; (2) if the parties have been helped to clarify goals, options, and resources, and then to make informed, deliberate, and free choices regarding how to proceed at every decision point; and (3) if the parties have been helped to give recognition wherever it was their decision to do so. If these specific objectives are achieved, then the more general objectives mentioned earlier will also be met, to the greatest degree possible. Parties will experience both strengthening of self and greater actualization of their capacity for relating to others, and they will advance in both critical dimensions of moral development. Successful mediation will bring out the intrinsic strength and goodness that lie within the parties as human beings, to the fullest extent possible.

Some Important Distinctions

Objectives such as finding good solutions or ensuring fairness, even if they sometimes prove elusive to define and measure in practice, are familiar enough that people can discuss them without worrying that they will be totally misunderstood. Not so for empowerment and recognition. Even though they are based on ideas that have been around for a very long time in the mediation field, the ideas themselves have rarely been presented in succinct and precise form to define concrete objectives for mediation. As a result, it is important to distinguish our use of the concepts and terms *empowerment* and *recognition* from other usages with which they might be confused.

Empowerment is a term used currently to mean so many different things that it is important to clarify what we do *not* mean by it. As we are using the term, empowerment does *not* mean "power balancing" or redistribution of power within the mediation process itself in order to protect weaker parties. Indeed, empowerment is always practiced with both parties. Of course, empowering *both* parties, in our sense, may indeed change the balance of power, if one party starts off with greater self-confidence and self-determinative ability. That, however, is a side effect of empowerment and not a conscious objective.

Similarly, empowerment does *not* mean controlling or influencing the mediation process so as to produce outcomes that redistribute resources or power *outside* the process from stronger to weaker parties. It does not mean using the mediation process—and the substantial powers of the mediator to influence how problems are defined and how solutions are chosen—to give more power to those who are members of defined "weaker" groups. While some mediators may in practice see this as their role, we do not endorse it, and it is not what we mean by empowerment.

Finally, empowerment does *not* mean adding to the strength of either party by becoming an advocate, adviser, or counselor. We acknowledge that the distinction between empowerment and advice giving, or empowerment and advocacy, is sometimes difficult to draw in practice (Bernard, Folger, Weingarten, and Zumeta, 1984; Folger and Bernard, 1985; Bush, 1992). Still, the objective of empowerment does not require or support the mediator's taking sides, expressing judgments, or being directive, all of which are central aspects of advice giving and advocacy. In fact, empowerment in a transformative approach to practice requires *avoiding* all these behaviors. Therefore, even if there are questions at the borders, the general concept of empowerment remains quite distinct from advice giving and advocacy.

Recognition, unlike empowerment, is not a term in wide use, so confusion over language is less likely here. However, a number of concepts common to discussions of mediation and dispute resolution may be confused with recognition in the transformative sense. As discussed previously, recognition means *giving* recognition *to* another, not getting it *from* another. Beyond this, several other distinctions are important.

Recognition, first of all, does *not* mean reconciliation. It should be clear from the illustrations given earlier that the parties do not have to become fully reconciled—have their relationship fully restored or fully accept the other—in order for recognition to have occurred. Of course, recognition may sometimes go so far as to bring about reconciliation. But this need not happen for recognition to be achieved. This distinction is very important, because if recognition is the goal, it is very easy to argue that it is simply unattainable in all but a tiny fraction of cases. While that may be true, it is certainly not true for the objective of recognition. Recognition is a much more modest, practical, and attainable objective, in a wide range of situations. And this modest objective has very real and substantial value. It is a mistake to accept a "threshold of value" argument that suggests that nothing short of complete reconciliation has any value, in terms of how the parties relate to each other. This argument misses the point that, in transformative, moral growth terms, there is a continuum of value. Reconciliation may stand at the top, but it does not obviate the value of every lower point on the continuum. The recognition objective is concerned with the whole continuum.

At the other extreme, recognition does *not* mean the mere realization of one's enlightened self-interest, the experience of interdependence in instrumental terms. When one party sees how she can get more of what she needs by giving the other some of what they need, this is a fundamentally self-referential awareness and experience. In it, the consideration of the other stems essentially from concern with oneself. The hallmark of recognition is *letting go*—however briefly or partially—of one's focus on self and becoming interested in the perspective of the other party as such, concerned about the situation of the other as a fellow human being, not as an instrument for fulfilling one's own needs. The experience of interdependence, in fact, is a key part of problem-solving mediation. It is not the same as the recognition objective of transformative mediation.

Both empowerment and recognition, as objectives of transformative mediation, should be distinguished from the objectives of different forms of therapy. Some therapy has as its objective the working out of the client's unresolved feelings about parents or early childhood or the working out of conflicted feelings about some current situation. Many therapists, in pursuing these objectives of resolving conflicted feelings, are highly directive and relatively unconcerned with clients' giving recognition to family members or others, except as it helps their own emotional state. In effect, this type of therapy is a form of problem solving, concerned with solving emotional problems (Haley, 1987; Roberts, 1992). It is not concerned with empowerment or recognition, and the distinction of objectives is fairly clear.

Other sorts of therapy, however, focus more on the process of learning *how to handle* the problems the client faces, whether from the past or in the present, as a strengthening process for the individual (Haynes, 1992). There is a similarity between the objective of this type of therapy and empowerment, and the term is sometimes used in the literature of therapy in a similar sense. The distinction to be drawn here is that in transformative mediation empowerment is never a sole objective; it is always linked to recognition. In therapy, empowerment is often an objective unto itself—the client's attainment of a state of adjustment, well-being, autonomy, and so forth.

Finally, in some forms of therapy, usually with couples or family members in close relationships, the objective seems to encompass not only empowerment within the individuals themselves but also recognition between them (see, for example, Boszormenyi-Nagy and Krasner, 1986). The objectives envisioned by this kind of therapy are similar to those of transformative mediation. However, this connection between mediation and some forms of therapy should not be seen as problematic. If the objectives of empowerment and recognition as defined make sense and are of real value, and if an approach to doing mediation exists that can attain them, then we should not be concerned if mediation encompasses some of the same objectives as some forms of therapy. Many astute mediators in the field have seen these linkages but have hesitated to suggest they were there.

The field has been hypersensitive to preserving strict divisions among mediative and therapeutic processes—drawing lines that have at times been ignored in practice and at times held mediation back from realizing transformative objectives (Forlenza, 1991).

This discussion brings up a broader point. The objectives of empowerment and recognition are indeed considered important today in many fields outside mediation, and therapy is only one of them. Management experts in both the private and public sectors stress participatory measures that empower individual employees and citizens as the key to effective enterprises (Osborne and Gaebler, 1992; Rosen and Berger, 1992). Educators see students' achievement of confidence and self-reliance, not just acquisition of knowledge or skills, as a key objective of the teaching process (Bouman, 1991). Political theorists observe that in order for democratic institutions to be healthy, individual citizens must develop the power to define and address their own needs (Lappé and DuBois, 1994). Public health professionals document the importance in treating serious illness of fostering empathetic recognition through patient support groups (Spiegel, 1993). Social theorists argue that recognition and empathy in everyday life are crucial in maintaining healthy social institutions (Kohn, 1990; Bellah and others, 1991; Scheff, 1990). In sum, there is widespread acknowledgment across many fields that empowerment and recognition are concrete and important objectives. This acknowledgment reinforces our suggestion that they deserve greater attention in the mediation process, where there are such rich opportunities to achieve them.

The Processes of Empowerment and Recognition: An Overview of Transformative Mediation

Thus far, we have looked at empowerment and recognition as objectives; now we look briefly at empowerment and recognition as processes that transformative mediators employ to achieve these objectives. Transformative mediation practice can be captured by reference to three overall patterns of mediator conduct, each of which contrasts with one of the patterns of problem-solving mediation we described in Chapter Three. First, mediators adopt a microfocus, concentrating on the presentation of the conflict by the parties that takes place in the mediation session itself. Second, mediators take conscious steps to encourage parties to engage in deliberation and choice making. Third, mediators consciously invite and help the parties to consider each other's perspectives. We will briefly discuss each of these patterns, noting how they contrast with those of problem-solving practice.

Microfocusing on Parties' Contributions

In a transformative approach, mediators focus, from the very outset of a session, on the details of how the case unfolds before them. They scrutinize parties' individual moves—their statements, challenges, questions, narratives—for the possibilities each affords for transformative opportunities. Disputants' individual moves and exchanges are seen as significant in themselves, because they are the places where mediators can locate opportunities for empowerment and recognition that are presented by the parties' conflict. Mediators look for points where choices arise that the parties can be empowered to make, and they search for openings that afford disputants the chance to give recognition by acknowledging each other's perspectives. In general, mediators enter the session looking for, and expecting to find and capture, myriad opportunities for empowerment and recognition as the case unfolds in front of them. This "microfocus" is in sharp contrast to the more global or "macro"-outlook adopted within the problem-solving approach, in which mediators try to reach global assessments about the definition of the parties' problem and view all the parties' contributions in terms of inputs into this global problem-assessment effort.

Encouraging Parties' Deliberation and Choice Making

In keeping empowerment central in the process, mediators employing a transformative approach try to clarify parties' available choices at all key junctures and encourage parties to reflect and deliberate with full awareness of their options, goals, and resources. The parties' goals and choices are treated as central at all levels of decision making. Mediators consciously try to avoid shaping issues, proposals, or terms for settlement, or even pushing for the achievement of settlement at all. Instead, they encourage parties to define problems and find solutions for themselves, and they endorse and support the parties' own efforts to do so. This characteristic also stands in sharp contrast to problem-solving mediation, in which mediators' directiveness and influence over parties' decision-making and settlement terms is widely documented.

Encouraging Perspective Taking

In keeping recognition central, mediators actively explore each party's statements for openings that allow one party to consider the other's situation or self. Starting with parties' opening narratives, mediators look for places that would allow each party to consider the other's point of view. Mediation becomes less future oriented than in the problem-solving approach, since past events can be as important as future choices in offering opportunities for recognition. To aid perspective taking, mediators reinterpret, translate, and reframe parties' statements—not to shape issues or solutions but to help make each party more intelligible to the other. They then ask parties to consider the significance of such reformulations, pointing out opportunities for recognition without forcing them. Instead of dropping relational issues, mediators mine them for recognition opportunities. As a result, settlement terms can include a broader range of accomplishments than those in problem-solving agreements, such as statements of misunderstandings that were removed or more positive views of the other party that were developed.

Different Patterns and Different "Maps"

Each of these major patterns of the transformative approach to mediation practice will be explored in greater depth and with specific case examples in Chapters Five and Six. What is evident here is that as a matter of practice the approach directly reflects the transformative orientation—by viewing a conflict as a field full of opportunities for empowerment and recognition, and then concentrating on helping the parties take greatest possible advantage of those opportunities.

In practice, empowerment and recognition are often interdependent and reinforcing. That is, as a result of the mediator's helping one party to be more empowered, that party may become more able and willing to give recognition to the other, because it is easier to consider the other's situation when we feel less desperate about our own. Similarly, as a result of the mediator's helping one party to give recognition, the other party may be empowered, because it is validating and empowering to get recognition. Thus there can be a symbiotic relationship between empowerment and recognition in practice, with each aiding in achieving the other, and a sensitive practitioner can take advantage of this to build a momentum in the mediation session that maximizes achievement of both objectives.

This overview gives some idea of what transformative mediation looks like and how different it is from the problem-solving approach. One good way of summarizing the picture, and the contrast, is to imagine the general expectations with which a mediator comes to a mediation session, under each approach. Of course, every case has its own unique twists and turns. But practitioners know that there are common patterns in the way cases flow and unfold in mediation sessions. Based on their sense of those patterns, mediators carry an internal "map" that gives them a sense of familiarity with the general terrain and the direction they are going, even if the details are new each time they travel the road.

The problem-solving mediator comes to a session ready to hear a barrage of factual and emotional information, which can be sorted and organized into negotiable issues that are parts of a problem faced by the parties. The mediator expects that, once this information is organized, options can be found or constructed that will address the various issues, and the options can be considered and rated by the parties as more or less desirable. Eventually, after some attempts at persuasion on the mediator's part to "generate movement" by each party, the disputants will either reach an agreement that solves the problem or get stuck at an impasse. Despite great differences in the particulars, the problem-solving mediator knows that this is how any case will generally unfold—from opening, to information, to organization and definition of issues, to search for options, to persuasion and movement, to agreement or impasse (see Stulberg, 1987; Folberg and Taylor, 1984).

The "map" carried by the transformative mediator is very different. This practitioner comes to the session ready to witness an intense interaction and exchange between the parties that, because it involves difficulties faced by each party as well as hostile perceptions of each by the other, is filled with myriad opportunities for empowerment and recognition. The mediator expects that those opportunities will begin to present themselves right from the start of the session and that he or she must be ready to seize them and work with them as they come up. The mediator has a certain idea of the kinds of interactive patterns that may give rise to empowerment and recognition opportunities and how early or late in the session they might occur. Still, there is no firm rule of order in this regard.

The transformative mediator also expects that a certain cycling back and forth between empowerment and recognition will take place because each to some extent sets up and flows from the other. However, the mediator is also aware that parties may resist responding to both empowerment and, especially, recognition opportunities. Finally, he or she expects that, at some point in the session, the opportunities for empowerment and recognition will be exhausted, and the session will end. Sometimes, in the process, a settlement will have been reached and sometimes not, according to the decisions made by the parties. Either way, the parties will have changed and grown to some degree.

These two "maps" of how mediation unfolds look very different because the objectives and purposes of transformative mediation, when put into practice, lead to considerable differences in the practitioner's approach and conduct. The differences between problem-solving and transformative mediation are not simply at the conceptual level. Rather, the important conceptual differences between the two lead to major differences in the way mediation is actually practiced.

Solving the Problems of Problem Solving

Adopting the transformative approach to mediation holds several important advantages. Some of them relate to the issues of directiveness and mediator influence, as difficulties with problem-solving mediation; and some of them go beyond these issues to the question of ultimate purpose and values.

Recall the difficulties with mediator influence. Mediators, as intervenors in conflict, necessarily carry their own interest with them. In problem-solving mediation, given the underlying view of conflict and resolution, the mediator's interest is in finding a good solution to a problem that is blocking the parties' satisfaction. This interest leads mediators to be directive in shaping both problems and solutions, and they wind up influencing the outcome of mediations in favor of settlement generally and in favor of terms of settlement that comport with their views of fairness, optimality, and so forth. But such influence threatens the core objective of satisfaction itself, since it often produces settlements that do not satisfy anyone.

From within the problem-solving orientation, this problem appears unsolvable. But changing orientation and adopting a transformative approach to mediation produces a solution. It does so not by eliminating the tendency for mediators to influence (which is impossible, given the real dynamics of third-party intervention in conflict) but by changing the nature of the influence. In the transformative orientation, mediators simply have no incentive to influence *outcome*, in any way whatsoever. Reaching settlement, or any particular terms of settlement, is not something that *matters* to the mediator, because it is not a direct objective of his or her intervention into the conflict. Instead, the mediator's interest is not an interest in outcome at all, but an interest in *making sure that the outcome remains in the parties' hands*, in a very explicit way. This is the mediator's interest because, given the underlying view of conflict and resolution, this is a central objective of the intervention. In effect, what happens to the influence problem in the transformative approach is that the inevitable tendency to influence is *channeled* in such a way that it becomes harmless. On the contrary, it is enlisted in a valuable service—empowerment.

As a consequence, adopting the transformative orientation produces a new and more realistic definition of "neutrality" in the mediator's role. Recent critics have noted that claims of "neutrality" by mediators are dubious, given the evidence and apparent inevitability of mediator influence on outcome (Cobb, 1991). But many suggest that, rather than abandon the whole concept, what is needed is a new conception of neutrality that makes sense given the reality of mediator influence. Still, no one has articulated such a conception, because it cannot be done from within the problem-solving orientation.

Shifting to a transformative orientation, however, opens up the possibility of a new conception of neutrality. The meaning of mediator neutrality, in the context of inevitable influence, is *commitment to use influence only for the sake of keeping the ultimate decision on outcome in the parties' hands*. Neutrality means that the mediator's only interest is the interest in using his or her influence to make sure that *the parties maintain control* of decisions about outcome. This type of interest is not neutral in the sense of noninfluential. It is influential. But it is influential in one way only, and that is a way that does not attempt to influence outcome, whether through shaping how the conflict is framed or by directing how the issues that get framed are decided. As a result, the mediator stands a very good chance of *not* indeed influencing outcome in these ways. We suggest that this is a very useful—and realistic—conception of mediator neutrality. By adopting the transformative approach, the mediation movement gains a solution to the problem of the inevitability of influence, and a new and meaningful conception of mediator neutrality emerges.

In addition, adopting the transformative approach produces a greater likelihood that, when settlements are reached, they will be settlements that serve the parties' interests rather than the mediator's. That is, when reached through a transformative approach, settlements are more likely to actually satisfy both parties rather than satisfy neither or satisfy one at the expense of the other. The latter effects are what the problem-solving approach tends to produce—despite its stated goal of party satisfaction—because the mediator's outcome-related interest enters and distorts the discussion.

Under a transformative approach, by contrast, the parties themselves make outcome-related decisions *without* mediator influence on the content of the decisions themselves. And the parties are unlikely, especially with the mediator monitoring their decision-making process for empowerment, to make agreements that do not truly satisfy them (within whatever external constraints they face). In other words, adoption of a transformative approach eliminates the problem of "illusory settlements" (which satisfy no one) and "unjust settlements" (which satisfy one party at the expense of the other), because it empowers both parties to decide for themselves whether and on what terms to settle.

At the same time, the transformative approach produces the likelihood that, although the mediator does not focus on this objective (and perhaps *because* he or she does not focus on it), mutually satisfying settlements are going to occur anyway, wherever they are really possible. That is, *a transformative approach does not disregard the value of settlement*. It simply acknowledges that even if settlement is important, there is no effective way to approach it directly without creating the risk of doing more harm than good. As discussed earlier, seeking settlement directly, as the problem-solving approach tries to do, leads mediators to become overdirective and, as a result, undermines the value of settlement itself—satisfaction.

The transformative approach, through empowerment, avoids illusory or unfair settlements, but it also facilitates genuine and balanced settlements. To put it differently, wherever the possibility exists for a genuine settlement, empowerment and recognition, if practiced effectively, are likely to bring it about. When no settlement is reached, it is because no settlement is truly acceptable to both parties; in that case, no settlement is desirable. Therefore, despite first impressions, the transformative approach does not ignore the settlement objective. Rather, it provides a different way of meeting that objective, and one that does not work against its own ends.

In all these ways, adopting the transformative approach to mediation would help solve the problems of problem solving: by offering a solution to the problem of mediator influence; by articulating a new conception of neutrality; by providing a way of avoiding illusory and unjust settlements while capturing genuine and balanced ones. Yet, though these are major advantages, none describes the strongest reason for adopting the transformative approach. Its greatest strength is that it opens up the possibility and the real likelihood of accomplishing a profoundly important objective that the problem-solving approach does not consider: capturing the priceless opportunities for moral growth that are inherent in conflicts between human beings.

Through concentrating on empowerment and recognition and on moral transformation as an ultimate purpose, transformative mediation directly pursues and captures those opportunities. Because of the value we see in that accomplishment, this remains for us the most compelling reason for making the transformative approach central to mediation practice. This is especially so because, while transformative mediation effectively, if indirectly, achieves the objective of satisfactory settlement, the converse is not true. Problem-solving mediation, as recent research demonstrates, rarely if ever achieves the objectives of empowerment and recognition. Thus, a shift to the transformative approach means losing nothing while gaining something of immense value. For this reason, transformative mediation presents not just a different approach to practice but a sounder and more fruitful one.

Different Elements or Different Approaches?

For some who are attracted by the vision of transformative mediation presented here, the natural response may be to look for ways to achieve an integration of the two approaches, for example, by adding to the problem-solving approach an emphasis on empowerment and recognition. It might appear that there is no inherent obstacle to doing this, no inherent contradiction between the two approaches. In this view, the transformative dimensions of mediation can help strengthen current practice, but they do not suggest or support a discrete new approach to mediation or necessitate a choice between two distinct approaches.

While some may take this view, there are good reasons to believe that it is mistaken and that the transformative and problem-solving approaches are fundamentally distinct and inconsistent, especially at the level of concrete practice. To begin with, although individual mediators certainly vary, problem-solving practice in general presents a very different picture from the transformative approach. That picture, as documented and analyzed in Chapter Three, is one of directive, settlement-oriented practice that focuses on defining problems and producing solutions, without much regard for either empowerment or recognition. Moreover, this picture is not the result of the deficiencies of individual mediators. It is *the approach itself*, and especially its conception of mediation's aims, that lead mediators to be directive and solution focused in practice. Thus the internal logic of the problem-solving approach makes it difficult to integrate transformative practices into it, because those practices are tied to an entirely different view of mediation's ultimate purpose.

Indeed, the minority of mediators who currently avoid the pit-falls of the problem-solving approach do so because they *depart* from this approach and actually practice a form of transformative medi-ation, even if only intuitively. That is, implicitly valuing transfor-mative objectives above solving problems per se, they move toward a transformative approach, focusing more on empowerment (and sometimes recognition) and less on finding solutions to problems. Doing so both safeguards them from the pitfalls of problem solving and also helps them achieve transformative effects in their cases. However, these mediators' achievements do not mean that elements of transformative mediation can be integrated with a problem-solving approach, and they do not represent such an integration. Rather, the essential step that these mediators take to attain their results is shifting their view of ultimate objectives, putting trans-formation first and not focusing directly on problem solving and sat-isfaction. This is not an integration of transformative elements with problem solving. It is the adoption, however intuitively, of a differ-ent, transformative approach, driven by a different view of ultimate objectives.

By contrast, integrating the two approaches presents enormous practical and conceptual difficulties. From the earlier discussion of the three major patterns of practice in each approach, it should be evident that the core practices of each are inconsistent: it would be effectively impossible for mediators to employ both sets of prac-tices together. For example, if the mediator takes a macrofocus, con-centrating on the parties' *situation* in order to grasp the nature of the problem and possible solutions, this will work against taking a micro-focus and concentrating on the parties' *interaction* in order to spot opportunities for empowerment and recognition. The reverse is also true. In practice, adopting one type of focus necessarily means ignor-ing the other, so they cannot be integrated effectively. Similarly, if the mediator steers away from intangible relationship concerns and emphasizes the future in order to work towards a concrete settle-ment, this will work against exploring the parties' perceptions of each other's past conduct in order to surface opportunities for recognition. Again, taking one approach means doing the very opposite of what is called for in the other.

At a more general level, because the objectives of the two approaches are so different, it is very hard in practice to keep both in equal focus, and one or the other inevitably winds up being given short shrift. For example, when mediators try to add empowerment and recognition to a problem-solving approach, they may attempt to foster these objectives as a session unfolds; but they will usually abandon them and move to a more directive approach if this is necessary to achieve a settlement or to ensure that the settlement is fair and optimal.

To suggest an analogy, switching from transformative to problem-solving mediation in the course of a session is somewhat like a decision-making group switching from consensus to voting during the course of a discussion. This happens in some groups when members test for consensus on an agenda item and, if it is not achieved, rely on majority vote to settle the issue. If a group is dedicated to consensus—to preserving group unity and truly valuing the concerns and objections of every member regardless of how tough the issue—then leaving an escape valve (a vote) is inconsistent with the fundamental goals of consensus. Although good decisions may still get made and the voting process may be democratic, the group knows it is not using consensus and gaining the advantages that a consensus process offers.

Similarly, when empowerment is difficult or recognition fails, switching to the directive moves of the problem-solving approach may produce a settlement, but the value of transformation has not been achieved. In the end, the two approaches have not been integrated. Nor can they be. To create the alternative vision of practice described in this book, mediators need to adopt the transformative vision as a whole and not abandon it when the going gets tough. This means seeing empowerment and recognition as central objectives in a distinct and altogether different approach to mediation practice.

Rather than looking for ways to integrate the two approaches, mediators may find it more realistic and helpful to view them in a developmental perspective, seeing the transformative approach as distinct from but continuing a direction begun by the problem-solving approach. This view maintains that the distinctions in conceptions of purpose and in practice are real, and yet it acknowledges that the problem-solving approach as a whole *is*, in a larger sense, a move toward the transformative view.

Chapter Three described the distributive orientation to conflict. In relation to that framework, and dispute resolution processes like adjudication and arbitration that are based on it, problem-solving mediation does represent a partial move toward a different approach to dealing with conflict. Indeed, its departure from the distributive orientation is certainly one of the things that has made problem-solving mediation so appealing. And to some degree, problem solving represents not only a shift away from the distributive orientation but a shift toward a transformative one. All of this must be recognized and appreciated, and perhaps seen as part of a continuing evolution of conflict resolution institutions.

Nevertheless, problem-solving mediation does not—and cannot—reach the same destination as the transformative approach, because although it is a move away from the distributive view, it is only a partial move. It is a move from win-lose to win-win, which is certainly a major change. But problem solving remains within a framework that sees conflict as concerned with winning or losing rather than something entirely different—*growing*. Perhaps this explains why the transformative dimension of practice has not been articulated more clearly in the literature of the field to date. The transformative dimension *cannot* really be articulated clearly or consistently put into practice without leaving the framework of problem solving altogether.

The picture of the transformative approach presented here tries to go beyond that framework and to articulate the intuitions of many about what an alternative and more fruitful approach to mediation looks like. As clarified here, the approach we are setting forth *is* indeed such an alternative. By describing that approach fully enough that others can refine, study, and follow it, a first step is taken toward putting a different picture of the mediation movement into practice.

5

Rethinking the Process:
A Case Example of
How Mediation Might Work

In constructing a different approach to mediation practice, moving from the general picture to the details of actual practice is an essential step. But it is not an easy one, partially because good examples of transformative practice are hard to find. We were not surprised to find that virtually no case studies in the literature, across divorce, community, labor, and business settings, are offered as concrete illustrations of transformative mediation. However, in many published accounts of mediation cases, the transformative routes mediators *could have taken*—the opportunities for fostering empowerment and recognition—were readily apparent. There were places in the move-by-move descriptions of unfolding sessions where mediators could have made alternative choices—phrased comments differently, helped parties explore each other's outlooks and build their own capacities for handling problems. In short, mediators and disputants in these cases had many opportunities before them to pursue conflicts transformatively, opportunities that were most often ignored or overlooked. So even though the existing case study literature does little to provide positive examples of transformative mediation in practice, it does present cases that allow us to describe clearly and in detail how transformative mediation *might* be practiced. The result is quite useful in adding detail to the picture of the transformative approach.

We will discuss one of these cases in depth in this chapter. The case, published by William Felstiner and Lynne Williams in 1978 in *Law and Human Behavior,* is entitled "The Case of the Adjacent Gardens." We have chosen this particular case because in some ways, it provides a revealing comparison with the Sensitive Bully case we described in Chapter One. The Adjacent Gardens case also involves a neighbor dispute and centers around charges and fears of violence. Unlike the Sensitive Bully case, however, the Adjacent Gardens mediation illustrates how transformative possibilities can be left untapped by disputants and mediators.

We will present the case as it was originally summarized by Felstiner and Williams. We have broken their summary of the case into a series of ten short segments and have underlined those parts of each segment that will be the focus of our analysis. After each segment, we offer an analysis of the major moves that were made by the mediator in the segment. In this analysis we first comment on what the mediators did in particular moves they made, explaining why, for the most part, these moves are not transformative. We then offer an alternative approach that could have been taken for each move. These alternatives comprise the transformative route through this dispute and exemplify the details of the transformative approach to practice. Table 5.1 summarizes the mediator's moves that are described and analyzed here.

Table 5.1. Mediator's Moves in The Adjacent Gardens Case: Missing Opportunities for Empowerment and Recognition.

Move 1	Removing a Procedural Decision from the Parties' Hands
Move 2	Defining Mediation as Getting Agreement
Move 3	Ignoring an Assertion That Agreement Already Exists
Move 4	Allowing Parties to Think That Mediation Is Adjudicative
Move 5	Refusing to Share Control of the Agenda with the Parties
Move 6	Overlooking the Potential for Recognition in an Apology
Move 7	Overlooking an Opportunity for Recognition in Response to a Description of Self
Move 8	Missing Possible Grounds for Recognition in a Caucus
Move 9	Failing to Pursue Issues a Party Raises
Move 10	Planning to Pursue the Mediators' Definition of the Problem
Move 11	Missing Possible Grounds for Recognition in a Caucus
Move 12	Suggesting Unprompted Terms for the Agreement

The Adjacent Gardens Case

SEGMENT 1

C (complainant), a black woman in her 40's or 50's, had complained to the police that R (respondent), a white man about 30, had threatened her and had fired a gun as a threat. When the police arrived, they were unable to find a gun and told C to file a complaint in court. She did, and when the case came before the judge he referred it to mediation. Two younger sisters of C, W1 (witness 1) and W2 (witness 2), were present at the mediation, as was W3 (witness 3), the boyfriend of W2 and the owner of the land adjacent to the house in which R lived. W3 was black, in his 40's and from Barbados. The mediators were Mf (mediator female), a black woman, and Mm (mediator male), a black man, both in their 20's. Before the session began the mediators were informed by project staff that R did not want W1, W2, and W3 to be present in the hearing room. The witnesses and C were arguing that they should attend the hearing since they were concerned with the dispute as neighbors of R, because W3 owned the property on which the alleged shooting took place, and because W1 was with C when the incident occurred. The mediators did not discuss this question, and ushered everyone into the mediation room.

Move 1: Removing a Procedural Decision from the Parties' Hands

Comment: Even before addressing any substantive issue, the mediators had to address a procedural concern: Who should participate in the session? The mediators knew that R objected to allowing the witnesses to participate, but this concern was never put to the parties. The mediators chose instead to avoid discussing this issue with the parties and decided for themselves to allow the witnesses to attend. This move fails to empower and in fact disempowers the parties. An expectation is established at the outset that the mediators, alone, decide whose information is relevant to the case.

Alternative: To foster empowerment, the mediators could allow the parties themselves to address the issue. To do this, the mediators would have to accept the possibility of several potentially troubling outcomes, including a considerably longer session, a delay in addressing substantive issues, and termination of the mediation if the participation issue is not resolved. But in giving the issue to the parties, the mediators would acknowledge R's potential discomfort with the situation and open up the possibility for a decision on this point that is acceptable to all, thereby empowering the parties from the first move in the session.

To be more specific, the mediator could address the issue by saying, "Before we begin, we understand that there is a disagreement about who should attend the session. Please give us a chance to explain to all of you what this process is all about. Then the very first thing we are going to deal with is who should attend the meeting. So don't think we are not going to get to that, but in order for it to make sense to talk about that, let us first explain what the process is about. Then we'll discuss who should attend, so that you can decide on that."

After giving the opening statement describing the mediation process, the mediator could then return to the participation issue, saying, "This is your problem. It is up to you to decide who should be here. Can each of the disputing parties describe how they see this issue? First, C, please give us your feelings."

Obviously, any number of outcomes might ultimately result. R might accept the witnesses' participation or agree that witnesses can stay but only the parties would be allowed to talk. Or the witnesses might leave at first and come back later in the session, perhaps during caucus. Or, it may be that the parties ultimately fail to agree on the issue altogether. If the mediator has clarified what the consequences of not proceeding with the session will be, and if the parties still disagree on this participation issue, then the mediator would end the session. Any of these outcomes would produce empowerment.

SEGMENT 2

At 10:30 A.M. all the parties were ushered into the hearing room. R made it difficult for the mediators to present the standard introduction. Mf's efforts to explain mediation were interrupted by R's aggressive declaration that "You are the judges, they (pointing to C and the witnesses) are the Union and I am the arbitrator" and "Mediation is the second-hand thing to the loser. . . . I'd win in court. . . . I've done everything I can. . . . I can't do any more." When Mf said that mediation helps people reach an agreement in an unhappy situation, R said that he and C had already reached an agreement, and that is why he wanted to talk to C along with W3 who had previously upset matters in court by raising an old incident about his, W3's, dog. At this point the session became chaotic. Mf, C, R, and W3 were all talking at once. Mf tried to avoid the old incident by sticking to the current charge. C was saying that the relevant charge was the one she wrote, not W3's complaint. W3 was accusing R of growing and smoking marijuana. R was asking about the assault and battery charge (which he never got a chance to pursue), declaring his fear that W3 would sabotage peace efforts between him and C and asserting that: "I could stop this any time. I could beat it in court. I don't want to."

Move 2: Defining Mediation as Getting Agreement

Comment: In response to R's interruptions during the mediator's opening statement, the mediator says that "mediation helps people reach an agreement in an unhappy situation." From a transformative viewpoint, this is a misleading explanation of the mediation process. The entire focus in the mediator's comment is on the goal of reaching agreement, with no reference to empowerment or recognition. Moreover, this statement leaves in place the disputants' perception that mediators act as judges, a perception that was reinforced by the way the participation issue was handled earlier.

Alternative: The mediator could attempt to correct the misperception that mediators act as judges, could clarify that the parties create their own agreements, and could do so in a way that puts reaching agreement and not reaching agreement on equal footing as options. More generally, the mediator could explain mediation in terms of empowerment and recognition.

For instance, the mediator could have said, "I'm not the judge. I don't want you to have that mistaken idea. It is not my job to render a decision or make an agreement for you. Mediation is not like going to court. What mediation does, and what I can do, is help you understand the situation—and each other—better, and help you decide how you want to handle the situation. You really have to be the ones to work out a solution and to decide if you even want to. I can help you decide what you want to do—whether you want to reach some kind of agreement here, and if so what kind, or whether you want to do something else. But I want to make it clear that I do not make that decision, you do."

This alternative move also points up that transformative mediation requires an opening statement from the mediator that avoids focusing on reaching settlement as the primary or only goal of the session. In the transformative approach, mediators have to give an opening statement that makes empowerment and recognition, explained in simple language, the goals, with settlement as one possible outcome.

Move 3: Ignoring an Assertion That Agreement Already Exists

Comment: R claims that an agreement has already been reached. Neither mediator checks to see whether C feels the same way. Rather, the mediators assume that there is no preliminary agreement between the parties.

Alternative: The parties could have been allowed to decide whether there is still a dispute to be discussed and thus a need for the mediation. The mediator could have said, "If you both have reached an agreement, we may not need to go through the whole process. C, what do you think about what R has just said?"

Note that our discussion of these first three moves indicates that empowerment is not limited to giving the parties control over outcomes. It includes giving disputants control over process issues (such as, who will attend the session, what issues will be discussed). Since empowerment includes developing the capacity to handle disputes on one's own in the future, these kinds of moves are important. If mediators simply run the process entirely, without explaining it or involving the disputing parties, opportunities for this type of empowerment are easily lost.

SEGMENT 3

Mm tried to restore order, to give Mf a chance to explain the process. R would not be quiet. He asserted: "I'm on the offensive. . . . I have to be on the offensive. . . . Anything taken down can be held against you. . . . You're a spanker, a naughty kid has to be spanked. . . . I'm looking at the legal aspects . . . the humanitarian aspects. . . . I must be on the offensive even if it was accidental. . . . I'll win in court cause there is no case, no proof." R then subsided a little. Mf doggedly went on with the introduction. She met R's interruptions directly and finally finished. What normally takes 3 or 4 minutes had taken 10.

At last, C was asked to explain what had happened. She said that she was working in her garden with W1. The garden is on W3's land which sits directly behind R's garden. C does not live on this block, but comes there often because W2, who apparently lives with W1 and W3, looks after C's children while she is at work. C and

W1 heard a bang, a shot, and saw R walk into his house with a gun in his hand. A few minutes later, they heard a second shot. R and his wife were then on their porch. C and W1 then left to call the police.

W1 told roughly the same story. C and W1 said there were no prior incidents with R. R interrupted to say that the prior incidents had been with W3. R said W3 should talk about these incidents. Both mediators said no, let's deal with this matter first. Mf then asked R to speak.

Move 4: Allowing Parties to Think That Mediation Is Adjudicative

Comment: In response to R's continued interruptions, the mediator tries to restore necessary order and continues with the introduction. Although completing the introduction is important, R's outburst indicates that he still sees mediation as an adjudicative hearing—a view that has probably been reinforced by several of the mediators' moves already discussed. The mediators do nothing to correct this misunderstanding.

Alternative: The mediators could take time to establish the fundamental difference between adjudicative hearings and mediation, in similar fashion to that already suggested. Disputants often need repeated explanations of the purpose of mediation and the nonadjudicative role of the mediator, because they frequently enter the process expecting judgments or decisions from the mediator. Without overturning this expectation, accomplishing empowerment is impossible.

Move 5: Refusing to Share Control of the Agenda with the Parties

Comment: The mediator allows W1 to speak. Then, when R interrupts to ask that W3 be allowed to talk about "prior incidents," both mediators insist on keeping the focus on the first issue. At this point the mediator limits the agenda (or at least the order of discussion), despite R's desire to add (and put first) another issue. Even if the mediator's comments are aimed at keeping the process orderly, saying "no" to R's request without adequate explanation is disempowering, and fails to uncover the problem that matters most to him.

Alternative: The mediator could help the parties stay on track while not disempowering R. For example, the mediator could say to R, "I understand that you are concerned about some other incidents that you see as related to the present matter. You will certainly have a chance to bring those up here. But in order for us to be able to help all of you clarify your concerns and look for ways of addressing them, we find that the most effective thing is to work on just one thing at a time. So, R, would you be willing to stick for now with discussing the present matter that C has been talking about?"

This move would explain the reason for keeping the discussion orderly, which is itself empowering. Moreover, this move would give R the chance to decide whether to accept the process advice. If, after hearing this advice, R still wants to place the other incident on the table, the mediators could allow this to occur. Such a move would be expedient as well as empowering, because it is unlikely that progress can be made on the first issue if R is adamant about addressing a different one. Most important, however, this would put R in the decision-making position, which is a central part of empowerment.

SEGMENT 4

R's recital was confusing. He denied he had shot a gun at C, but "a firearm was discharged at the dog." He spoke at length about the difference between a human being and a dog, a "mere beast," with "no brain, no sympathy, can't relate like a human being, a dog has no constitutional rights." Mm asked R to be clear. R said he had no intent to hurt C or the children. But a dog is different. He said there was a third party involved. He heard a bang, but he is not an expert. He can't tell the difference between a firearm and a firecracker. Kids let off fire-crackers all the time. On the 4th of July. He then said that because this recommendation is going to the judge, he had to be on the offensive. He referred to the incident as an accident, that he was sorry and that it would not hap-pen again. R agreed that he would be willing "to write that." C would also; R then asked: "But what about him?" pointing to W3.

Move 6: Overlooking the Potential for Recognition in an Apology

Comment: R's statement that "the incident was an accident, that he was sorry and that it would not happen again" is a clear opportunity for evoking recognition, probably on both sides. Yet, despite R's clear admission and apology, the mediators do nothing to explore and capture this potential recognition. Although R indicates that the apology could be put in writing, it is dropped at this point and never becomes part of the final agreement.

Alternative: The mediator could foster recognition by framing the exchange and stating, "Let's get to W3 in a minute, but before we do, let's understand if we're hearing you right. It seems by the apology you are offering that you (R) understand that the incident was distressing to C and understand to some extent how C feels. C, do you see that R is saying this? Based on this understanding, where do you want to go with this? You said, R, that you wanted to write this apology. Would that be helpful to you C? Should we work on the wording of that for the agreement? Can we do anything else based on this understanding between you?"

Comments along these lines capitalize on a moment of recognition by framing it—marking that it occurred and giving the parties the chance to decide whether they want to do anything with it. This may lead to something further, or it may just stand on its own.

Either way, the key transformative move illustrated here is *framing* a statement that gives recognition—here, an apology. By doing so, the mediator helps the party giving recognition to do so consciously and to go as far as they are willing in expressing it to the other. This is what expresses the transformation embodied in giving recognition, and it is up to the mediator to help the parties experience it as fully as possible. Unless such recognition-giving statements are highlighted for the parties, they can easily be lost in the rush of the session.

SEGMENT 5

W3 now reported that during the previous year R had become angry at W3's dog, showed W3 a gun and said that if the dog did not stay away from him and his children he'd shoot it. W3 then described the shooting incident. He added there "was something else." A week after the shooting a cab belonging to a friend of R's blocked W3's driveway. A gang of R's friends were drinking there at the same time. W3 accused R of bringing his friends there "to start a riot."

R told his version of the driveway incident. Earlier in the evening R had become angry at the dog. A friend of W3's had then jumped over the fence, told R's wife that he was going to blow R's head off and showed her his gun. After this threat, R asked some friends from a veterans' club to come over with some beers. The cab driver was one of those friends. When Mf noted that the purpose of mediation was to see that these incidents did not happen again, R said: "This is my problem—I was in Vietnam at 18." He noted that he sees a psychiatrist every week, that men come back from Vietnam with no jobs, no home, "no one to relate to . . . simulate [sic] themselves." C accused R of being childish and W3 criticized him for using the psychiatrist as an excuse for his behavior. The mediators then broke through and said they were going to caucus [recess to discuss the case by themselves].

Mm began by interpreting R's circumlocutions about the gun. Since the police did not find the gun, R believes he can beat any gun charge in court. Thus, although he does not deny that he fired a gun, he will not admit it for fear that mediation will break down and he would be confronted with an admission in court. Mm then said that the dog is at the root of the problem; they must "remove" the annoyance of the dog.

R was asked back for a solo session (party caucus). Mf immediately asked him about the dog.

Move 7: Overlooking an Opportunity for Recognition in Response to a Description of Self

Comment: R's description of himself, as a Vietnam vet who had severe adjustment problems, is a clear opening for recognition. R is asking to be seen in a certain light. It is his first direct statement about who he is and why he lost control during the dog incident. He is trying to explain himself and in so doing is asking for recognition. This bid for recognition is rejected by C and W3; and it is ignored by the mediators, both when they discuss the case by themselves and when they subsequently caucus with R and focus on what to do about the dog. A potentially important opportunity for recognition is missed.

Alternative: The mediators could act to help C and W3 hear, and thus give them a better opportunity to respond to, R's plea for recognition. For example, the mediators could caucus with C and W3 instead of R. They could focus on what has just been said in joint session, "translating" it for C and W3 into more "recognizable" terms. One approach could be to say, "You know, what R was saying about the driveway incident and his being in Vietnam—I understand you saw that as being not really to the point or as some kind of excuse. I can understand why you took it that way but it might be heard somewhat differently. Perhaps R was admitting that he felt out of control or threatened in the driveway incident and reacted as he might have in a situation in Vietnam by calling on his buddies. He was saying that he really hasn't learned how to make the transition to life back here. You know a lot of vets have had that problem so it could be possible in his case. In other words, maybe he was trying to explain how he felt and how it happened, but not really denying what happened or excusing himself for it. Do you think this is one possible way of understanding what R was saying?"

This alternative move serves two functions. First, it offers C a safe and private opportunity to think about acknowledging R and his situation. If C takes this opportunity, it begins a process of recognition that could be extended into the joint session at some point. But even if nothing is said explicitly in joint session, C has given recognition to R in some degree, by considering R's perspective, and possibly also acknowledging it to the mediator, in caucus. Second, in offering an alternative translation of R's statement, the move is empowering to C, in an educative sense. It is a clear demonstration of a skill—the ability to construct and consider alternative interpretations of the same behavior or statement—that is often useful in conflict and that C can carry out of the session, no matter what the outcome of this particular dispute.

The general point is that, in transformative practice, the mediator looks for statements by each party that can be used to evoke recognition from the other—implicit or explicit appeals or bids for recognition—and then helps "translate" them to the other party in terms they can relate to, so as to present that party with the chance to respond and give recognition. These statements come in many guises, including, as here, the direct appeal, but also including others, such as statements of positions, arguments, and so forth.

Another way of describing this move of "translation" is to look at it as "reinterpretation": Whenever the opportunity arises, the transformative mediator offers parties the opportunity to reinterpret statements or past behaviors of the other party in a more positive light, in view of information and explanations offered by that party in the mediation. If accepted by the listening party, the reinterpretation is itself one form of giving recognition to the speaking party.

Whether described as translation or reinterpretation, this move is fundamental to the recognition objective and can be repeated often in a mediation, as illustrated in the next segment.

SEGMENT 6

[Caucus with R continues] R said that last year the dog had bitten his daughter through the garden fence. R told W3 that if it happened again "the dog would die." He then related the current incident about the dog. R was returning from dinner at a local restaurant with his family. He raced an older daughter home while carrying a smaller child. When he ran past W3's fence, the dog jumped up, startled him and caused him to drop the baby, which he caught in time. He was very angry, swore at the dog, called it "a black son of a bitch," pointing out that the dog happens to be black all over. Then there was "the discharging of firearms," but at the dog (presumably in the direction of, or to frighten, the dog), not at human beings. R said he was jumpy these days because he had been shot "in three places" in another part of town a year before. The mediators then explored with R the conditions of the dog's confinement and whether it was necessary for him to pass by the yard in which the dog was kept. These issues were not clarified very well. R said he would not fire the gun again. He then explained how the gun (which he spoke about obliquely as if its existence were still in question) had been dismantled, partly buried and partly thrown out with the garbage. He was very sorry about it. His wife does not want any guns in the house ever again.

Move 8: Missing Possible Grounds for Recognition in a Caucus

Comment: R is saying in effect, as he indicated earlier, that he is sorry for what happened, that he felt scared and threatened, and that he did not want to hurt anyone. He is asking to be seen, not as a violent or bad person, but as someone who made a mistake and wants to do the right thing. R's statements here both offer recognition *to* C and ask for recognition *from* C, in indirect fashion. The mediators largely ignore this entire dimension of what R is saying, continuing to focus (in segment 7) on the mechanics of separating R and the dog. They miss entirely the possibility presented here for encouraging greater recognition among the parties after the caucus with R.

Alternative: The mediators could emphasize the possible grounds for developing recognition that were implicit in R's comments. One approach would be to say, "You seem to be saying that you are really sorry about what happened, that you felt somewhat worried or threatened yourself in the situation and maybe got carried away, but that you certainly didn't and don't want anyone hurt. Is that close to what you're saying? If so, then let me say that I don't know if C and W3 really understand that so clearly. Would you be willing to say that to them again, in so many words, or maybe let me try to convey that to them? If it's put to them in the right way, I think they might understand, and it might help work things out. There doesn't seem to be much to lose by trying it. Is this something you would be comfortable with?" Even this much serves to help R express recognition for C's situation, as in the earlier move in connection with the apology. Beyond this, it opens up the possibility of working with C and W3, translating these comments of R to evoke recognition of R from them.

SEGMENT 7

[Caucus with R continues] <u>Mm asked what R thought could be done about the dog.</u> R suggested a shorter leash. If the dog worried him or his children again, he wouldn't shoot it; he would strangle it through the fence. After further inquiries about the physical layout, the discussion shifted to the cab and the "guys." R said that W3 had an unemployed friend who would sit around W3's place and who had threatened to blow R's head off after R had threatened the dog. After being told "I'll beat your white ass," R called his veteran friends "to show the power structure." They had a few beers and joints but made no threats. Mm tried to get R to say that he was making a show of force because he was expecting a "beef." Mm then switched back to the layout and R complained about the deterioration of the neighborhood and the fall in real estate values. R then began a speech about why he must be on the defensive, then the offensive, because the jails are full of people who are there by mistake. Mf cut him short and asked whether he wants the dog's leash shortened. R then said the leash should be taken away, that the dog should not be left out in all weather, that the dog is man's best friend, that it should be in the house.

Mf appeared exasperated. She asked whether R wanted anything else in the agreement. R said no, he did not feel this really was an agreement. Mf replied that he must feel he wanted an agreement. R then went off again. He said that if it is a question of feelings how do we know what people are feeling. Mf did not respond. R said that a fence is going to be built which will partly curtail the dog's running area. Mf then started to cross out the part of the agreement she had written about the dog. This session with R ended. It had lasted for 40 minutes.

Move 9: Failing to Pursue Issues a Party Raises

Comment: Despite the mediators' efforts to get R to talk about the dog and possible solutions to this "problem," R keeps raising other topics that seem important to him. R's comments about "the cab and the guys," the threat to "blow his head off," and the concern about jails being "full of people who are there by mistake" all reflect issues that R considers relevant and important in some sense. The mediators treat these comments as sidetracks, ignoring them or cutting them off, and instead focus on a solution to the "dog problem." Mf feels exasperated because R will not stick to one point. There is little attempt to figure out what issues R wants to address and help him get there.

One issue that was clearly of concern to R was the way these incidents, both past and present, escalated from minor clashes to major and potentially violent confrontations. R was clearly concerned about, and scared by, this escalation. And, although the dog was the flashpoint for these incidents, even its removal would not necessarily prevent other clashes from occurring and escalating.

R is also clearly concerned about whether he might go to jail on the gun charge. His apologies and explanations are directed toward this, and his comments about judges and jails show his level of concern. Recognizing this fear, and letting R know that it could probably be alleviated if concerns of the other party were met, would have been more empowering and responsive to R.

Alternative: In hearing R repeatedly interject other points into the dog issue, the mediators could respond by saying, "You know, it sounds to me like, even if the dog is one of your concerns, there are other things you want to talk about too. The firearms incident is one thing, and the interaction with W3's friend is another. Is that right? Because we can certainly deal with all these things, we just need to take them one at a time. I thought it might make sense to first look for ways of solving the question of the dog. But if you want to go into one of these other points first, let's do it." The mediators would then listen to what R really wants to talk about and move in that direction. Such a response would empower R in at least two ways. First, it would help R to "organize his case," clarifying his concerns and his priorities. Second, it would leave the choice of which issue to pursue first up to R—it would let him make that choice. In transformative practice, shaping the agenda is not a job for the mediator on the way to solving the problem but an opportunity for the parties to experience empowerment.

SEGMENT 8

The mediators caucused [recessed] to discuss the case by themselves for about 5 minutes. They wanted to do something about the dog, but were hesitant to talk to W3, given R's attitude. They also considered trying to persuade R to warn his family not to go too close to the fence, but they were reluctant to say this to R. Without deciding what to do about the dog, they invited C to a private session.

Move 10: Planning to Pursue the Mediators' Definition of the Problem

Comment: In this recess, the mediators continue to focus on the dog. The mediators established this focus earlier when they caucused with each other and concluded that the "dog was the root of the problem" and that "they must remove the annoyance of the dog." (See segment 5.) Here, the mediators continue to assert this conception of the problem they see before them. They consider suggesting, as part of the solution, that R "warn his family not to go close to the fence." The whole thrust of the mediators' planning centers on deciding what is going to solve the dog problem and thinking about how to persuade the parties to accept possible solutions.

Alternative: The mediators' discussion and assessment of what to do at this point in the session could have been cast much more broadly. They could have discussed the way in which the dog seemed only to be the trigger for deeper concerns and issues that the parties raised. They then could have planned for ways to discuss these other issues while still taking into account specifics about the dog, if the parties felt specific commitments were needed.

SEGMENT 9

[In Caucus with C] C was upset that R would not tell the truth about the gun. He has admitted to her in private, but would not confess in court, to the police or to the panel in public session. She said that she didn't want him to go to jail or be convicted, that he had kids just as she did. She also was worried about his friends and hers: that there would be trouble if R went to jail. She would, however, like him to be on probation. She said that other neighbors know him and were afraid of him. Mm pointed out that an agreement will lead to dismissal of the charges against R only if he lives up to it for 90 days. In a sense then, he would be on probation. C said she was still worried that R would get high, forget and start shooting again. The mediators tried to reassure her and said they wanted to work on the agreement. C left. This session had lasted 15 minutes.

Move 11: Missing Possible Grounds for Recognition in a Caucus

Comment: Because the mediators failed to grasp the possibilities for recognition in R's earlier statements, they are unable to build on this recognition when clear openings arise in this caucus with C. C wants an admission from R and is worried about his stability. But R has actually already made the admission and apologized, and he has offered some explanation for his volatility. C has clearly not "heard" this because the mediators failed to translate and help her do so. C also acknowledges in this caucus that she understands R's fears about going to jail. She indicates that she has kids just like he does and implies that going to jail might put them in jeopardy. All this could be used here with C, to communicate and evoke recognition to the greatest degree possible. The mediators make no attempt to help or encourage the parties to build on these opportunities.

Alternative: The mediators could acknowledge C's concerns and then bring in R's earlier statements in relation to them by saying, "Clearly you want to see R take some responsibility for what happened in the firearms incident, and you are concerned about this for the future. I think I understand your position and fears. Actually, I think some of the statements R has made, at least the way I heard them, show a willingness on his part to meet your concerns. For example, even if R hasn't made a signed admission about the shooting, I heard him apologizing for what happened, not once but twice. I heard him say he'd never fire the gun again, that he had actually gotten rid of it. And he did offer to put the apology in writing. Would you see that as taking some degree of responsibility for what happened?

"As far as the future and your fears about that, some of what R said seems related as well. It seemed like R felt scared when these incidents happened—maybe in part because of his past experiences. He just lost control somewhat. I'm not excusing that, and he doesn't seem to be, either. In fact, he seems to have real concerns about the possible consequences of his actions. He has real fears about going to jail, should he lose control again. These are fears you indicated you understood, especially since there are kids involved. But if you agree that that's what happened—that R loses control at times— rather than anybody really wanting to hurt anybody, then maybe there are concrete things you and R can do to reduce your concern about the future. We can discuss what kinds of things might help with that. But to start with, you might want to let R know that you understand his fears about going to jail and that you actually would like to help him avoid that if at all possible. I doubt he understands that right now. Maybe there are other things—if you see that R is in fact sorry about what happened and wants to avoid these things in the future. Maybe there's even something specific you and R could come up with about the dog. What do you think?" By this move, the mediator both conveys recognition from R to C and provides C with the opportunity to give recognition to R.

SEGMENT 10

In caucus [recess], the mediators decided to refer in the agreement to both firearms and threats. The dog was not discussed. Mf said that she was afraid that R would make them change the wording of the agreement, that he was a very prickly man. Because they were concerned that the agreement not be one-sided, they inserted a provision that C would not provoke R.

C and R but not W3 returned to the room. Mf read the agreement to them. R objected to the part about C since C had never provoked nor incited him and he did not think that she ever would. C agreed that she would not, but thought that she wanted some statement in the agreement. Mf said that she thinks that C meant that she does not wish him ill in any way, does not want him to go to jail and that is why she wanted something in the agreement about her future conduct. R said alright. The agreement was signed. The mediation lasted for 2 hours and 15 minutes.

The agreement provided that:

1. R agrees to do the following:
   A. Not to threaten or assault anyone on the property of _____ Street.
   B. Not to discharge any firearms within the vicinity of _____ Street.
2. C agrees not to verbally or physically provoke or incite R in any manner.

Move 12: Suggesting Unprompted Terms for the Agreement

Comment: In a discussion among themselves, the mediators begin to discuss threats and firearms—aspects of the problem that the parties raised but were not been pursued on their own terms by the mediators. Given their continued focus on the dog problem throughout the session, it is surprising that the mediators turn away from any concerns about the dog at the last minute and instead formulate stipulations in the agreement about future threats and provocations. Although concerns about assaults and provocations have been raised by the parties, the mediators have not explored these with the parties in any depth. In fact, as we have indicated, they have sidestepped broader bases of these problems throughout the session. As a result, the commitments to avoid assaults and provocations seem unearned, because they have not been sufficiently explored or worked through. They have not been achieved by the parties through their own efforts at understanding each other and considering deliberate choices they might make to improve the situation.

It also appears that in their recess, the mediators decide to include a provision in the agreement—C's promise not to provoke R—primarily because they are concerned about achieving an equitable settlement. They are concerned that they may be asking R to make several promises or commitments and not C, so they suggest that C should promise not to provoke R. Although R had raised important concerns about W3's friend's provocations, R has not raised specific complaints or concerns about C and the mediators have not pursued C's provocations during the session. Although equity may be important in the final agreement, including this particular provision in the agreement seems strained. It is as if the mediators are looking for some way to achieve the appearance of equity even though the settlement terms may not be initiated or requested by the parties. Even R, when he hears about this provision, argues that this promise seems unnecessary; he says C has not provoked him in the past, and he does not believe she will in the future. C says she wants to include it. R may feel it is put in to appease him, while not addressing other concerns he has raised.

Alternative: The way in which the final agreement was developed and the terms it included would have looked quite different in a transformative approach. The mediators would not have developed the settlement terms in a caucus that excluded the parties themselves. Rather, they would have allowed the parties to describe the agreement they thought they had constructed, and they would have relied on the parties to choose the language that best suited their understanding of the settlement. Most importantly, the mediators would not have included terms that the parties themselves were reluctant to support. Without pursuing a transformative route throughout the session, it is difficult to know exactly how the final settlement would have turned out in this approach. But given the range of concerns the parties raised (and the mediators could have pursued) throughout the session, the agreement in this case might have included a written apology, a promise from R to pursue counseling, provisions about how to restrain the dog, or a range of other commitments. Regardless of what specific terms were included, these terms would have grown from the parties' concerns and the understandings they reached with each other.

On Missing Transformative Possibilities

What is striking about this case is that from the time the parties entered the room through the writing of the final agreement, numerous opportunities arose to empower the parties and foster recognition. Yet these opportunities were repeatedly missed by the mediators as they guided the process, interacted with the disputants, and sought a workable agreement.

What is missing in this case, from a transformative perspective, is a focus on the here and now during the mediation—on what the parties are saying about themselves and how they see each other, on the opportunities the unfolding interaction affords for allowing the parties to strengthen both their sense of how to work on life's problems and their ability to relate to others. The mediators did not encourage the parties to deliberate about options, weighing the pluses and minuses and making self-conscious choices about why they might move in one direction rather than another. Nor did they encourage them to consider each other's particular perspectives or common human predicaments. Despite the many opportunities presented in the session, the disputants do very little to express consideration for each other or to make clear and informed choices about their situation. And the reason is that the mediators devote little or no effort to helping them do these things. The net effect is that while a promise to reduce hostilities has been made, the disputants probably leave mediation essentially unchanged as human beings, without having grown stronger in themselves or more responsive to others.

The moves the mediators did and did not make suggest that they approached this case as a problem-solving endeavor. Throughout the session, for example, the mediators pull back from the individual comments the parties offer and make a *global assessment* of what the dispute is about. Almost from the outset the mediators seem to be asking themselves, "'What can be done with a case like this? What kind of outcome is possible?'" (Shapiro, Drieghe, and Brett, 1985, p. 112). They grasp for a unified whole that will make sense, in problem-solving terms, of what they are hearing from the parties. They are primarily concerned with finding ways to shape the parties' stories into something manageable, something that ensures that "incidents like this never happen again." More emphasis is placed on identifying the shape of the problem—the global issue—than on finding transformative possibilities that might be explored in each of the parties' comments, concerns, or moves.

The mediators come to believe fairly early on that what the parties are telling them can best be treated as a "what can be done about the dog" problem. This is the "boilerplate," the "kind" of case they come to see before them. However, although the dog is clearly pivotal in the history of events and prominent in the parties' stories, this is clearly not the only level at which these issues can be addressed. The parties themselves resist the mediators' attempts to define the dog as the epicenter of their dispute. Their reactions to the mediators' moves suggest that they may be resisting the mediators' efforts to simply classify the dispute as a packagable problem.

In addition to the "problem" of the dog, the parties' exchange also points to the understandings and misunderstandings, the interpersonal bridges and chasms that lay between them. And it points to their confusion, uncertainty, and frustration at how to deal with the difficult and escalating situation in which they find themselves. These relational and decisional concerns are not just parts of a tangible "problem"—they are key elements of the interaction *as it unfolds* during the mediation. In other words, there is a whole set of possible considerations that have to do with what the parties are saying and doing at the moment—the decisions they are analyzing and making, the views they are offering about themselves and forming of the other, their fears about what they know and do not know, about both themselves and each other. In this mediation session, the mediators make few moves that land on this transformative plane of the dispute—the kinds of moves we have tried to suggest in the alternatives we offer.

The global focus that leads these mediators to search for a recognizable and solvable problem also leads them to *influence settlement terms* in ways that seem out of touch with what the parties are comfortable agreeing to. Besides pressing the parties to consider possible ways of dealing with the dog, the mediators push for a clause in the final settlement that C will not provoke R in the future. But, just as they resist the mediators' focus on the dog, the parties seem unconvinced that such a promise needs to be made. It is more the result of the mediators' need to add something that makes the agreement less one-sided than it is the result of the parties' sense of what will contribute to a workable arrangement for them. The mediators' influence on settlement terms is clear, and so too are the parties' efforts to resist this influence.

Evident throughout this case is a clear sense that the mediators are willing to *drop concerns that cannot be readily treated as problems*. The mediators keep an almost exclusive focus on future commitments the parties might or might not be willing to make—regarding the dog's behavior, the use of the gun, the verbal threats and assaults. These are central to packaging the dispute as a solvable problem. The parties raise several concerns, however, that the mediators either ignore or explicitly reject as possible topics for consideration during the mediation. These include whether R's Vietnam experience matters, R's fears of going to jail, the meaning and impact of possible apologies, and how each party's friends contributed to the conflict. These issues are, at least on the face of it, less tangible and certainly outside of the dog-as-problem focus. They are more related to issues of trust, deep-seated fears, images each party holds of the other, understandings of broader worldviews, and the pressures friends and relatives exert. None of these are explored in any depth during the mediation.

All of this suggests that the mediators walked through this case with a problem-solving view of the process and that, as a result, many opportunities for fostering empowerment and recognition were missed. A transformative approach to this mediation would have focused the parties' attention on these opportunities and encouraged and helped them to respond in ways that exploited their potential for growth and transformation. This would have meant allowing the parties to deal with the issues that lay at the heart of the matter for them. Rather than the settlement produced here, it might have produced terms that dealt with these concerns and that rested on new understandings and commitments. Such a settlement could have strengthened their ability to relate to one another, and others, and left them with increased awareness of their own capacity to deal with problems of all kinds. Even without any settlement, however, the experience of the process could itself have produced these effects to some degree, and at least the outcome would reflect the parties' concerns and decisions rather than the mediators'.

The next chapter presents an analysis of a case in which a concern for empowerment and recognition was kept central throughout the mediation and, as a result, the transformative opportunities presented were consciously pursued by the mediator's specific moves and captured to a much greater degree than in the Adjacent Gardens case.

6

. . . .

Capturing Opportunities for Empowerment and Recognition: A Case Analysis of Transformative Mediation in Practice

The case we will discuss in this chapter is a landlord-tenant dispute that one of the authors mediated at the Queens center. This case is not offered here as an ideal or perfect illustration of transformative practice. It is, however, highly instructive in several regards: it captures the range of opportunities for empowerment and recognition that can arise during a mediation session, it illustrates how a mediator can work with these opportunities, and it offers a sense of how these opportunities build on each other over the course of a mediation session. We will summarize the case in a series of short segments, underlining those parts of each segment that will be the focus of our analysis. After each segment, we discuss how the mediator's moves and the parties' interaction illustrate a transformative route through this dispute. For some segments, we also comment on the transformative possibilities that the mediator missed or gave insufficient attention to. Table 6.1 summarizes the mediator's moves that we analyze.

The Landlord-Tenant Case

SEGMENT 1

The complaining party (C) was the landlord, a man in his fifties. He spoke with an accent and had a Greek surname.

**Table 6.1. Mediator's Moves in the Landlord-Tenant Case:
Capturing Opportunities for Empowerment and Recognition.**

Move 1	Defining Mediation in Transformative Terms
Move 2	Allowing Parties to Decide Whether They Will Participate
Move 3	Allowing Parties to Decide on Commitment to Ground Rules
Move 4	Probing Past Events to Elicit a Party's Views of the Other
Move 5	Allowing Parties to Decide on Commitment to Ground Rules
Move 6	Probing Past Events to Elicit a Party's Views of the Other
Move 7	Providing an Inclusive Summary of the Parties' Concerns
Move 8	Focusing Parties on Choices for Their Decision Making Without Imposing "Boilerplates"
Move 9	Deciding to Caucus to Foster Empowerment and Recognition
Move 10	Helping a Party Clarify Goals and Options in Caucus Without Being Directive
Move 11	Probing in Caucus to Elicit a Party's Views of Self and Other and Surface Opportunities for Recognition
Move 12	Offering Possible Reinterpretations of the Other Party's Behavior to Evoke Recognition
Move 13	Allowing a Party to Control Discussion of Options
Move 14	Allowing Each Party Equal Control in Defining Options
Move 15	Probing for Views of Other/Offering Reinterpretations
Move 16	Keeping Evaluation/Choice of Options in Parties' Hands
Move 17	Helping Translate Party Proposals in Joint Discussion
Move 18	Helping the Parties Respond to the Opportunities for Recognition Surfaced in Caucus
Move 19	Translating Between the Parties to Evoke Recognition
Move 20	Reframing Parties' Differences on Substantive Issues to Maintain Recognition
Move 21	Asking Questions to Help Parties Clarify Their Options and Make Choices
Move 22	Summarizing the Parties' Tentative Agreement
Move 23	Allowing Last-Minute Concerns About Settlement to Surface
Move 24	Encouraging Parties to Consider Alternative Options
Move 25	Preserving Recognition in the Face of Impasse
Move 26	Preserving Empowerment in the Face of Impasse
Move 27	Framing the Value of a Party's Parting Argument

The respondent (R) was the tenant, an African American woman in her forties. The mediator (M) was a white male in his forties.

The session began at about 2:00 P.M. with M ushering the parties into the mediation room and asking each to take a seat on opposite sides of the table. M sat at the head of the table and gave a brief opening statement. He explained that "this is not a court and I am not a judge. I'm not going to order anyone to do anything or decide what should be done here—I don't have the power to do that." Instead, he said, the object of the session is "to help each of you better understand your own position and options, as well as the other person's position," adding that "I can help you do that, but all the decisions are up to you." He said that if the parties decided on steps that they agreed would resolve the situation, he could help them put their agreement in writing. Even if not, he concluded, "each of you will at least have a chance to understand better where the other is coming from and the options that are available to you in the situation." M also explained the ground rules for the session. At the end of his introduction, M asked both parties whether they had understood his comments and whether they had any questions.

Move 1: Defining Mediation in Transformative Terms

In introducing the goals and objectives of the process, the mediator emphasizes the importance of empowerment and recognition. He stresses the aim of empowerment by explicitly indicating that all decision-making power is left in the parties' hands and that, as a mediator, he will not step in to settle their problem or dictate terms of an agreement. He points to the goal of recognition by suggesting that the process offers an opportunity for the parties to achieve greater understanding of each other. The mediator suggests that a settlement is one possible outcome of the process, but he does not make settlement the sole or primary objective. He implies, instead, that mediation can be worthwhile even if settlement is not reached, because of new insights parties gain about their own situation and about the other party. Using simple language, the mediator frames the process in distinctly transformative terms.

SEGMENT 2

During M's introduction, R had been inattentive. When M asked whether she understood his explanation, she indicated she did but said she was concerned about how long this might take, because she had to get to work and didn't see that this was going to be worthwhile anyway. She really didn't want to be here, she said, and wouldn't have come except for the "summons" she got from the police. In response, M stopped and told her that while the "summons" stated correctly that if she didn't come, some court action might be taken—for example, by R—this was a completely voluntary session, and she didn't have to participate unless she wanted to. Then he said, "But you are here at this point and it's up to you to decide whether you think there are things disturbing you at this moment and whether this might be a useful chance to see if there are ways of dealing with them right here. It's up to you." Hearing this, R indicated she wanted to go ahead, and it was agreed that the session could go until 4:00, and the parties would decide again at that point whether it made sense to continue if need be.

Move 2: Allowing Parties to Decide Whether They Will Participate

The mediator fosters empowerment for R by clarifying that the summons she received does not mean she has to stay in mediation and by indicating that *she* can choose whether she wants to continue with the process. These comments set a tone for the entire session: the mediator suggests to both parties that they will decide on their own level of involvement in the process and that he will not pressure them to participate or otherwise act against their wishes. When parties realize that they are genuinely being given decision-making power, it has a strong empowering impact.

SEGMENT 3

M then indicated that the party bringing the case usually speaks first and that if R had no objection, he would ask C to begin and describe the situation from his point of view. R did not object, and C started to speak. C said that he brought the case because R was way behind in her rent. She now owed him $3,800 and hadn't paid him anything since October. (It was now the first week of February.) R interrupted and said it wasn't anything like $3,800, more like $2,800 tops. <u>M turned to R and reminded her that she would have ample time to respond to C and to say everything she wanted to but that it would be easier for him to understand the situation and help both her and C if each person took turns. M asked whether she could wait until her turn and then bring this point up, according to the ground rules mentioned earlier.</u> R agreed; M turned back to C.

Move 3: Allowing Parties to Decide on Commitment to Ground Rules

The mediator's concern for preserving a ground rule of not interrupting is balanced here with a concern for fostering empowerment. The mediator reminds R of the ground rule but *asks* whether she is willing to abide by it, thus explicitly leaving the choice up to R. Again, the mediator shows the parties that his commitment to giving them decision-making power is real. In addition, by giving the reason for the ground rule as he asks for R's commitment to it, the mediator is also empowering both parties by clarifying effective conflict resolution skills that the parties can use outside of mediation. In a small way, explaining the importance of ground rules begins to give the parties a sense of what is entailed, behaviorally, in developing effective conflict resolution skills for themselves.

SEGMENT 4

C continued by saying that now R was also leaving lights on and turning up the heat just to run up the bill (utilities were included in the rent) and hurt him. He had not pressed R for the back rent right away, but when it went on so long with no payment, he went over to the house to see why she hadn't paid. This was in mid-January. Instead of talking to him decently, he said, R called him names, spat on him, slapped him in the face, and then turned around and pulled her trousers down to insult him. "This is not nice," he said, and it made him very angry. So he decided to call the police and file assault charges and to evict her. He just didn't want to deal with her anymore after this incident.

M asked C whether he wanted to add more, and C said no. M then asked C several questions. Had C already started a legal action to evict R? The answer was, not yet, though he had spoken to his lawyer. M asked how long had R been a tenant in C's building. C said two and a half years; R interrupted and said it was really three and a half, and C agreed. M asked C whether R had generally been on time with rent in the past, whether this was the first time something like this had happened. C indicated that R had usually paid on time, or a little late, but he had never complained or pressured

her when she was late. In fact, he said, one time she got
$2,500 behind, and when she told him that she just didn't
have the money, he waited until she could get it together.
In fact, he'd helped her in lots of ways over the years,
taking her kids to stores and buying them school sup-
plies, sometimes even lending her money.

M interjected here, asking C, "So you are saying that
you've been willing to wait for the rent in the past and
help R out in certain ways; but you're also saying R has
generally been pretty reliable as a tenant in the past, in
paying rent and so on?" C responded that this was true
and that R had been reliable; even with the $2,500, he
knew she would eventually pay him, and she did.

Move 4: Probing Past Events to Elicit
a Party's Views of the Other

By asking C about R's past actions, the mediator elicits information
about the way C sees R—how he viewed her in the past and
whether her current actions are consistent with his general sense of
her. Although the mediator has no idea how C will respond when
the questions are asked, probing for information about the parties'
perceptions of each other usually surfaces opportunities for recognition, which can then be explored during the mediation.

Here, these questions about the parties' history begin to lay the
groundwork for recognition in two important ways. First, in responding to these questions, C suggests that R has not only been a reliable
tenant but someone whom he was inclined to befriend. Thus, C's
response itself gives some measure of recognition to R. C acknowledges that R has positive characteristics—that she is not entirely
malicious or untrustworthy—despite the facts recounted in the story
he has just told. Second, C's statements also suggest the kind of
recognition he may value or want *from* R. He sees himself as an
understanding landlord, one who is willing to give people "a break"
and treat tenants as potential friends. These are the characteristics

he presumably would want R to acknowledge. This suggests points that can be explored later, on which R might give recognition to C.

Thus, the open-ended questions the mediator asks about past events encourage C to consider alternative ways of viewing R and allow C to offer statements about himself that R might acknowledge at some later point. Without pursuing this line of questioning about past events, the mediator would have missed possible grounds on which recognition could be built. Instead, in his comments at the end of this segment, the mediator is able to summarize C's positive perceptions and offer him the opportunity to acknowledge explicitly these perceptions in front of R. C does so and thus gives recognition to R even at this early point in the mediation.

SEGMENT 5

Then C added that now it was different. Before, he could at least talk to R and find out what was going on. Now, she was $3,800 behind, and she wouldn't even talk to him. And when he came to find out the story, she hit him and insulted him. Too much had happened now, he said. And R had changed. She didn't want to pay what she owed. He was sorry, he said, but he couldn't afford to go on like this and didn't want to be so insulted. Now he felt R should just leave and pay the money she owed him.

Before the mediator could turn to R and ask her for her comments, she interrupted again, sounding quite angry, and said that she didn't have any money to pay him, and C could go ahead and do whatever he wants. M did not cut R off but allowed her to continue. R went on and said, "Actually, I have a good job and paycheck, but I'm not paying any rent because there are holes in the walls and ceiling of the apartment, and C hasn't repaired them even though I reported them months ago. That's why I haven't paid." C started to disagree with R here and protest that she had never asked him to make repairs, but M stepped in and reminded C that he would have plenty of time to respond but that it would help matters if each party spoke in turn. C had a turn and now it was R's, so would he agree to let R continue for now? C agreed to let R continue.

R then said that she had called C's wife about the repairs, and if she hadn't told him, that wasn't R's fault. And as for her supposed "assault" on C, what really happened was that he had come over at night sometime in December, around the holiday, and stood in front of her building yelling names and insults at her window from the street, embarrassing her. Then he came a few weeks later to her door and pushed her into the hallway, so she defended herself. "I'm a human being," she said, turning to C, "and you can't do that to me." She continued, addressing C directly, "You and I used to talk about religion, about helping each other, but now I see that was just slick. You're like everybody else. But if you try to hurt me, you'll only hurt yourself. You and I both know that house is not legal, the way you have three families living there, and one in the basement, with no separate meters. You better get yourself legal, before you take me to any court!" R got increasingly angry through this statement. Then she changed her tone and said, "I know I owe him some money, and if he wants to work something out, I'm willing—but I don't want anybody threatening me." She then stopped.

M stepped in as R paused and asked her some questions. What was the rent she paid per month? R said the basic rent was $750 per month, with $45 for utilities and $40 extra for water for her washer, for a total of $835 per month. Just how much money did R think she owed, if it was different from C's figure? R said that it was more like

$2,400, or maybe a bit more, but certainly not $3,800. She said, "C even admitted that I've always paid my rent, even when I got behind. But I don't have to pay if he won't do repairs." M asked whether the condition of the apartment was ever a problem before, or had C kept it up in the past? R said that really it hadn't been a problem before, that C had been a pretty good landlord, and it was true he had helped her out in the past like he said. But, she ended, things were different now.

Move 5: Allowing Parties to Decide on Commitment to Ground Rules

This move is parallel to that of move 3, now directed to C rather than to R. The point and impact is similar.

Move 6: Probing Past Events to Elicit a Party's Views of the Other

This move is parallel to that of move 4, now directed to R rather than C. Probing for information about the parties' perceptions of each other is the kind of move that can and should be repeated when appropriate. Certainly it can be used with both sides, and it may be appropriate to use it more than once with each, if it seems that surfacing further perceptions would create new opportunities for recognition.

SEGMENT 6

M leaned back from speaking to R and looking at both parties said, "You have differences about a number of points. One is the question of the amount of rent that is due and whether R will leave or stay in the apartment; another is the condition of the apartment and need for repairs; another is the question of how each of you wants to be treated by the other. But what I am hearing is that

both of you feel that something might possibly be worked
out without needing to go to court. Also, from what you've
both said, it seems that you agree that, up until these differences arose this past fall, for three years or so, you
got along pretty well and thought well of each other; but
the events of the past few months have changed your
feelings about each other. Is this a fair summary of what
you've both said? I don't want to put words in your
mouths, so correct me if I've got it wrong."

Move 7: Providing an Inclusive Summary of the Parties' Concerns

In this summary of the parties' statements, the mediator recaps the
discussion thus far, but in a way that fosters empowerment in two
important senses. First, he summarizes the issues without reducing
or significantly reshaping what the parties have said about the situation in which they find themselves. He does not, for example,
frame their comments solely as a "what to do about the rent problem" in the way that the mediators in the Adjacent Gardens case
reduced the disputants' concerns to a "what to do about the dog
problem." Instead, he mentions the rent and repairs issues but also
notes relationship concerns they have expressed. This inclusive
summary fosters empowerment because it stays true to where the
parties have headed in the mediation thus far. This move contrasts
with the tendency of some mediators to shape conceptions of the
problem and drop the more elusive relationship concerns. In fact,
the mediator could have been even more explicit about including
these concerns in the summary, by mentioning not only "the question of how each of you wants to be treated by the other," but also
"what kind of relationship, if any, you want to have in the future."

Second, the summary is empowering because of the way it is
worded. The mediator does not assume he has provided an accurate
statement of what has transpired thus far. He checks with the parties
to see whether the summary is a fair and accurate representation of

what they have said, and he gives them the opportunity to edit or reject his version. The mediator is careful only to assist, not direct, the disputants' discussion of concerns. He keeps allowing the parties to define these concerns for themselves.

SEGMENT 7

C and R seemed to nod their assent to this summary. But then C went back to an earlier point, saying that he had made plenty of attempts to communicate with R, but she had ignored him. Calling R by her first name, C said, "R, why didn't you call me directly about the repairs? You know I always handle this directly, not my wife. I never got any message from you. And why didn't you ever return my calls when I called to find out about the rent?" R responded, "Because I found out your true colors, that's why. You're just out for the money, like everybody else. And I don't have to deal with that." C and R continued for a few minutes to talk back and forth, sometimes addressing their comments to each other and sometimes to M, first about the money owed and then about the hallway incident. C said to R, "You know what you did, and it wasn't nice." R looked away, and then said, "Whatever I did—and it wasn't like you said—you had it coming." C sat back at this response, seemingly offended and angry.

M stepped into their exchange, going back to the summary. He again mentioned the points of difference but also reminded the parties of what they'd said about their past relationship, noting that C had said positive things about R as a tenant and vice versa. He then asked, "At this point, given all that has been said, what do you both want to do about the situation as it stands at present? Do you want to try to put things back on the same footing as before—is there a way to do that? Or if not, what do you want to be done instead?"

In response to M's question, R spoke first and said, though without the same degree of anger as before, that she didn't know whether she wanted to stay in the apartment at this point. She said she thought she could get a better place somewhere else. C immediately said that if so, she should move. But then R said she needed time, both to look for another place and to save up money for the move. She said she really needed a bigger place, because she just had a new baby. But she really liked the location of C's apartment because of its convenience to her workplace and the safety of the area. She said she didn't want to have to lower her standard of living at this point. If so, C responded, and she wanted to stay, she had to pay the rent she owed. She couldn't just keep living in his apartment without paying rent. M asked C whether this meant that, assuming they could work out the rent issue, he would be willing to talk to his attorney to stop any eviction action, and C said yes. But R then said that she didn't see how they could work out anything, because she just didn't have the money, and anyway, she really had to find a new place.

M stepped in at this point and said that, if neither party objected, he wanted to speak to each privately. He asked to talk to R first.

Move 8: Focusing Parties on Choices for Their Decision Making Without Imposing "Boilerplates"

In the opening exchange between the parties in this segment, C and R make several accusations that reflect their concerns about how they see each other. This is, in effect, a continuation of the discussion of relationship issues, which had been prompted by the mediator's earlier questions about past events. However, sensing that there is not yet a sufficient foundation to deal constructively with these issues, the mediator intervenes. He reminds the parties of the positive comments they had made about each other earlier, but then points them for the moment toward consideration of options and decision making, regarding what they want to do about the situation. In effect, the mediator is being sensitive to the interplay between empowerment and recognition: Helping the parties clarify options may create a foundation on which further recognition can be built. Moreover, simply putting to the parties the question of what to do reminds them of their decision-making power, like the earlier questions regarding participation and commitment to ground rules. Their realization of this power may itself help to strengthen them.

Furthermore, when the mediator asks how the parties might handle the situation, he does not direct them to one preferred definition of the problem. He does not ask, for example, "Do you want to figure out how and when R can move out of the apartment and how much R will have to pay?" or "Do you want to figure out how much R would have to pay in back rent to be able to stay in the apartment?" He does not attempt, in other words, to offer "boiler-plate" definitions of what their problems are and what choices they might make in dealing with them. Instead, the mediator fosters empowerment by giving the parties the power to define the nature of their dispute.

Move 9: Deciding to Caucus to Foster Empowerment and Recognition

The decision to caucus at this point, like the previous move of turning the focus to options and choices, is in part a response to the parties' unsuccessful attempt to deal with the difficult relationship issues they raised earlier, to which they implicitly return in their round of accusations at the beginning of this segment. Some recognition has already occurred, as the parties gave their opening statements and responded to the mediator's questions about past events.

However, exploring delicate relational issues and laying further groundwork for recognition is sometimes easier in caucus, especially in the early stages of the process. Parties often find it difficult at first to give recognition directly to the other party, because it is difficult to give recognition to another person when feeling vulnerable one-self. Vulnerability is usually greater early on in the process; it is also greater when parties are uncertain of their own positions. All of this seems to be going on with R at this point. Fostering empowerment, by helping parties gain greater clarity about their own situations and views, can strengthen their sense of self and lay a foundation for giving recognition later. In caucus, the mediator can help parties gain their footing in this way.

SEGMENT 8

M opened the caucus by saying to R, "I'm not sure I understand, from what you said in our joint discussion, what you want to do, what you feel is best for you to do in this situation. Maybe it would help to start out talking about that some more." R responded to this by saying that she really wanted to move and should have done it sooner, but since C's apartment is convenient to her work and comfortable, it had just been hard to face moving. She needed to move, but she needed time and really didn't know how or when she could pay C anything if she was going to have to save up money to move into a new place.

M simply listened to R, nodding and mm-hm'ing from time to time, but not interrupting. R continued, introducing a different line of thought. Actually, the reason she was concerned about moving was that she'd learned C was trying to sell the house. And then she'd be thrown out by the new owner. At this point, M asked, "So are you saying that you'd really like to stay in the apartment if that were possible? I'm not sure I get what you're saying." R responded to this by bringing up the repairs that needed doing. "How can I live in this place when there are holes in the walls and leaks?" She said that the leaks were actually fixed last summer, but the holes weren't, and that's why she decided to withhold rent. M said, "So are you saying that, if the holes and so on are fixed, you want to stay?"

R responded by repeating that she really had to move, because the place was just too small now that she had another kid. But, she added, she can't pay C now, because she needs all her money to finance the move. And it will be hard to find an affordable, safe place, as nice and convenient as C's apartment but bigger. She won't live where there are drugs and crime, she said, because she doesn't want to expose her kids to that. M said, "So it sounds like you're saying a number of things: You like C's place, and the location, it's near your work and a good environment for your kids. But you need more room. So you want to find a place like this one, but bigger, in a similar area. And to do that you feel you have to save up your money, so you don't see how you can pay C the back rent. In fact, you need to stay on in C's apartment until you can find the place you need. Is that close to what you're thinking?" R responded by saying that M had got it right, that's what she thought.

Then M asked, "If that's what you want, what do you think you can do to bring it about? If you need more time in C's place, do you think he will let you stay without paying anything? Is there any way you can pay him something, even part of what you owe, so he will let you stay until you find a new place?" M also asked R again what she thought she owed C. R now said that, despite her disagreement earlier, she actually owed him pretty much

what he said, close to $3,800. But she didn't have it. M
asked whether she had any money saved, and R said
she had about $900, but she couldn't give any of that to
C—she needed to save it for moving. <u>M asked, "So your
idea is to just stay in the apartment, without paying, until
you can find a new one, or until C evicts you?"</u> R
responded that she couldn't see what else to do. And
anyway, she said, given how C had treated her, he would
be getting just what he deserved if she stayed a few
more months and moved out without paying him anything. <u>M asked whether she thought she could realistically do this.</u> She said she knew that it would take him at
least two to three months to evict her. M asked her how
she knew this. She said she'd been to landlord-tenant
court before, as had friends of hers. She would get time,
and what she owed would be cut way down because of
his building violations. She'd wind up paying very little.
She said she was very sure of herself on this strategy.

Move 10: Helping a Party Clarify Goals and Options
in Caucus Without Being Directive

In this first part of the caucus with R, the mediator fosters empowerment by helping R clarify what her goals and options are. R's statements in joint discussion have indicated that she is not completely
clear about what she wants or what choices she can make to deal
with her current circumstances. The mediator's opening question
about what she thinks she would like to do, his summaries of her
statements, and his attempt to "reality test" by asking whether the
options she focuses on are feasible are all efforts to empower R.
These moves help R clarify her own goals and options, thereby
allowing her to realize that she has control over the choices she ultimately makes.

Although R tends to ramble quite a bit as she tries to articulate
her options and preferences, the mediator is careful to follow and

not lead her thinking. Rather than becoming impatient with R's changes of direction and trying to get her to stick to one point, the mediator "follows her around" and mirrors her statements as she considers and reconsiders her options. The result is empowerment, as R gains considerable clarity about her situation and ultimately defines her goals and options for herself.

Nevertheless, while the mediator asks several questions to help R consider fully the consequences of her choices, there are points he overlooks in this regard. For example, when R first starts focusing on the option of leaving C's apartment and looking for a larger one elsewhere, the mediator could and should ask her to consider the risks of exchanging C, with all his faults, for a new landlord. Has she considered that, despite her current disappointment with C, other landlords might be even worse by comparison to C overall? Has she asked herself whether gaining more living space, assuming she can find it, is worth giving up a landlord who has been good in the past for a new one who is an unknown quantity? These kinds of questions must be framed in a way that gives R ample room to answer them either way. Nevertheless, while pushing R to answer the questions a certain way would be directive and disempowering, helping her consider them before making up her own mind is not. On the contrary, it empowers R by helping her make informed and deliberate choices. Here, the mediator doesn't ask all the questions he might to empower R in this sense.

SEGMENT 9

M went back to R's statement that C deserved this because of how he had treated her. Earlier, M said, R had agreed with C's statements that he'd helped her out in the past, that they had a good relationship. It seemed that things had really gone sour sometime last fall. How did that happen? M asked. R said that it was true—C had helped her out quite a bit in the past. He'd given her time to pay when she needed it, and even fronted her money. He'd been nice to her kids and even driven her to work sometimes. And she helped him too, looking out for the house, warning him if it looked like other tenants might damage the place. They used to talk to each other about family, religion, and so on. She felt like he treated her like an equal, a real person. Then he showed his true colors, that he was just out for himself and money like all landlords.

M asked whether R could say more about what she meant by that, that C showed his colors. R said, her voice changing tone and becoming a bit husky, that she had been going through some bad personal problems last fall, that pulled her way down. For days on end she didn't even get up in the morning, and she missed work quite a bit. She had finally pulled herself out of it, but it was really hard. In the middle of this, when she was only behind a month or two in rent, C came to her door and wanted to know why she was behind and when she would pay. She told him she was having problems and just couldn't talk to anyone, and he went away. She thought he'd understand and let her be until things straightened out. But then he kept calling every few weeks and came over again in December. "A real friend would have seen I was in trouble and waited. He knew I'd always paid him before. But when it came down to it, he was just interested in his money. He showed his colors," R concluded.

M asked, "So you felt, when C kept trying to talk to you, that it was because he didn't trust you, and so you felt let down at a crucial time by somebody you'd considered your friend—is that it?" R confirmed that was how she felt: "I saw he wasn't really the way he had seemed, so I decided the hell with him from then on." Then she asked whether this caucus was really confidential, and when assured that it was, she added, "That's why I lost it a few weeks ago when C came over and asked me again about the money. I did spit and hit him, and moon him, like he said, but I felt he deserved it because of the way he'd treated me. Really, it was wrong what I did. But I felt like he had it coming."

M commented that R had obviously gone through a terrible time. Then he added that it still seemed odd that, given all C's help and understanding in the past, this would suddenly change so sharply. He asked R whether she thought it was possible that the reason for C's continuing to call her was not that he didn't trust her but that he honestly didn't and couldn't understand how serious her situation was, because he just didn't have enough information and couldn't get it from her or anyone else. After all, she hadn't told him when the problems started, and she refused to talk to him when he first inquired. R rejected this suggestion, saying that if C really trusted her, he could and would have just waited for her to pull out of it.

M then asked whether R thought that perhaps, since it was wintertime, C felt more pressed himself to find out about the rent, because his bills were higher, so he couldn't be as flexible as he might have wanted to be. R said no, he was a greedy landlord like the rest of them. She'd seen him treat others like this; now he'd done it to her too. All the talk and favors in the past must have been done for his own sake. He was never interested in her. She added that she didn't want M to tell C what she had said now about her problems. M assured her he would say nothing she didn't want him to. He then said, "But maybe if C heard directly from you how things were for you last fall, he would understand what's been going on and react differently than you think. But it's up to you."

R didn't respond to this directly but explained there was another reason she couldn't believe this was just a misunderstanding on C's part and why she'd "lost it" when he came over. Because the week before he last came over, he had reported her to the Bureau of Child Welfare (BCW) for neglecting her child. As a result, a caseworker came out and did a whole investigation of her. Of course, they found nothing, because there was nothing to find. But it was a vicious thing to report her falsely. The caseworker had told her that it was someone connected with her building that made the report. It must have been C, and this showed the kind of person he really was. He was willing to threaten her family and violate her dignity because of his filthy rent money.

M said he understood that the BCW incident must have been extremely distressing, on top of everything else. He then asked R whether she had confronted C with her suspicions. She said that he'd just deny it. M asked whether, despite her suspicions, someone else in the building might actually have been the one that made the report. He asked whether any of the other tenants— one of whom she'd mentioned having some fights with— might have done it. R said she couldn't be sure, but she still believed it was probably C. But then she said that, if someone else did it, they certainly must have wanted to "set it up" to look like C did it.

Move 11: Probing in Caucus to Elicit a Party's Views of Self/Other and Surface Opportunities for Recognition

Having accomplished a good deal of empowerment in the first part of the caucus with R and thus laid some foundation for recognition, the mediator turns now to recognition. He does so by picking up again on an earlier remark R made about how she sees C—as someone worthy of "getting what he deserved." Like the questions the mediator asked of R in her opening statement while C was present, the mediator now asks a series of questions exploring past events that shaped R's views of C. R recounts several things C did in the past that she was quite pleased with, thus reminding herself of her former, more positive view.

As R talks, she not only reveals how she sees R but also how she wants to be seen. She valued, for example, the times when C treated her like an equal and talked with her about topics that mattered to her. She also wanted C to recognize that she was going through a tough time and needed to be left alone, at least until she got over the hump. In short, she wanted his trust in her to continue and felt she was deserving of it.

By focusing on R's views of C at this point in the caucus, then, the mediator surfaces new opportunities for recognition. R's statements reveal a range of opportunities—potential places the mediator and the parties can return to—for R to give recognition to C and vice versa. Without the mediator's probing, these opportunities would not have been revealed. The extent to which these opportunities will be realized is unclear at this point in the session, but the possibilities have at least been uncovered. Sometimes opportunities for recognition arise by themselves, but mediators can intentionally help surface opportunities that don't arise on their own, as the mediator does here.

Move 12: Offering Possible Reinterpretations of the Other Party's Behavior to Evoke Recognition

As R talks about past events in this caucus, she makes several charges against C. She claims, for example, that he refused to take into account her serious difficulties and that he had inappropriately reported her to the Bureau of Child Welfare. Without insisting on the alternative views he offers, the mediator asks R to consider whether there are plausible alternative explanations for C's actions in both instances. The mediator goes so far as to suggest that R might test these alternative explanations in the mediation by seeing whether C's response is different if he is given the whole picture—if he knew, for example, how tough a time R had been through lately.

The mediator's goal here is not to convince R that she was wrong about her interpretations of C's behavior—to force recognition—but to indicate that there are possible other ways of understanding these past events, which might be more sympathetic to C's perspective. This puts before R the choice of whether to give recognition by considering or accepting one of these explanations. Thus, in offering possible reinterpretations of C's prior behavior, the mediator presents R with a clear opportunity for recognition, which is the meaning of evoking recognition. R is made aware that, if she chooses, she can let herself explore and question assumptions she holds and decide to take a more sympathetic view of C. Note that at this point R rejects these opportunities, at least openly, and refuses to give recognition. However, as the case unfolds, they percolate, and R eventually returns to them.

Segment 10

At this point, M returned to the question of what R now wanted to do. Coming back to R's plan of staying and paying no rent, M asked, "Even if you believe the court will give you the time, won't a court case mean taking time off from work and create even more animosity between you and C? If you could work something out with C here, would that be better for you than having C go to housing court?" R said that, if C would agree here to give her time and not ask for money, certainly that would be better. M said, realistically, C will want at least some payment from her. Then R said that there was one possibility she'd thought of: She could go to the city welfare department, as some of her friends had, to get what she called a "one-shot" aid grant that was available to working people with rent payment problems, to help them avoid homelessness. She thought that, with the right documents from C, she could get such a grant. And, if C would cut a deal with her, she could use part of the grant to pay him off and part of it to finance her move. M asked whether R knew for sure that this program was in effect and whether she could qualify. She said her cousin had just done it a few weeks ago, and she knew she met the guidelines too.

Then R backed off from her own suggestion. She said that in fact, she might need to use this grant program in the future if she got docked at work for the days she'd missed. Since it was a one-time grant, she didn't know if she wanted to use it up now. So she didn't want M to tell C about this possibility. Instead, she said, M should find out if C would accept her security deposit and another $300 to let her stay for another three months. She also said that M should not mention anything to C about the BCW report. The caucus closed.

Move 13: Allowing a Party to Control Discussion of Options

Having opened up opportunities for R to give recognition to C by reinterpreting his past actions, as explained in move 12, the mediator now backs away when R rejects these opportunities. He lets them percolate and avoids forcing recognition, which would in itself be disempowering and a contradiction in terms. Instead, the mediator returns to the question of what R thinks her options may be at this point and discusses their viability. Once again, the mediator is careful not to cast a specific option as the best or preferred choice, not to unduly influence the choices R makes. An important empowerment move here is the mediator's refusal to pressure R to present the "grant" option to C, although it is a very attractive bargaining chip. Instead, he lets C decide whether and when to present this, which she eventually does.

SEGMENT 11

M then caucused with C. M started by asking C whether he wanted to say anything here privately that he had hesitated to say earlier. C's first comment was that, besides paying nothing and running up the utility bills, R had broken the storm doors and windows. He doesn't know what to do. He has expenses on the house and really needs the rent to meet them. And what repairs is R talking about? He always makes repairs when needed. M told him that R specifically mentioned holes in the kitchen ceiling and bathroom walls. C said he knew what she meant, but these were holes made to fix the leaks R had mentioned. Openings had to be left for access to the pipes, but they could be covered; he could take care of that right away. But what was he supposed to do about the money R owed him?

M asked R to clarify exactly how much was owed. C said R owed rent from October until the present (February), five months' worth. The total was about $4,000, including utilities and water. M said that, based on talking to R, it seemed that they could probably agree on the amount she owed. So, C asked, then would she also agree to give him the money, and when? M said, "Let me just ask you first, apart from the back rent, do you basically want R out of the apartment now? Or is your main concern the rent, and if R gets paid up you'd want to let her stay? From what I heard before, I wasn't sure what you want overall, because you mentioned that R had been a pretty good tenant before now."

C answered that, up until the hallway fight, he just wanted to have R pay the rent she owed. He didn't necessarily want her to leave. And it was true, she was one of the better tenants he'd had, because she was reliable.

Even if she got behind, he knew she'd pay; he didn't have to fight or run after her. But now it was five months, and he just couldn't afford anyone living rent-free. Anyway, now he wasn't sure whether she should stay no matter what. He had been nothing but patient and good to her, and then she hit and insulted him. He thought maybe she was going crazy. She was normal before, and then something happened to her. Now he just didn't know if he wanted to have her there anymore at all.

M asked C whether he knew whether something happened to R to make her change and whether he'd asked her about it. C said he tried to talk to her, but she refused. Then he said, in a low tone, he thought she probably got involved with drugs. That's another reason, he added, that it might be good if she left. He didn't want that in his building. M said: "Do you think it's possible that R just went through a very bad, rough time for some reason, and maybe now she's pulling out of it, getting herself back together, and needs some time to pull herself back up onto her feet? Like you said, she was solid and reliable before, even if she got behind sometimes. Maybe this is just a temporary thing?" C answered that he didn't know whether this was the case, maybe yes and maybe no. But still, how much time would it take, and when would he be able to get any of the money she owed? If she didn't pay soon, he would have no choice but to go to court.

Move 14: Allowing Each Party Equal Control in Defining Options

In questioning how C might want to handle the situation, the mediator intentionally allows C to define what he wants, *independent* of what R has said about how she sees her options and preferences. For example, given R's focus on moving out, the mediator could easily have built on that to construct a settlement, by directing C toward some sort of "move out and pay" deal. Instead, the mediator here "starts from scratch" with C, allowing him to define options in his own way. Perhaps he really would prefer R to stay after all, which would lead to an entirely different outcome. The mediator empowers C by encouraging him to independently define his interests and choices. He refuses to let his own assumptions rather than the party's true preferences control the agenda.

Move 15: Probing for Views of Other/
Offering Reinterpretations

Just as the mediator probed with R to surface her perceptions of C and encouraged her to consider possible alternative explanations for C's past behavior (in moves 11 and 12), here the mediator does the same with C. Again, the mediator makes it clear that he is not trying to convince C that one explanation of R's behavior is necessarily "true." Notice that the mediator does not really argue or push for the interpretation he suggests. Rather, the mediator simply opens the possibility that C might want to consider other reasons why R's behavior changed so radically. Like R, C makes no commitment to explore these explanations further. Nevertheless, the mediator's move does bring C to consider R's perspective for at least a few moments during the caucus, and it allows the opportunity for recognition to percolate with C as the mediation progresses.

On the critical side, the mediator does very little in this caucus to draw C out regarding his own feelings about the situation, especially the confrontation with R. Allowing a party to articulate these feelings in caucus (as M did with R in her caucus) empowers the party both by helping them learn how to express these concerns and by giving them some recognition (albeit only from the mediator). It is then easier for the party to seek recognition directly from the other party in joint session and also to offer recognition to the other from a position of increased strength. Here, after C mentioned how patient he had been with R and how she then "hit and insulted him," the mediator could have acknowledged C's distress and then invited C to talk more about how these events affected him, before going on to possible reinterpretations of R's behavior.

A further point is that the mediator could probably do more than he does here to suggest possible reinterpretations of R's behavior to C. On the one hand, R requested at the end of her caucus that the mediator not tell C "what she had said about her problems." Thus the mediator can only suggest in very general terms that R may have been through a very rough time; otherwise he would be violating confidentiality. Still, the mediator might pursue a different kind of reinterpretation while keeping the "problems" confidential. Thus, he might ask C, "Do you think it's possible, since R obviously came to think of you not just as a landlord but as a friend, that she expected that as her friend you would understand she just needed to be left alone for a while to work things out? So that when you called her and came over, she felt let down by you, her friend, and that's why she got angry and reacted as she did? Of course, this doesn't mean her actions were proper, but could it help you see them in a different light?" Focusing the reinterpretation on R's feelings of friendship for C rather than her "problems" avoids the confidentiality problem but offers an opening for C to recognize R's actions as consistent with rather than contradictory to their past relationship.

In general, there is some sense that the mediator does not pursue recognition opportunities as fully in the caucus with C as he did in the caucus with R, perhaps because of R's relatively greater capacity or willingness to verbalize. Mediators need to be able to work with each party at their own level in fully developing empowerment and recognition opportunities.

SEGMENT 12

M asked C whether he had already started the eviction process, and he said no. Then M asked whether C knew how long it would take and how much it would cost—had he done it before? C said he knew it could take several

months and was costly, but what else could he do? M
asked whether C would rather extend R some time to
pay and accept less than the total owed. Would that be
better for him than going to court? He had helped R in
the past—did he want to give her a break now? And
would it wind up being better for him than spending the
time and money to go to court? C responded that this
was possible, but it depended on how much of a wait and
how big a loss he was looking at. What was she offering
to do? M said that this wasn't clear yet, but the question
for C was what he felt he would be willing to accept, what
would be better for him than going to court?

C said, "I'll do whatever you say. What do you think I
should do?" M told C, "I'm not here to tell you that. I'm just
asking questions to help you consider your choices and
decide. It's your decision. But I can go over the figures
with you." M and C reviewed the figures, and C said that
as of May 1, R would owe $5,600. C said that he'd be will-
ing to let R stay until then and pay him $4,000 total, tak-
ing a $1,600 loss. M asked whether C thought this would
be better than going to court. C said he thought it would,
but he asked, "What happens if I agree to this and then R
doesn't move by May 1? I'll have to start in court then and
wait even longer." M said that this was a good question
and that, if the discussions got that far, C could check with
his lawyer and see whether there was a way to cover that
situation. M asked C if he wanted to propose this offer to
R to start the discussion when they resumed joint discussion in a moment. C said he would.

Move 16: Keeping Evaluation/Choice
of Options in Parties' Hands

The mediator helps empower C by summarizing several possible
options C has available to him. But in doing so he places the
options on equal footing and leaves the evaluation and choice

squarely in C's hands, refusing explicitly to advise C of what to do when asked. Instead, he reminds C of his own decision-making power. Furthermore, when C raises an important objection to one option, M does not discount or downplay the concern in order to encourage C into a particular settlement. Rather, he takes C's doubts seriously and encourages C to find out more about this option. This segment of the case offers the mediator a clear opportunity to direct things toward settlement and even specific terms of settlement. The mediator resists this opening and redirects control back to the party.

In this part of the caucus, the mediator also fosters empowerment by asking numerous questions that help C consider the consequences of different responses to the situation. However, the mediator misses some important questions in this area. In particular, although he asks C about the possible time and expense involved in a court action to evict R, he does not raise questions about how each side's case is likely to fare in court. It is always proper, and helpful, to ask each side to look realistically at how it may fare in court, if that alternative is being considered. Are the local courts typically sympathetic to tenants like R? Are there any problems with the legality of the rental unit? Like questions to R about the likelihood of finding a better landlord, these questions to C about prospects in court would more fully empower him by helping him make clear, informed decisions about what to do.

SEGMENT 13

M called in R to resume joint discussions and said it was his sense that there were some points of common ground. He said that each had expressed their ideas of what could happen now. For example, he said, R said she would be willing to leave the apartment after some period of time and pay some amount of back rent, with part of this being covered by her security deposit. Maybe the best place to start was by C indicating his view of this. M turned to C to allow him to speak.

C first said that he could certainly repair the holes R mentioned, putting covers over them to allow for access to pipes. He said he didn't know it was a problem, that R should have called him personally. But he would have it done the next day. R responded that this was fine, but what about the time she needed before moving out? M asked C to relate to R the terms C had decided on in caucus, and C then said he was willing to have R stay until May 1 and pay $4,000 total. M said, "So you are saying that R can stay for two more months, and instead of paying the total of $5,600 that would be due by then, you'll accept $4,000, including her security deposit. So that would reduce the amount due by $1,600. Is that right?" C agreed that was what he was saying.

Move 17: Helping Translate Party Proposals in Joint Discussion

When the parties return to joint session after caucus, even if some foundation for recognition has been laid (or even if some recognition has been given), they have not been communicating directly. As they start to do so, the possibility for misunderstanding or not hearing each other fully is very strong. The mediator can ease the transition by acting as translator between the parties in joint discussions, if need be. Here, C conveys his proposal very tersely, so that R may not even realize what he is offering and how it contrasts with what he originally claimed. By expanding C's language, the mediator translates the proposal to make sure that R hears what is being offered and can clearly decide on her response.

SEGMENT 14

Despite her position at the end of caucus, R did not reject C's position out of hand. Instead, she and C began to discuss things directly. The tone on both sides was somewhat friendly, bantering, definitely not antagonistic. R said that $4,000 is too much and wanted C to give her more of a break. C said he gave her breaks, and that this is a break, but she can't just stay rent-free. R said the rent had always been too high; she'd been overpaying for years, so he should cut this down some more. C responded, "You knew the rent when you moved in, and it's not high for this area. You yourself said it was a good place, and I have to pay my expenses too." R ended this discussion by saying that it didn't matter, because she had to move to a bigger place anyway and would need all her money to do that, so she couldn't pay anything.

At this, C got angry and said, "So you just want to stay and pay nothing! Is this fair, after how I've treated you? I always helped you out, you even said so. And your kids, I've been like a grandfather to them, they even call me 'Uncle.'" At this point, despite her earlier refusal to disclose this to C, R brought up the child neglect charge: "Is that why you reported me to BCW, because you want to help me so much?" C said he didn't know what she meant, so she related what happened and said she knew it was C who reported her. C said that was ridiculous and R knew it; he knew she was a good mother. It was probably the tenant upstairs that R fought with at times. M interjected and asked C, "So you're saying you had nothing to do with this at all, that you wouldn't do anything like this to R?" C said of course not, and R knows that. M added, "But you can understand how upset R would be over such a false accusation." C said that sure he could, but he had nothing to do with it. Then R backed off, saying maybe not, but someone had certainly tried to make it look like C did it.

C suddenly asked R directly, "What did I do that you accuse me of this kind of thing and that you refused to talk to me? You don't tell me you're thinking about moving until we come to this meeting? Maybe you had problems. So what, you could have told me. We talked before, I helped you before. What did I do to you that you react like this? And then the way you treated me when I came to find out what was going on! You spit on me and insult me! I just don't understand any of this."

There was silence for several moments as C's questions hung in the air. Then R answered, "Well, I guess it was wrong the way I reacted when you came over, and I'm sorry for that. You don't understand because you haven't been there, and you better hope to G-d you never are! I hope I never get in such a place again, where things get so bad that you turn to things that you think will help you get through it but they make it even worse. And you just can't talk about it at the time, and no one understands. You didn't either, and I expected you to, so I got angry." M waited a few moments after R finished. Then he said to R, "So you're saying that you just wanted C to wait until you got through this period, and when you thought he wouldn't, you felt let down by a friend at a very tough time? And you were reacting to that?" R said that was it.

C said he just didn't know what was going on because she totally stopped talking to him and turned him away. He really had no idea what was happening. He was sorry that she had been through such a rough time. But he didn't see how he could have figured this out at the time. R made no verbal response but nodded her head at this in a gesture of acceptance.

Move 18: Helping the Parties Respond to the Opportunities for Recognition Surfaced in Caucus

During this part of the joint session, the parties turn away from the issues of R's payments and occupancy and return to their concerns about how they see themselves and each other and the past events that have shaped their perceptions of each other. That is, they return to where they were prior to the caucuses. The mediator allows this shift of focus to unfold and does not attempt to bring the discussion back to the occupancy, payments, or repairs topics. He intervenes only to provide summaries that highlight the recognition the parties are choosing to give to each other, based on the foundations laid in caucus.

In the earlier joint session, the parties' attempt to discuss these relational concerns led only to an escalating cycle of accusations (segment 7). The mediator decided at that point to focus the parties' attention on decision making, questioning what they wanted to do about the rent and apartment occupancy (move 8). Then the mediator broke for separate caucuses. In the caucuses, he worked on empowerment and on surfacing opportunities for recognition, first by helping each party explore and clarify their goals and options, and then by helping each party explore alternative interpretations of the other's past behavior.

Now, after the foundation laid in the caucuses, the parties return to the opportunities for recognition surfaced there and give each other considerable recognition—despite their rejection of those opportunities earlier. The mediator's probing about past events and his suggestions of other explanations for past behaviors have percolated in the parties. Now they have decided, *on their own,* to raise again the questions about how they see each other and to listen and respond to each other in a more sympathetic and positive way.

They address, for example, R's suspicions about the report to the Bureau of Child Welfare and her resentment of C's failure to understand her personal difficulties. They also address C's suspicions about R's lack of response to his calls and his distress over their confrontation in the hall. At this point, however, recognition is given by each party to the other. C acknowledges that R could have been legitimately upset if she had been correct in thinking that he had reported her to the Bureau. R acknowledges that it may not have been C who did the reporting. R also acknowledges that the way she treated C was inconsiderate and she apologizes for it. C acknowledges that he did not know how serious R's problems were and expresses his sympathy for her difficulties. And R gives an indication nonverbally that she accepts C's explanation.

This flow of recognition is no accident. It is the consequence of the foundation laid by the mediator from the beginning of the session, and especially in the caucuses with each party. It shows how the transformative approach, by consciously capitalizing on the possibilities for recognition that are inherent in mediated discussions, can open up a realm of new understanding that would otherwise be lost. In fact, it is possible that the mediator could have done even more to promote the flow of recognition here.

Perhaps most important, beyond summarizing and highlighting the statements of each party that either seek or offer recognition, the mediator here could directly invite each party to elaborate on their feelings and the reasons for their past conduct, just as he did in the caucuses. Doing the same thing here would further open up the possibilities for recognition, as each side directly heard the other party's perspective more fully and with more willingness to listen. Thus, after C's questions to R about her refusal to talk to him and about their confrontation, the mediator could say to C, "It's clear that these things you just mentioned were very disturbing to you; do you want to say more about how they affected you, after your previous relationship with R?" Or, after R has mentioned her "bad times" in response to C's questions, the mediator could ask her, "Do you want to say more at this point about the problems you were facing last summer? Do you think that might help C understand just how tough things have been for you?" Clearly, the mediator has to be sensitive to respect the parties' sense of privacy and dignity and not to pressure them. At the same time, merely inviting honest expressions of feeling can give parties needed support to say what they really want to. And those expressions, once articulated, may then evoke greater expressions of recognition from the other party, either immediately or later in the mediation.

SEGMENT 15

After a few moments, M commented that it seemed this conversation had helped to clear up some of the things that had been bothering both of them. There was still the question of what each of them wanted to do about the situation right now. This started another round of argument. R said that she'd try to move out soon but couldn't pay anything if she was going to have money to move. C said it wasn't his job to pay her rent; he couldn't give her the place for nothing; he had to pay his expenses. R said she didn't want the place now because it was too small.

M stepped in then and said, looking from one party to the other, "You're both basically saying what you've said before, but let me ask you something. Can each of you hear a bit differently at this point what the other is saying? R is saying she wants a decent place to live, safe for her kids, big enough for the family and not too far from work, and she's worried about how she can find that and pay off her rent at the same time. And C is saying he needs to have the rent in order to make his payments and keep the place up. Otherwise he risks losing the building, and maybe even his other property, and can't rent to anybody. So, does what either of you is saying seem out-of-line or unreasonable to the other? Or is the real question whether there is some practical way to handle things that might work for both of you? What do you think, does this way of looking at it make sense to you at this point?" Both C and R indicated it did. M then asked them, if so, what ideas did they have on what to do?

Move 19: Translating Between the Parties to Evoke Recognition

The mediator sees that the parties have gained considerably more sympathetic views of each other and may have cleared up several misunderstandings they have had about past events. So he encourages the parties, at this point, to return to decision making and discuss the payment and occupancy issues. But the parties seem to make little initial progress on these issues, probably because their new perceptions of each other have not firmly taken hold. The mediator is aware that, even if recognition occurs in a mediation session, backsliding is to be expected because of the history and weight of old perceptions. He realizes that recognition needs reinforcement. So the mediator gives a summary translation of each party's substantive positions for the other, framing them in a way that tries to make each party's goals and reasons understandable to the other, in light of their new perceptions of each other. This move builds on the recognition that has been achieved in discussing past events, making it a fulcrum for discussing the challenging issues that still divide the parties.

SEGMENT 16

C spoke first, saying maybe he could ask some other owners he knew about a place for R. But they were in more rundown areas, so R said she didn't want that. Then R asked, what about other apartments in her own building, but C said they were all the same size or smaller. M interjected and noted that C had said he had other buildings—was there anything available there? C said they had bigger units but in other areas that R wouldn't want. Then he added that he had one other building on R's block with a larger apartment opening up, but it was more rent than R's present place. M asked him how much and how big was it. It was $100 more but had an extra bedroom. R said that was the right size, but it was too much money. Then she said to C, "I'd take that place, but you have to lower the rent."

C didn't reject this idea, and the parties started bargaining directly about it. The tone became bantering, almost friendly. R said, "Come on, C, give me a break, you can afford to help me out," and C replied, "What am I supposed to be, your father?" and R said, "Well, that's what you said my kids thought, right?" In the discussion, C first agreed to lower the rent $25, then $50. But he said utilities were her business. M interjected periodically to summarize the figures each time they changed and keep comparing them to R's current expenses. Then C added that he didn't want a washer in this place. R said with the baby she had to have a washer, so C said then it's another $40 for the water. R got angry then, saying C didn't care about anything but money after all. C bristled and shot back that he'd already lowered the rent and R as usual wanted everything for nothing.

M stepped in at this point: "Wait a minute. Just because you don't agree about everything doesn't mean either of you is trying to take advantage of the other. R, you're saying you need the extra space and washer because of the kids, and it's not that you don't want to pay, but it's hard to fit it all into your budget. Is that right? And C, you're saying that it's not that you want to keep R from having a washer, but the water bills from the city are higher then and the city is tough on payment, just like the bank with the mortgage, right?" Each party indicated their assent. "So each of you has good reasons for what you're saying, why it's hard for you to go further." Both parties agreed that this was so, and they resumed discussion. They agreed on the rent/water figure at $840 ($5 above her current rent and utilities), with utilities extra. Then C raised the issue of the back rent.

Move 20: Reframing Parties' Differences on Substantive Issues to Maintain Recognition

Note first of all that the impact of the mediator's summary translation in move 19, to reinforce recognition, is quite noticeable—it opens up a free flow of bargaining between the parties that moves quite far in dealing with their concrete situation. Again, however, when they hit a snag, the effects of earlier recognition tend to fade. So the mediator steps in again to translate and reframe the parties' differences on the financial arrangements to help them avoid negative interpretations of each other's motives and behavior. In essence, the mediator suggests that the differences over the payments may be due to honest differences in needs and not attempts to cheat each other. This recasting of their differences offers the parties a chance to preserve and continue the recognition they had given each other and still engage in tough bargaining over difficult financial matters.

In effect, both this and move 19 are recognition "booster shots," helping the parties to remember their decisions to give each other recognition and allowing them to ratify those decisions in the face of new tensions. Maintaining recognition is as hard as giving it in the first place, so the mediator has to keep offering the opportunity to continue giving recognition as the circumstances require.

On the other hand, here the "booster shots" may not be all that was needed. Instead, the mediator in this case might have done more to strengthen the recognition exchanged between the parties, right when it was first given (in segment 14). Look specifically at the beginning of segment 15: there, before going back into the other issues, the mediator could have summarized more fully the new perspectives each party had gained. Instead of simply observing that the conversation seemed to help "clear things up," he could have expanded his comment, saying, "Let me see if I understand what you've said. R, you realize now that C never accused you to BCW and that when he tried to talk to you it wasn't because he didn't trust you. He just didn't have any way of knowing that you were going through so much trouble. C, you realize now that when R didn't respond to your calls, it wasn't because she was ignoring or avoiding you. She simply couldn't talk to anyone until she got through that rough time. Is this what you've said, and how you see things now?" Such a summary would frame for the parties the recognition that they had in fact exchanged, making it easier to hold on to it as they continued discussing other issues.

In addition, beyond simply summarizing the exchange, the mediator could have given a general "translation" to help make the parties more understandable to each other, such as saying, "It seems as though each of you had different ideas, as many people do, about communicating. C thought communication and talking showed trust and respect, and silence meant rejection. But, at least at this time, R thought that accepting silence would show trust, and insisting on talking meant suspicion. So it was like you had two different languages, talking and silence meant opposite things to each of you, so you didn't understand each other's behavior. It often happens that a way of acting means different things to different people and leads to misunderstanding, when in fact no one means anything bad by what they're doing. Does this make any sense to you as a way of seeing what happened between you?" Again, this kind of translating comment could have cemented the shift of perspectives that had occurred, helping the parties maintain the recognition they had given each other.

Segment 17

C asked when will R move, and when will she pay the $4,000 back rent? She can't move into the new place until she pays that off, and the place is opening up next week. R was silent, so <u>M asked C whether he would be willing to accept a partial payment before the move, with the rest over time, since he was originally willing to give R two months rent-free before moving out.</u> C asked how much would he get up front, and M turned it back to him and asked him to come up with a figure that would be acceptable. C said he wanted at least $2,000. R said she would need some time to get that amount together, but C said he couldn't hold the apartment open for long; he would lose too much on it. M asked C, in order to get R into the new place and recoup his back rent, was it worth it to hold the place open a few weeks? Didn't it normally take a while to rent apartments? After some discussion, C agreed to wait for two weeks. Then R would pay him the $2,000 and move to the new place at the new rent/water figure. But she'd also have to give him advance rent and deposit for the new place then. That would make a total of about $3,500 due within two weeks.

M asked R whether this was acceptable and possible for her—would she be able to raise the funds necessary within this time? At this point, R raised the idea that she had mentioned in caucus and asked M to keep confidential, about the one-time emergency housing grant. M helped her explain it to C and asked whether C would provide R with the needed documents to apply. C agreed that he would. R said that once she knew she would get the grant, even if it took more than two weeks, she could pay C the $3,500 before moving in. She would pay the rest of the back rent when the grant came through.

Move 21: Asking Questions to Help Parties Clarify Their Options and Make Choices

The mediator asks a series of clarifying questions in this segment, encouraging the parties to consider the viability of several possible options. Notice that the mediator refrains from defining the specific terms of these options and instead keeps decision-making responsibility on the parties themselves. He also does not ask about options that the parties mentioned in caucus but were hesitant to bring up to the other party (e.g., the possibility that R could get an emergency housing grant). The mediator does, however, help clarify these options once the parties raise them for discussion.

SEGMENT 18

M said that it looked as though a way of resolving things might be shaping up. <u>He said that he would summarize what he heard the parties saying, so that they could check if this was what they meant, and then work out the remaining details.</u> As he summarized orally, M made a written outline. He said he understood: R would contact the welfare office to confirm the documents necessary; C would provide documents; R would apply for the grant; if welfare indicated it would make the grant, R would pay C $3,500 and move from the old to the new place at the end of two weeks, at a rent of $840 including water (utilities extra). C and R confirmed that this was what they'd said. <u>M said that both of them had worked very hard in the discussions, listening and speaking to each other, and working toward this point.</u> Everyone agreed to take a short break. R asked C whether he could give her a ride to work when they were done, and C said he would be glad to. Two and a half hours had elapsed.

Move 22: Summarizing the Parties' Tentative Agreement

The mediator steps in to summarize the terms parties seem to be agreeing to at this point, checking with the parties so that they can make decisions clearly and deliberately and edit or reject his summary. As with defining the issues (move 7), defining the terms of settlement is for the parties, not the mediator.

One important element that the mediator overlooks in this summary is the progress the parties have made in understanding each other's perspectives and past behavior. In effect, beyond agreements on measures to deal with occupancy and payment issues, their discussion has also entailed "agreements" on how to see and understand each other. The mediator's indirect reference to "listening and speaking to each other" does not adequately capture the importance of these new perspectives. Instead, he could include them explicitly in his summary of what the parties have said, in terms similar to those suggested in the comment on move 20. Although the real impact of recognition is in the interaction of the parties (including the moves toward each other they make on other issues), articulating them explicitly can help strengthen the parties' commitment to maintaining new perspectives of one another.

SEGMENT 19

After the break, everyone reconvened. They started to review the plan and numbers. Then C raised a concern. Was it really going to be possible, he asked, for R to come up with this lump sum in two weeks and to handle an even larger monthly rent/utility payment than she had been making in the past? <u>M said that this was the time to raise such questions and turned to R, asking her whether she felt confident about this or whether she wanted to think about it some more.</u> He summarized the figures again, comparing her current monthly payment of $835 total (including water and utilities) to the new one of $840 without utilities. R considered the figure again, saying that with utilities she'd probably be paying close to $900 per month. She hesitated, frowned, and said that she didn't know whether she could really do it, $900 really was too much for her, and it just wouldn't work. Then she turned to C and said, "Why can't you come down some more on the rent or the water? You know you can do it."

C was exasperated by R's response. He said that they'd just spent two hours going over all this and that he couldn't reduce things any more. M stepped in and asked him to consider whether, given the $2,000 amount he'd been willing to write off to start with and the legal expenses he would save by reaching an agreement here, he could afford some further reduction. But C said he didn't want to talk any more about reductions; he'd spent enough time on this already. He would just go to court. R's reaction to this was equally strong. She accused C of being just another greedy landlord, like she said earlier, and of thinking he was better than her, even though she was an American and he was a foreigner. C reacted angrily that he was as American as her, had been here forty-five years, was a citizen, and so forth. The tone of the interaction reverted to the earlier hostility. As the agreement seemed to fall apart, so did the parties' more positive views of each other.

Move 23: Allowing Last-Minute Concerns About Settlement to Surface

When C begins to question whether R can meet the financial requirements of their tentative deal, the mediator encourages these concerns to enter the discussion. After C expresses second thoughts, the mediator asks R whether she believes she can swing the deal. This move preserves empowerment, even at this key stage of the process. A mediator who was focused on settlement rather than on the empowerment objective might very well squelch or downplay C's last-minute concerns and pressure the parties to go ahead, in an effort to preserve the tentative agreement the parties (and mediator) had worked so hard to reach. Here, the mediator allows the agreement to unravel even though it is clear at this point that the parties may not have the time or energy to work much more on the issues. One of the hallmarks of a transformative approach is the willingness to slow down and back up in response to concerns the parties raise rather than turn up the pressure and minimize concerns.

Move 24: Encouraging Parties to Consider Alternative Options

When it appears that the tentative agreement has fallen through, the mediator raises a second option that the parties had been considering. Specifically, the mediator asks C whether he would consider reducing the rent further in a settlement, because of the expenses he might incur if he has to go to court. The mediator does not push this but raises it with C to determine whether he has considered all angles and understands the consequences of the choices he is and is not willing to make.

It might be suggested that the mediator actually should have pushed somewhat harder here, with both C and R, to think through the alternatives before abandoning their tentative agreement altogether. Another caucus would have allowed each to consider calmly the choice between making some further adjustment, however difficult, and facing the consequences of nonagreement. The mediator could have asked C to consider more fully whether reducing the rent a bit more would in fact be better for him than going to court and finding a new, perhaps less reliable tenant. He could have asked R to consider more fully whether she could in fact find some way to afford the new rent or perhaps offer C some nonmonetary consideration to offset a lower rent. The conclusion might not have changed, but the parties would have made the decision with a greater sense of control and clarity, and fuller empowerment.

However, empowerment also includes allowing the parties to decide for themselves when they have given the matter sufficient time and consideration. In this case, the mediator seems to have sensed that both sides had reached that point. It is not empowerment to keep the parties in the room until they break down and reach agreement simply to escape the session.

SEGMENT 20

At this point, M stepped in and said, "Look, this happens sometimes; it's very frustrating and disappointing to everyone not to be able to reach an agreement when it looked so close, especially after all the hard work you put in. And when you're frustrated and disappointed, it's natural to lash out." R interrupted M and said, "I'm not frustrated; it's really the way C is—a greedy landlord who doesn't care about people." M continued on and said, "Well, that's one way of seeing it. Another way of seeing it is, like we said before, that neither of you is taking their position because of meanness or greed; both of you are acting in good faith. It's just that both of you have real limitations that you can't ignore: R has to stay within her budget, and C has to pay his bills. If you see it this way, what both of you want is reasonable, but the situation just makes it hard. Right at this point, it may be hard to see it this way, but I think that at other points this afternoon both of you have seen this."

M continued, "In any event, it seems the option of the new apartment doesn't look workable to both of you at this point. But let me remind you, earlier on you were talking about another option, for R to move out within two months and pay C a certain amount. Do you want to go back and consider that option, since this other one isn't working out?" Both C and R indicated that they had no interest in further discussion at this point.

M then said that this was OK but that they didn't have to regard the session as wasted time. They had done a great deal of work. For one thing, they had identified several different paths they might take to handle the situation they were in, and it was worth summarizing those now, because they could consider these options further on their own. M summarized: One option was the new apartment deal—each of them could look over the figures again, maybe with more consideration R can see a way to cover the payment, or maybe C can see a way to reduce it more.

Another option was the lump-sum deal discussed earlier—
R would get a limited time to stay, and then would move
and pay some portion of the back rent due. A third option
was to take steps to handle the situation through attorneys
in court. All three options were at least clarified in the discussions today, M said, and the parties could consider and
discuss them further on their own or, if they thought it
would help, come back to the mediation center again.

M concluded, "Just because no agreement has been
reached today, you don't need to wipe away the things
you did accomplish in this session. I think you both got a
better understanding of what you wanted out of this situation and what options are open to you to accomplish
those things, as we just summarized. And you also both
listened to each other and learned more about each
other's perspectives on the situation. This is a real accomplishment, and it counts for something regardless of what
comes next." Both C and R, despite their fatigue and
frustration, listened attentively to these closing remarks
and seemed somewhat buoyed by them.

Move 25: Preserving Recognition in the Face of Impasse

As the prospects for reaching a settlement on the rent and occupancy issues dim, the mediator reminds R and C that they need not
think the worst of each other and revert to the most negative
explanations of each other's behavior. The mediator's goal here is
to remind the parties of the recognition they have given each other
and to encourage them to preserve it, even if they do not settle on
some of the difficult issues that still divide them. At the very end of
this discussion, he explicitly asks the parties to recognize what has
been accomplished in the session: it allowed for an exchange of
information and perspectives that cleared up misunderstandings and
restored a more sympathetic view of each other. In fact, in an ideal
scenario, the mediator here could have actually described again the

new perspectives the parties have gained. Just as he specifically mentions the practical options open to them as they leave the session, he should give the relationship dimension equal weight by being concrete about what they have accomplished in this area.

Move 26: Preserving Empowerment in the Face of Impasse

The mediator keeps empowerment central in the process at this point in the session as well. Through summarizing the range of options the parties had discussed, the mediator reminds R and C that they can continue to think of options and make choices on their own in the future—they can continue the process started here, even if they are too tired or frustrated to continue at the moment. This point is underscored when the mediator makes it clear that the accomplishments of the session were due primarily to the parties' efforts, not the mediator's. (He does suggest, however, that they could consider coming back to the mediation center, if they wanted to. But this, again, is cast as one of the choices the *parties* could make.)

Both moves 25 and 26 are indicative of the unique strength of the transformative approach. Faced with impasse and lacking any possible solution, a mediator's impulse is usually simply to close the session. For a transformative mediator, however, the absence of a settlement does not negate the progress made in empowerment and recognition, and it is well worth doing something to frame that progress, independent of settlement. In fact, the mediator might have gone even further here, helping the parties compose some sort of written "memorandum" of understanding that summarized both the decisions made and the new understandings reached in the session. The mediator here may have sensed that the parties were too tired and frustrated to do this but he could have suggested it to them.

SEGMENT 21

Just as M was about to close the session, R launched into a heated tirade directly at C. First she said, "Don't tell me you can't go down more on the rent—you can if you want to. You could take less, but I can't pay any more. I know we both got kids, but if you don't get as much profit, maybe your kids have to go to a different college. If I pay you more rent, my kids don't eat! If you were really my friend, you'd help me out." C said he was doing all he could—he couldn't do any more. R then got up out of her seat and launched into a description, in some detail, of how, if the case went to court, the housing court would favor her as tenant and R would wind up getting to stay months more and pay nothing. M did not interrupt R's argument. When she finished, M turned to C and said, "Even though R sounds angry when she says these things, what she is doing could be useful for you. She's giving you a chance to ask yourself, how will all this sound to a housing court judge, and what is the court likely to do? That could be useful for you to think about in considering this further, even if you don't want to discuss things any more right now."

M thanked the parties again for their patience and efforts and closed the session.

Move 27: Framing the Value of a Party's Parting Argument

Although the parties are clearly tired and ready to end the mediation, R feels compelled, perhaps out of pure frustration at this point, to argue further. The mediator allows R to make her points, in part because the case she is making is slightly different from anything she argued previously. R suggests that C might look at this as a financial equity issue in which he should consider giving her a financial break because he has a stronger financial base than she has (essentially an income redistribution argument). She also warns C that things could turn against him if he went to court.

By letting R make her case and by summarizing the gist of R's statements to C, the mediator encourages the parties to continue the dialogue that occurred through the session and to listen to each other for information and views that might help them make useful and clear-headed decisions in the future. The mediator's final moves suggest to the parties that they can continue talking and listening as they have done over the past several hours. These moves leave a final impression that the session is ending but the kind of interaction that the parties have engaged in is not.

The next chapter offers an overall analysis of how the mediator's moves in this session followed a transformative route through the mediation, followed by a discussion of some general guidelines that can help in applying this approach to other cases.

Part Three

· ·

Practicing the
Transformative Approach

7

. . . .

Identifying Patterns for Practice:
The Process of Transformative Mediation

The transformative opportunities identified in the Adjacent Gardens and Landlord-Tenant cases, and the mediator moves that work with these opportunities, are not unique to any particular type of dispute. The kind of transformative route taken through the Landlord-Tenant case could equally be taken through disputes involving businesses, managers, professionals, families, agency representatives, and so on. The specific examples we offer in the preceding and following chapters were chosen for clarity and consistency. The substantive issues would vary in different contexts, but the transformative opportunities would be similar.

Involvement in conflict affects all parties in similar ways. No matter what the context, disputes make parties fearful, confused, and unsure of what to do. As a result, they feel vulnerable and out of control. Moreover, in the heat of conflict, disputing parties typically feel threatened or victimized by the conduct and claims of the other party. As a result, they are defensive, suspicious, and hostile to the other party, and almost incapable of looking beyond their own needs. Thus, across all contexts, conflicts engender in people the experience of relative weakness and relative self-absorption. It is the experience of conflict itself, whatever the context, that creates transformative opportunities for empowerment and recognition. The transformative approach illustrated in the Landlord-Tenant case can be used to surface and work with those opportunities in any context. And indeed some mediators are already using it in many different contexts. The only limitation is the mediator's ability to recognize and follow a transformative route through conflict and mediation.

Reviewing the course of the Landlord-Tenant case is a good way to summarize what that route looks like. This case is particularly instructive in understanding how and when opportunities for empowerment and recognition arise in mediation and, even more important, how a mediator works with and develops them. The mediator in this dispute uncovered, evoked, and worked with a range of different opportunities to empower the parties and foster recognition. Although such opportunities were occasionally missed, as noted in the case comments, they were never intentionally ignored by the mediator as he guided the process and interacted with the disputants. The desire to achieve settlement never became a substitute for keeping empowerment and recognition the primary objectives of the process. The result, in our view, was that the parties left the session with greater capacities for addressing life's difficulties, stepping outside of themselves to consider another's perspective, and realistically confronting their own (and each other's) options, resources, and limitations. Ironically, although a settlement was not reached in this case, the *parties* moved much closer to constructing one here than they did in the Adjacent Gardens case, in which an agreement was signed.

Tracing the Transformative Route

Looking back over the Landlord-Tenant case, it becomes clear that the mediator's moves follow and exemplify the defining patterns of transformative practice as described in Chapter Four. First of all, throughout this session the mediator avoids making any global assessment of what the dispute as a whole is about and instead keeps a *microfocus on the parties' contributions*. The mediator is always focused on what the parties have just said, what they are doing in each move as the dispute unfolds. During the entire session, the mediator remains in a *responsive* posture. When he makes a move, he does not know what his next move will be. Each "next move" depends on what the parties do in response to his prior move and on what possible opportunities for empowerment and recognition arise at that point. Although the mediator probably has a general idea of the kinds of things that may happen as the session unfolds, he knows that the specifics of the parties' interaction differ in every case, and he keeps his attention on responding to those specifics.

This means that, in a sense, the mediator "follows the parties around" as they explore and clarify their options, challenge each other's views, and consider possible points of settlement. In each of the caucuses, for instance, the mediator asks one or two general questions about past events that shaped R's and C's views of each other or about what steps they are considering in the current circumstances. But after the questions are asked, he essentially pursues R's and C's lines of thinking, summarizing and reframing what they have said, or else asking more questions to help them consider things fully—but not directing the discussion toward an inevitable conclusion or a preferred settlement option. The reason is that he is not pursuing settlement per se but seeking to surface and capture opportunities for empowerment and recognition.

Taking this responsive posture means that the mediator is comfortable not knowing where things are headed, that he can move through the process without having a sense that all of the interaction and discussion is aimed at solving a readily definable problem that is set in place early in the process. A student who observed this mediation session said afterward that if she had been mediating, she would have been very frustrated at many points, especially during the caucuses. She said the parties, especially the tenant, seemed to be "all over the place" and did not know what they wanted and what would rectify the situation for them. Looking back over the case, especially segments 7 and 8, this seems a fair description. At the same time, it is clear that if the mediator had gotten frustrated

194 THE PROMISE OF MEDIATION

with the parties' lack of focus, the most likely alternative would
have been to push for a specific definition of the problem and a specific solution. The mediator's frustration could easily have led, in
other words, to a global assessment of what the dispute as a whole
was about and a focus on settlement. And the inevitable consequences of this would be the mediator's loss of focus on the moves
the parties were making in the session and his failure to explore the
opportunities for empowerment and recognition they presented.

Beyond fostering empowerment and recognition, the microfocus
on the parties' moves and the ability to remain in a responsive posture are important for another reason. Allowing and encouraging
the parties to pursue their own sense of the issues and their own
views on settlement is perhaps the only way for mediators to ensure
that they are not pigeonholing the dispute to fit their own sense of
what the parties' problem is and what the best solution might be. It
prevents mediators from placing their own interests—in achieving
a settlement or adopting the "best" solution—on an equal footing
with the parties' views of the concerns that have brought them to
mediation. In this case, the mediator's moves clearly keep both the
definition of issues and the construction of possible solutions
squarely in the parties' hands.

A second general pattern visible in the mediator's moves in the
Landlord-Tenant case is that he fosters empowerment by *encouraging the parties' deliberation and choice making*. From the earliest moves
in the session, the mediator encourages and helps the parties clarify
their needs and goals and reflect and deliberate about options with
a full awareness of their potentials and limits. In the caucuses, for
example, the mediator makes a sustained effort to encourage the parties to articulate their concerns and to identify and evaluate the
choices they might make to deal with them. As noted, the mediator
could go even further sometimes in raising questions and leading the
parties to consider the feasibility or desirability of certain options.
Nevertheless, the mediator does do a great deal in this regard, and
as a result the parties gain considerable clarity on many key points.

For example, although R starts out being quite confused about what she wants and how to get it, she grows much clearer about her goals and options, including her desire to move to a bigger place but not in an unsafe neighborhood, her view that she needs a decent place to live for her kids, her belief that her current rent is too high for the quality of the apartment, and her plan to move out for a bigger apartment and save money by not paying arrears. She also develops arguments to support her possible courses of action, including what she might say if the case went to court, why C might be better off settling with her out of court, and that C should reduce her rent or give her the bigger apartment at a lower rate because he can afford to. In articulating these views and making these arguments, R gains substantial personal strength. She has a better understanding of her own interests, what she wants and does not want in the situation, and what she is willing and able to do about it. Even at the very end of the session when it looks like no agreement will be reached, R continues to clarify the way she sees her choices and how she will make her case. There is a strong sense that R will continue to use this new awareness after the mediation. Similarly, in caucus and in joint discussions, the mediator's moves help C gain considerable clarity on his key concerns and options for satisfying them—though again the mediator might have done even more to raise questions for C about the consequences of his choices.

The mediator supports the parties' deliberation and choice making in several other respects as well. For example, at the very outset, he encourages the parties to consider whether they want to engage in mediation and commit to the ground rules of the process rather than simply insisting on participation and compliance. Here and later in the session, he explicitly gives the parties the responsibility for making decisions—about participation, definition of issues, acceptability of solutions. By doing so, the mediator puts the parties directly in touch with their own control over their situation. He is also careful throughout the session to word summaries of the parties' views as questions, checking to see whether his statements accurately reflect the parties' positions and views. Although he cycles back and forth between different substantive and relational concerns the parties raise, he tries hard not to drop any issue the parties want to discuss. Sensitive points about how they see each other are as much a part of the parties' concerns as, for instance, how much back rent R will pay. These concerns remain part of the discussion because the parties keep returning to these issues *and* because the mediator encourages them to do so—although at certain points he could be even more careful about this.

Finally, toward the end of the session, the mediator pursues C's concerns about the tentative agreement that was reached, even though it means that the settlement quickly unravels. In some ways, this is the mediator's most telling empowerment move. He does not squelch last-minute doubts for the sake of saving an agreement that is almost within reach. To do so would reverse the empowerment he has fostered throughout the entire session.

The third pattern visible throughout the Landlord-Tenant case is that the mediator fosters recognition by *encouraging perspective taking* whenever an opportunity for it arises. The mediator looks for openings—places where one party can consider the other's situation or self from the other's perspective and where a more positive or sympathetic view of the other might be entertained. Sometimes, especially in the caucuses, the mediator himself creates these openings, by asking the parties to talk about events or views of the other and then drawing on these statements to help explain one party to the other in a new way. The mediator also listens for and invites each party's expressions of their own motives and sensitivities, statements that call for response and recognition from the other. He then helps each to hear and respond to what the other is saying about how they want to be understood.

This focus on achieving recognition means that the mediation is less future oriented than many mediators might consider "wise." Mediators often say that turning to the past is counterproductive or dangerous, because the mediator cannot judge the accuracy of parties' accounts and the goal of mediation is to find an agreement that specifies what the parties will commit to do in the future. In this view, mining the past does not do much to get you to the future. In this session, however, the mediator works with statements parties make as they discuss past events, not to get to the facts or determine the "real story" but rather to clarify misunderstandings and open up possibilities for new ways of seeing each other.

Indeed, much of the recognition that occurs in this session occurs around the parties' current reinterpretations of past events. The discussions of past events—whether C reported R to the Bureau of Child Welfare, what C did and did not know about R's recent difficulties, and why R treated C the way she did when C asked her to pay the back rent—all serve as the basis for the parties' developing new and positive perspectives of each other. The mediator uses the information that surfaces in these discussions to suggest to each party reinterpretations of the other's past behavior, and this strategy creates opportunities for each party to give recognition by seeing the other in a more positive light. These opportunities would have been missed entirely if the mediator believed that the discussion and interpretation of these events were not central to what the mediation was about, just as they were missed in the Adjacent Gardens case.

Thus the three primary patterns of transformative mediation—microfocusing on parties' moves, encouraging deliberation and choice making, and fostering perspective taking—are plainly evident in this session. Also apparent is the way that these patterns can combine in dynamic interaction to produce other, more subtle contours of transformative practice. As we pointed out in Chapter Four, empowerment and recognition are interdependent and reinforcing effects. This interdependence allows a mediator to build momentum in a session that maximizes the achievement of both. The interaction between empowerment and recognition, and the momentum it can build, are very much at play in the Landlord-Tenant case.

As the session begins, both parties are self-protective and accusatory, threatening each other (with eviction or irresponsible landlording) and ready to defend themselves against each other's damaging attacks. As both parties begin to clarify their views—what they want and do not want, what resources they have to address the situation—they are more able to give each other recognition. For instance, after R clarifies her interests and sees the possible resources she can bring to bear in the conflict, there is a sense in which she is empowered—she has stood up, thought through her options, and been taken seriously by the mediator and C. It is then that she is able to begin tossing off her defensive posture and starts to see things from C's perspective. Although she wavers back and forth on some key points during the session, she admits that he has been a good landlord in the past, that she hit him, and that some of what she did was wrong. She even goes so far as to apologize for some of her past behavior. These are major admissions on her part. R was able to offer this recognition because of the strength she gained as she clarified her goals and options and came to a clearer sense of what was important for her. Feeling empowered, R is then strong enough to admit weakness and open up to C.

This movement on R's part then influences C's reactions. Once R apologizes for her past behavior, C is strengthened by R's admission and he, too, becomes willing to admit his weaknesses. He tells R that he may not have realized how rough a time she has been through, and he offers his sincere sympathy for her recent problems. In a sense, with C's comments to R, a transformative arc has come full circle: the strength R gains in understanding her own views enables her to offer important recognition to C; C is then strengthened by R's expression of understanding of him and he, in turn, offers her recognition.

The mediator in this case helps create and advance this cycle by triggering the dynamic interplay between empowerment and recognition. This occurs through the shifts he makes in his own efforts during the session—shifts between empowering the parties by encouraging them to think through their options, resources, and choices and, on the other hand, laying the groundwork for and encouraging recognition between them. As noted earlier, throughout the session he follows the parties' leads on what they are ready to discuss and how they see the issues. Nevertheless, when the mediator is expected to initiate discussion (e.g., at the beginning of caucuses or joint sessions), he adopts a focus that builds the cycle of empowerment and recognition. Also, at key points within caucuses and joint sessions, he raises questions and frames summaries in ways that enable the parties to move back and forth between empowerment and recognition. In short, when he senses that the parties have moved as far as they can in offering recognition, he encourages a shift in focus to empowerment, and vice versa. Even the decision to caucus in the first place is built on a sense that the parties could not go further in giving recognition in joint session, without first gaining the strength that the caucuses could provide. Making these shifts in focus is important process work in the transformative approach to mediation. These shifts are always made in response to where the parties are heading and thus do not undercut empowerment. But they are important moves because they directly affect the way the transformative process builds over time—they help sequence empowerment and recognition efforts over the course of a session and build the kind of momentum and interactive effects that are apparent in the Landlord-Tenant case.

This dynamic character of mediation is important in understanding the overall mind-set mediators operate from in finding a transformative route through a dispute. Since transformative mediators consciously avoid shaping disputes into readily solvable problems, they remain closely attuned to the *ongoing* nature of the conflicts in which they intervene. They do not start by thinking that the dispute is a static item that can be easily packaged and that the role of the mediator is to find this package and seal the case. Instead, they remain aware that they are entering a stream of interaction, that the interaction among the parties began before the session and will, in most cases, continue afterward, whether a settlement is reached or not. They realize that even when agreements are reached, parties often continue to interact and points of conflict may persist. The parties may need to work out what the agreement actually means in practice, they may have to adjust to changing circumstances or new issues, or they may simply fall into old patterns of interaction over the same or different issues.

Therefore, the mind-set of the transformative mediator is that a settlement agreement does not define success in mediation, and empowerment and recognition do. That is why we chose to present the Landlord-Tenant case as an illustration of the transformative approach: because although transformative mediation often does lead to settlement, it can be successful even where it does not, if empowerment and recognition are achieved. While not every opportunity for empowerment and recognition was captured in the Landlord-Tenant case, a great many were; and the impact of this on the parties was significant and visible, despite their frustration at the close of the session. For this reason, in the transformative view, the Landlord-Tenant case represents successful mediation, although no settlement was reached, while the Adjacent Gardens case exemplifies failed mediation, despite the settlement produced.

This is *not* to say that the transformative approach ignores the importance of meeting parties' human needs. It only means not concentrating directly on this objective. By focusing on empowerment and recognition, transformative mediation can do as good a job or better than current practice in satisfying needs, because when settlements are reached, they are determined by the parties' genuine needs alone. In addition, even when no settlement occurs, the groundwork has been laid for further movement by the parties themselves on needs issues, after the mediation ends. In both of these ways, the objective of satisfying needs is not lost under a transformative approach. Still, this objective is not the primary focus, because there are *other* dispute resolution processes, such as arbitration, that can serve the goal of satisfying needs. However, *no* process besides mediation can serve the goal of transformation equally well, and this goal is a vitally important one.

The value of transformative mediation is that it helps parties change and experience new modes of behavior and interaction; and these changes and new behaviors can occur, and continue, whether or not an agreement is reached in any given session. These changes—transformations—can be far more lasting and transferable than the terms of any agreement, because they stem from changes in the parties themselves. They are built on the often slight but always significant ways in which parties are transformed as people through the empowerment they have gained and the recognition they have given in mediation.

Directions and Signposts for the Transformative Route

The review here of the Landlord-Tenant case summarizes the elements of transformative mediation, which can certainly be translated to other cases and contexts. However, generalizing even further about how transformative mediation works can be helpful in putting the approach into practice. For example, it is useful for mediators to have a general picture or model of how a mediation session typically unfolds, what directions a case typically takes, in the transformative view. In particular, it is important to have a sense of when and how opportunities for empowerment and recognition arise in mediation sessions. In addition, it is useful to have some idea in advance of what these opportunities tend to look like, in a general way, and what kinds of moves can be taken to exploit them and thus foster empowerment and recognition. In effect, this would offer mediators both a "map" of the direction transformative mediations generally take and "signposts" that mark opportunities for empowerment and recognition along the way. Together the map and signposts can provide a model to guide practitioners in their work, telling them what to look out for, in order to recognize and capture these opportunities.

Figure 7.1 offers a map of the transformative mediation process, a rough pictorial representation—not a scientific illustration—of the way sessions can be expected to unfold using this approach. In

Figure 7.1. Mapping the Transformative Process.

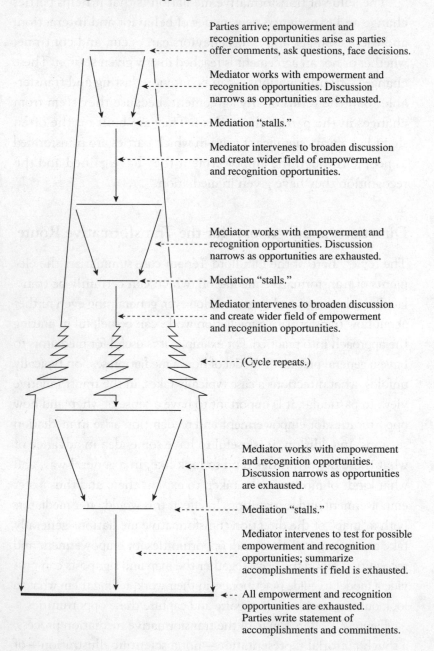

Parties arrive; empowerment and recognition opportunities arise as parties offer comments, ask questions, face decisions.

Mediator works with empowerment and recognition opportunities. Discussion narrows as opportunities are exhausted.

Mediation "stalls."

Mediator intervenes to broaden discussion and create wider field of empowerment and recognition opportunities.

Mediator works with empowerment and recognition opportunities. Discussion narrows as opportunities are exhausted.

Mediation "stalls."

Mediator intervenes to broaden discussion and create wider field of empowerment and recognition opportunities.

(Cycle repeats.)

Mediator works with empowerment and recognition opportunities. Discussion narrows as opportunities are exhausted.

Mediation "stalls."

Mediator intervenes to test for possible empowerment and recognition opportunities; summarize accomplishments if field is exhausted.

All empowerment and recognition opportunities are exhausted. Parties write statement of accomplishments and commitments.

the transformative view, mediation typically begins in a somewhat narrow field of opportunities for empowerment and recognition, composed of the initial comments of the parties (verbal or nonverbal) as the session starts. The mediator takes a microfocus on each comment the parties make from the time they enter the mediation room. The field of opportunities is narrow to begin with because, compared to the number of comments that will be made by the time the session ends, there are very few comments on the table. Yet each comment, as it is offered, becomes important in moving the transformative process along. Right from the start, even before the mediator gives an opening statement, the session presents choices for the parties to make—for example, about whether they want to be there at all, about what they want to say and how they want to frame issues, about whether they are willing to commit to the ground rules of the process. These choices offer possible opportunities for empowerment because they are points at which parties can make clear and deliberate choices regarding their involvement in the process. And right from the start, as soon as the parties start talking, each is presented with opportunities for seeing the other differently, opportunities for recognition. As the session begins, the mediator is poised to identify and work with any of these opportunities.

A set of possible opportunities for empowerment and recognition (like those just mentioned) typically present themselves at the beginning of a session. As the mediator responds to and works with these opportunities, helping the parties notice and exploit them one by one, the field of possibilities thins out and the mediation tends to "stall"—to settle into a noticeably slow period, in which further opportunities for empowerment and recognition are not apparent. At this point the mediator needs to make some move that opens up the interaction between the parties. Some of these moves are standard, some responsive to the particulars of the case.

For example, after choices have been made about whether parties will stay in the process and commit to the ground rules, it is standard for the mediator to ask the parties to give their views of the situation that brought them to mediation, their opening stories. This move encourages the parties to talk about a broad set of issues and thus opens up a wider field of comments/interactions and opportunities for empowerment and recognition than has emerged thus far in the session. The comments the parties make during this second period are then explored for the opportunities for empowerment and recognition they offer, and the opportunities are addressed one by one. When all of these opportunities are exhausted, the mediation will appear to "stall" again. Once again the mediator intervenes in a way that encourages further comments and interaction, for example, by probing about a particular set of statements that seem to carry implicit messages about how the parties see or want to be seen by one another or about what the parties want to do. Such a move creates a new and even broader field of comments and empowerment and recognition opportunities.

Thus in the transformative model, the process flows in cycles or segments. But, as suggested by Figure 7.1, the overall direction of the flow is broadening, from a narrow consideration of a few initial opportunities for empowerment and recognition to an increasingly wider transformative field. The field gets increasingly broader because once topics are opened up, they remain possible places to which parties might return. Even an initial concern, such as whether the parties want to participate in the process, might resurface at a later point in the session and offer a second opportunity for empowerment. In addition, each successive cycle tends to generate increasing numbers of comments and interactions by and between the parties. (There can be any number of segments or cycles; Figure 7.1 only suggests the general idea.)

The map signals to mediators that their work in mediation sessions will typically be twofold: first, to encourage the parties to cycle through a set of increasingly expansive discussions that allows opportunities for empowerment and recognition to emerge; and, second, to help the parties recognize and work with these opportunities one by one as they surface. Through this process, solutions to people's problems may emerge, but the real accomplishments of the session are a much wider set of understandings parties gain and choices they make about their options, as well as understandings they gain about each other's perspectives. When solutions to concrete problems are found during this process, they are built on the reassuring footing of these transformative accomplishments.

This picture of how a mediation session unfolds is not meant to dismiss as irrelevant the sense of many practitioners (and theorists) that mediation sessions typically move through certain stages, such as setting ground rules, making opening statements, defining issues, and generating and evaluating options (Stulberg, 1987; Folberg and Taylor, 1984). However, rather than seeing these "stages" as a defining structure or map of how mediation sessions unfold, the transformative model sees them as roughly marking some of the points at which certain kinds of opportunities for empowerment and recognition can be expected to arise. This point will be clearer after discussing the second element needed for a model of how transformative mediation works.

To be effective in practicing transformative mediation, mediators need more than a general map of how mediation sessions unfold. A model of transformative practice also needs to identify a set of typical events that mark opportunities for empowerment and recognition. Although such opportunities can arise almost any time a party speaks, there are events that tend to occur across many cases, transformative "signposts" of sorts, that signal their presence. These typical events are either comments made by one party or short interaction sequences between the parties. They tend to arise in predictable places during sessions, and, as markers, they tell mediators, "This is a place where empowerment or recognition might be fostered." Identifying these points in advance helps flesh out the general map of the process. This kind of advance notice enables mediators to keep transformative objectives at the heart of practice. If mediators walk into each session with even a small set of such signposts in mind, they are more likely to see the whole range of empowerment and recognition opportunities that surface as sessions unfold.

Table 7.1 summarizes a range of transformative signpost events,

Table 7.1 "Signpost" Events Marking Opportunities for Empowerment and Recognition.

Stage of Process	"Signpost" Event	Mediator Response
Early opportunities	Parties interpret mediation as an adjudicative process and expect mediators to give solutions to problems.	Clarifies nonadjudicative role of the mediator; emphasizes parties' responsibility in decision making.
	Parties disagree about who should participate in the process (such as whether friends or relatives should speak on behalf of disputants).	Holds discussion with the parties to decide who should participate and why. If no agreement, session may end.
	Parties challenge ground rules of the process.	Explains why ground rules are important to process; probes whether parties are willing to commit to each ground rule. If no commitment, session may end.
	A disputant says that he or she does not want to talk to the other party at all, but just wants to take the case to a hearing or judge.	In joint session or caucus, discusses why the disputant does not want to participate; encourages party to make a clear choice about why he or she will or will not open discussion.
Midstage opportunities	A party indicates that something the other has said is news to him or her.	Explores what this news is and how it might change the party's understanding of past events or the other disputant.
	A party's comment suggests that some way in which he or she sees himself or herself is important and that this image of self has not been fully considered by the other party.	Explores what is important about this image of self, discusses how this concern might be important in understanding the dispute.
	A party "rambles" from point to point in statement of concerns/goals, not clearly focusing.	"Follows" party's lead, mirroring concerns and asking questions, allowing and helping party to define his or her own priorities.

Late-stage opportunities	A party asks mediator, "What do you think I should do?" about a particular solution option.	Declines to offer advice/judgment; reminds party of his or her decision-making power; asks questions to help party evaluate option.
	A party speaks very emotionally, passionately.	Discusses what prompts the strong reaction; encourages party to state the basis for the strong views, to surface opportunity for recognition.
	One or more issues that were raised by the parties early in the discussion are no longer mentioned as the session progresses.	Asks whether these issues have been forgotten, or whether parties want to discuss them further.
	A party offers an explanation or account for past events that assumes "the worst" about the other party and his or her motives.	Offers possible reinterpretation of the past event that avoids negative judgment of the other; asks whether this or other interpretations are possible.
	When parties cannot think of any acceptable option for how to deal with situation, mediator offers a suggestion as a "last resort," but one party reacts sharply and negatively and rejects it.	Confirms party's power to decide to reject suggestion, then asks questions about reasons for rejection to help further clarify party's goals and surface perceptions of self and other.
	After an agreement appears to be reached, one or both of the parties indicate that they have doubts about whether the terms are going to work.	Indicates that the parties can rethink the agreement at this point; asks them about their concerns.
	The parties become angry and frustrated because they do not settle on terms that substantially alleviate their concerns and tensions.	Explores the basis for parties' frustration; summarizes understandings, points of recognition that may have been achieved; encourages parties to build on these in their own discussions after the session ends.

marking opportunities for empowerment and recognition, that occur over and over again in mediated discussions, together with the kind of mediator responses that help parties work with the opportunities presented. This is only an illustrative summary, but it can serve as a basis for further work identifying a more exhaustive list. These "typical events" are arranged by when they are most likely to occur in a mediation session—in the early, middle, or late stages of the process. (As implied earlier, the traditionally recognized "stages" of the process can be seen, in the transformative model, as useful in identifying the general "areas" in which certain signpost events tend to occur.) Not all of these events will occur in any one mediation, and they will not necessarily take place in the exact order in which they listed here. However, mediators can expect some of the events summarized in the table to occur in almost every case and can anticipate roughly the stage of the process where they are likely to occur. Most important, mediators can know that when one of these signpost events occurs, it marks an opportunity for empowerment or recognition, and they can respond accordingly. It should be evident that many of these signpost events occurred, in some variation, in the Landlord-Tenant case; and it was probably the mediator's awareness that they might occur that enabled him to recognize them and respond as he did. Across mediation arenas, transformative practice can be built on the mediator's ability to sense moment-to-moment opportunities for empowerment and recognition and to intervene in ways that realize their potential.

The Landlord-Tenant case illustrates how mediators can work to achieve the transformative objectives of empowerment and recognition, and this chapter has presented some general patterns and guidelines to help in applying the approach more broadly. It is also important to acknowledge that the transformative approach, together with its strengths, entails its own difficulties and potential pitfalls. Understanding these pitfalls and how to handle them is important in putting the transformative approach into practice. This is the subject of the next chapter.

∙ ∙

Avoiding Pitfalls in Transformative Mediation: The Connection Between Purpose and Practice

Following the transformative approach to mediation is no easy matter, even with a good model and clear examples. The approach is just beginning to be articulated, even though some mediators have long tended toward it intuitively in their practice. Therefore, even those who try to follow it consistently and conscientiously are bound to be imperfect in their practice, as was the mediator in the Landlord-Tenant case. In fact, the various principles and examples offered in this book must be understood as first steps toward a full understanding of how to implement this approach. As more people practice and study transformative mediation, more will be learned, which will almost certainly require modifications and extensions of the descriptions of transformative mediation practice offered here.

Beyond the inevitable difficulties of learning the contours of a new approach, however, a number of predictable pitfalls await those who try to practice transformative mediation. These pitfalls are predictable because of what is already evident about the elements of transformative mediation and their nuances. However, with advance warning and careful attention, it may be possible to avoid most of them most of the time.

Thinking Empowerment Means Mediator Passivity

Because the transformative approach emphasizes empowering parties and placing decisions in their hands, mediators may be hesitant about making certain moves, thinking that these moves may dis-empower the parties. Sometimes such hesitancy is a healthy guard against overdirective practice. However, mediators may become so concerned about avoiding disempowerment that they avoid initi-ating any positive intervention and instead adopt an almost pas-sive posture.

For example, mediators may feel obliged to use only the parties' exact words in repeating or summarizing what they have said; they may be reluctant to do anything that would "impose order," even if the discussions degenerate into a shouting match; and perhaps most serious, they may hesitate to raise tough questions that would encourage the parties to evaluate options carefully and consider each other's perspectives seriously. All these responses involve act-ing as though party empowerment requires mediator passivity, so that the mediator becomes a mere "convenor" of the discussions.

This pitfall involves a misunderstanding of empowerment. Empowerment means *encouraging and helping* parties to deliberate and make decisions, because this support from the mediator helps parties find their own strength. Simply standing by—while parties struggle, flounder, and exchange reflex reactions—does nothing to strengthen them at all. Instead, reframing the parties' language in ways that help them fully express themselves and understand each other is empow-ering—as long as the mediator checks to make sure the parties' mean-ing has not been changed or "lost." Intervening to raise questions that remind and help parties to consider the consequences of different options, instead of reacting reflexively and impulsively, is central to empowerment. Indeed, "[B]oth empowerment and recognition require . . . a mediator . . . to 'push' the parties . . . in the positive sense of inviting, supporting, encouraging, motivating, and urging the parties to work through the processes of self-determined choice and mutual acknowledgment" (Bush, 1989, p. 277).

Nevertheless, a hesitancy to push the parties at all, even in this positive sense, can result from misunderstanding the emphasis trans-formative mediation puts on party control of decision making.

Those just starting to explore the transformative approach may be particularly vulnerable to this pitfall. For example, in one housing case, in which the mediator had only recently begun to use the transformative approach, the tenant began by stating very angrily that, because the landlord had insulted and mistrusted him, he had made up his mind to "get even with" the landlord by staying as long as possible and moving out without paying a cent. Though the situation was very similar to the Landlord-Tenant case, the mediator here hesitated to raise any questions with either party and simply restated the tenant's position in much the same terms. The session was over very quickly, and the students who observed it questioned whether either party was really empowered, because the session essentially began and ended with these initial emotional accusations. The mediator did nothing to encourage either side to consider either their own options or each other's perspectives.

Carrying "Positive Pushing" Too Far

The second pitfall of the transformative approach is in effect the converse of the first. While the first pitfall is for the mediator to err on the side of not enough intervention, the second is for the mediator to go too far, in the name of empowerment and recognition, with "positive pushing." The warning to mediators here is that, like too little intervention, too much can also undermine both empowerment and recognition.

While raising tough questions is important to help parties fully consider their options, the mediator can carry the questioning so far that a party feels the mediator is "looking for" certain answers. Overly tough questioning can thus wind up conveying a directive message to the party, even though the mediator's real purpose is only to encourage deliberation and not to influence its direction. The effect may be disempowering, the very opposite of the mediator's intent. For example, in the Landlord-Tenant case, the mediator questions the landlord in caucus about his plan to evict the tenant (segment 12). After a series of questions that in effect ask the landlord to consider whether a "buyout" arrangement would be preferable to court action, the landlord says, "I'll do whatever you say. What do you think I should do?" Clearly, given the mediator's overall conduct in this case, his questioning is intended to encourage deliberation, not to pressure a settlement, and the questioning here is not even particularly tough. But the pitfall is there anyway, and the mediator must be on guard against it.

Avoiding this pitfall means that, even while questioning and inviting parties to consider options, the mediator must listen to himself or herself and stop short of being directive, in tone or substance. Moreover, since this is itself difficult and partly dependent on parties' perceptions, the mediator needs to be sensitive to parties' reactions and prepared to pull back quickly and clarify the point if parties get the wrong message. The mediator in the Landlord-Tenant case acted precisely this way, explaining that the questions were only intended to help the landlord clarify his choices. Beyond this, the mediator can guard against this pitfall by "framing" moves in advance, telling parties the purpose of the questioning and reminding them that all decisions are still up to them. And when a party does change views in response to a mediator's questioning, a further safeguard is for the mediator to pause and doublecheck that the new view is genuinely the party's choice.

As with inviting parties to consider and evaluate options, mediators can also err by going too far in encouraging parties to seek or offer recognition. For example, offering possible positive reinterpretations of past conduct involves active intervention with each side. But if a mediator goes too far in arguing for the suggested interpretation, it may wind up provoking even greater hostility, both toward the other party and toward the mediator for seeming to be an advocate for that party. Thus the mediator in the Landlord-Tenant case was careful only to suggest reinterpretations (in the caucuses), and not to argue forcefully for them, and he allowed the parties to reject them on first hearing (segments 9 and 11).

On another level, if the mediator goes too far in trying to open up opportunities for recognition—for example, by asking the parties to elaborate on statements already offered to describe their feelings or problems—this may also be counterproductive. Stepping in to ask for such elaboration may simply interrupt, and even short-circuit, a flow of recognition that is already under way. Or it may be unduly intrusive and invasive of the parties' sense of dignity and privacy, like stepping across the line that divides mediation from therapy. In the Landlord-Tenant case, the mediator avoided this pitfall by limiting his intervention in the joint discussion, once a flow of recognition began to occur between the parties (segment 14). Although the comment there suggested that he might have pushed the parties a bit further in this exchange, doing so might have risked going too far and bringing about the negative consequences just described.

In general, the discussion of the first two pitfalls suggests that transformative practice requires mediators to walk a careful line—between not doing enough to encourage empowerment and recognition and, on the other hand, going too far in working for these objectives. On either side of this line is a pitfall, and leaning over too far to avoid one may mean falling into the other. Keeping on the center course between the two is difficult but certainly not impossible. The better mediators understand each of these two pitfalls, the better they will be at walking this line.

Protecting Too Much, Protecting Too Little

Transformative mediators have to walk another line, between two opposite pitfalls. In one sense, these two pitfalls are variants of the two just discussed, but they are important enough to mention separately. On one side of the line, because transformative mediation emphasizes party choice based on full consideration of options, mediators may think they have a special obligation to ensure that parties have adequate information before making decisions. After all, if a party lacks information—factual, legal, or otherwise—how can that party make an informed choice about what to do? In this view, allowing people to make choices on the basis of partial information is not empowerment at all.

However, this view overlooks the point that party choice *includes* the choice of how much information to consider an adequate basis for decision making. While mediators can and should call parties' attention to the question of whether they think their information is adequate, it is possible to go too far on this point, as on others. When mediators do so, they can wind up discouraging decisions the parties themselves feel prepared to make. In effect, the mediator falls into the pitfall of "protecting parties from themselves," shifting from pursuing empowerment into protection—and disempowerment.

In one case, for example, a husband and wife were at odds because, after a decision to separate, the wife had left the house while the husband was at work, taking all the furniture with her. The wife maintained that she valued the furniture much more than the husband did, and indeed that she was prepared to have him take the house (jointly owned) if she could keep the furniture. The parties discussed estimated figures, which put the value of the house at roughly six times that of the furniture, and the wife still sought the exchange of furniture for house. The mediator suggested that she not make this decision without first consulting an attorney, accountant, and other information sources, but the wife insisted that whatever the value differential, this was her preference. The mediator, however, insisted that the mediation be discontinued until she got more information. Clearly, he saw this as encouraging "full deliberation," but in making this move the mediator deprived the wife of her freedom to make her own decision on what was adequate information even if she was "making a mistake." Self-determination includes the freedom to make one's own mistakes. Unless there is reason to believe the party lacks the capacity for decision making, protecting parties from themselves by insisting on more information is a pitfall that undermines empowerment.

On the other hand, this last comment points to the pitfall on the other side of the center line. In some cases parties do lack capacity for decision making, and if the mediator does not recognize this and discontinue the process, empowerment and recognition are both at great risk. Perhaps the most important example is when one party is the victim of past violence by the other. In this case, fear of future harm may negate that party's capacity to engage in genuine deliberation and decision making on issues involving the abuser, even if the party is otherwise completely competent. The pitfall is that, because of the supposed importance of leaving choices up to the parties, a mediator may feel reluctant to raise questions about capacity when the parties have not and they seem willing to proceed.

Avoiding this pitfall means that, if something suggests the element of violence and fear, the mediator needs at the very least to pursue this question in depth with the possible victim party and not proceed unless satisfied that nothing has occurred to negate that party's capacity for free decision making. A transformative mediator should not hesitate to do this, thinking that because it involves "protection" it is beyond his or her scope. When protection means ensuring that the fundamental condition of capacity is not lacking, what is being protected is the party's opportunity to participate meaningfully in the process. This kind of protection is part of empowerment.

A connected point is that, while protecting parties from their own decisions is a contradiction to empowerment, helping parties fully participate in the mediation process is not. For example, if one party is monopolizing the discussions, or cutting off the other party, or addressing abusive comments to them, the mediator might feel obligated to refrain from intervening, so as not to take control away from the parties. Again, the pitfall is mistaking passivity for empowerment, and help with participation for disempowerment. On the contrary, in such a situation the mediator can and should intervene, although not by "imposing control" on the session.

Instead, as illustrated in the Landlord-Tenant case, the mediator can ask questions that help both parties decide how they want to proceed and whether they think the present course of the discussions is productive (i.e., will it get them where they want to go). With the "quiet" party in particular, the mediator can ask whether that party feels their concerns are getting sufficient attention and whether they find the tone of the discussion acceptable. If the answers are negative, the mediator can explore what each party is willing to do to alter the tone and course of the discussions, and then help them pursue this to the satisfaction of both, before proceeding further. Helping both parties to participate fully in the discussions is itself empowerment and can lead to further empowerment in dealing with the substantive issues.

Again, the discussion here suggests that taking the transformative approach requires avoiding pitfalls in two opposite directions: going too far to protect parties from their own decisions, and not going far enough to protect parties' opportunity to participate meaningfully and fully in the mediation.

Focusing on Empowerment Alone or Recognition Alone

As discussed in Chapter Four, the transformative approach sees empowerment and recognition as linked. Neither is really valuable without the other, because neither alone produces transformation. Recognition without empowerment involves no freely made choice to reach beyond the self. It is simply a forced concession, a grudging admission unaccompanied by any real change of perspective or heart. It accomplishes no transformation of the "giver," because it is not really given at all but taken.

Conversely, empowerment without recognition, while it certainly involves development in one dimension of moral growth, is just that: one-dimensional. If not employed as the foundation for relating to others, for recognition, empowerment simply transforms weak and selfish people into strong and selfish people. It accomplishes a transformation but one of questionable value, and certainly not the one envisioned and valued by the transformative orientation.

Nevertheless, empowerment and recognition can be treated as separate, independent objectives, and pursued in isolation from one another. Another pitfall of transformative practice is doing just this. Forgetting about the invaluable connection between the two, mediators may not make the effort—a considerable one—to work constantly for empowerment and recognition together. Instead, they may focus only on one or the other.

Thus mediators may make the mistake of trying to evoke recognition between parties without any concern for empowerment, by forcefully telling them how they should see and treat each other, and then lecturing them about the need for empathy and consideration. This approach loses sight of the crucial difference between the parties' choosing to give recognition and being shamed or pressured into it. The most it is likely to produce is forced recognition, which has little transformative value.

For example, in one case involving a dispute over noise between upstairs and downstairs apartment dwellers, the mediator told the upstairs party,

> You have to realize that the people below are not hypersensitive—they're being driven crazy by the noise from your apartment, with its bare wood floors. Imagine what your music and walking sounds like to them, and be more considerate. I know you think wood floors are very nice, but when you live right on top of somebody like this, you have to understand what it's like for them. It's just not right not to put down a carpet.

In another case involving a couple who had threatened a woman with whom their teenaged son was having an affair, the mediator told the couple,

You have to understand, your son is legally an adult, and adults have the right to choose their own friends, male or female. This person he's chosen to associate with has done nothing unusual for this day and age. She didn't force him into any-thing—she's just acting as she might with anyone else on your son's level. You may not like your son's choices, but you obviously can't tell him how to run his life, and it's not fair to hold other people responsible for his choices.

In both cases, the mediator was focusing on having one party "recognize" the other's perspective, but he was trying to force the recognition rather than inviting the parties to see and respond to each other in more positive terms, and then letting them decide for themselves whether to do so.

On the other hand, mediators may make the converse mistake, taking care to empower parties but then doing nothing to foster recognition. In one landlord-tenant case, for example, the landlord complained against a longtime tenant for keeping her shopping cart and overshoes in a common hallway/foyer. The tenant was adamant that she had a right to use the area and would not move her things unless a judge forced her to. Each party was indignant at the other, whose behavior and attitude they saw as offensive and inexcusable. The mediator reviewed the options and their consequences with both parties thoroughly but made it clear to each that decisions were in their hands. Indeed, at one point the tenant turned to the mediator and said, "I see what you're doing; you're not telling me what to do, you're helping me to think out what I really want to do. I appreciate that." Eventually, the parties reached an accommodation.

Afterward, however, a trainee who observed the case voiced her disappointment with what had happened, because despite empowering the parties, the mediator did practically nothing to foster recognition between them: "I understand that he didn't need to do more in order to help the parties decide what to do; but there was so much these parties didn't really understand about each other, and could have understood more of, if the mediator had only focused some effort on recognition." The trainee put her finger right on the point: Empowerment could be accomplished alone; but when this was done, it seemed a somewhat empty achievement. The failure to build on empowerment by pursuing recognition left the transformative potential of the interaction largely untapped.

Avoiding these twin pitfalls—pursuing empowerment without recognition and vice versa—requires that mediators always practice on *both* levels, seeking both empowerment and recognition together. They must always try to foster empowerment, so that there is both a strengthening of self and a real foundation for recognition. And they must also always try to take every opportunity to encourage parties (without forcing them) to use the foundation of empowerment to give recognition. It is essential to work on both in every case, to the fullest extent possible, because only this can tap the full transformative potential of the parties' interaction. Avoiding the pitfall here means attending to both empowerment and recognition, because both are essential to transformation.

Losing Sight of the Transformative Orientation Entirely

The last pitfall to be guarded against in transformative practice is the most serious of all. Because of the fundamental shift of orientation that underlies the transformative approach, it is often difficult for a mediator to keep the new orientation clearly and firmly in mind, especially in the pressurized atmosphere of an actual session. However, when the orientation wavers, it is possible to forget about both empowerment *and* recognition—not just one or the other—because the mediator loses sight of the underlying purpose of transformation altogether.

For example, a group of mediators were discussing how the transformative approach could have been applied in a case that one had recently mediated: Complainant (C) and respondent (R) were lifelong best friends who had an argument at C's wedding, at which R was a bridesmaid. C threw R out of the wedding party, and their friendship broke up. But R refused to return the dress C had given her as bridesmaid, and the ensuing complaint came to mediation. The mediator said that she sensed R wanted to reestablish the friendship, but C just wanted to be paid for the dress and call it quits. The mediator asked her colleagues, "I felt C and her new husband would regret their choice later on—R was a life-long friend, and people don't have many such friends. But how far do you go in pushing them to see this, if you're using a transformative approach?" Someone suggested that empowerment would involve asking C if she'd considered the value of the friendship, if she'd firmly decided that the argument was too serious to overcome, and so forth. But if C had considered these things, empowerment meant letting her make her own choice and not pressuring her into a different one. At this point, another mediator in the group burst out excitedly:

> What kind of mediation is that? She's going to sacrifice a life-long friend over a stupid argument and a dress, and you're telling me I should sit there and let it happen? If I see people about to drive off a cliff, and I can stop it, are you telling me not to? Why not? I can understand letting people decide things themselves, but at a certain point you have to step in to stop them from hurting themselves, or help them see and do what's best for them. I can't see what's wrong with doing that. That's the whole reason I'm there!

This was an unwittingly perfect statement of the pitfall in question. The mediator who made it, at some point in thinking about the case presented, lost sight of the aim of transformation altogether and slipped from a transformative into a problem-solving orientation. When he did so, empowerment quickly ceased to matter, in comparison to the objective of avoiding suffering by solving the problem. Without a firm foothold in the transformative orientation, "letting people decide things themselves" is fine up to a point; but if things go too far off track, the mediator must "step in" to make sure the problem is solved in the best way.

Even mediators who have made a conscious attempt to follow the transformative approach to practice have experienced how easy it is to lose a transformative focus. They have found that the demands of some cases—and their own emotional reactions to them—can lead them to lose sight of the transformative orientation itself.

Consider the example of one mediator who is explicitly committed to using the transformative approach. He was mediating a case involving two sixteen-year-old high school girls that started over a "dirty look" at a basketball game. The look had led to two physical fights, one with several of the girls' friends involved. The girl who was attacked last said she had to get even before the fighting would stop. This was a frustrating and frightening case for the mediator. His attempts at empowerment seemed to go nowhere—the girls kept restating their desire to continue fighting until things got settled. And they adamantly resisted seeing things from the other's point of view. In fact, there was only one instance when recognition occurred. One of the girls had been attacked by the other while holding her three-month-old baby. The attacker said she realized this was unfair, and she could understand the other girl's desire not to be attacked while she was holding the baby. She then said that "next time," the other girl should let her sister hold the baby, and the sister should then "stay out of it."

In the face of these tough stands, the mediator felt a strong pull to become directive. He found himself preaching to the girls, instructing them on the way in which the escalating violence was a game without end if both sides kept wanting "last licks." He pushed for one particular solution—having one of the girls move to another high school—even though the girls strongly resisted this option and would make no commitment to it. The session ended without an agreement and with the mediator feeling frustrated and worried because the violence seemed likely to continue.

This case is particularly instructive because it shows how easily a mediator can lose focus on transformative objectives, even when openly committed to them. During the course of the session, the mediator became worried about the violence, about what would happen after the mediation if no settlement were reached. This concern was clearly legitimate and, in many ways, unavoidable. However, because of the strength of this reaction to the dispute, the mediator became increasingly frustrated with the girls' resistance and the slight progress he seemed to be making in the session toward addressing this concern. As a result, he lost sight of the transformative potential of the dispute.

The desire to do something about the violence pulled this mediator away from watching for and working with opportunities for empowerment and recognition. Rather than building one step at a time on comments the girls made, he pulled back and looked for a solution that would address the real and alarming prospects of what would happen if a settlement of some kind were not reached. In retrospect, he saw many places where he could have probed about how the girls saw each other, how they wanted to be seen, and what choices they thought they might have before them. But he missed the chance to explore these opportunities because he became so concerned about ensuring that the immediate problem did not go unsolved. And ironically, his attempts to find a solution may have thwarted the chance to have the parties *construct one themselves*.

Trainees who observed this case said afterward that trying to persuade the girls to go to different schools, or to commit to some similar solution that at least diminished the chances of violence, was justifiable here. They argued that given the age of the girls and likelihood of serious violence, a more directive approach was necessary. The mediator himself, thinking it over afterward, disagreed. He said that although he had felt the same way during the session, and his own moves indicated he was being pulled in that direction, he should have resisted this pull. There would have been little point in imposing a solution that the girls had not constructed themselves. Separating the girls at school would not stop the violence from occurring on the streets, in shopping malls, or anywhere else their paths might cross. In fact, the girls seemed ready to seek each other out to continue the attacks. Unless a settlement was built on the choices the girls made and unless it was based on some degree of recognition for each other, there was little hope that *any* agreement would end the fighting. Most important, the mediator pointed out, simply stopping this fight would not, in any event, have *changed* either of the girls—made them stronger and less defensive, understanding and more tolerant of others. But without such change in the girls themselves, the overwhelming likelihood was that one or both would soon get involved in other fights, on other occasions, with other people. Violence would not be avoided in the long run, because the parties themselves had not changed. In short, the "justification" for a directive approach was illusory; the mediator simply fell victim to the pitfall of losing sight of the transformative orientation.

The mediators' reactions in this case and the bridesmaid case were not unlike the reactions mediators have in other types of cases and contexts. In divorce and family, public policy, business, and landlord-tenant cases, mediators often have strong reactions that lead them to be directive and to try to protect parties from their own decisions, including the decision to keep fighting. Moreover, at some point in almost every case they handle, mediators begin to sense the looming presence of the "unsolved problem" about which "something must be done." These are often visceral reactions, and they prompt mediators to advise parties what is best for them and to attempt to reach settlements at all costs. Mediators who try to follow the transformative approach are not immune to these kinds of reactions, which can easily undercut this approach in any conflict arena, by causing mediators to lose sight of the transformative orientation altogether.

It is worth noting, additionally, that the dangers posed by this pitfall are similar to those of trying to "integrate" the problem-solving and transformative approaches, a point made in Chapter Four. In fact, the examples presented here can help clarify the reasons offered there to explain why integration of the two approaches is, as a practical matter, impossible. Like transformative mediators who lose sight of the overall transformative orientation, mediators who try to integrate the two approaches will inevitably be pulled to abandon a transformative objective like empowerment, whenever doing so seems necessary in order to keep parties from suffering dissatisfaction or harm. The bridesmaid and basketball cases clearly illustrate what is likely to happen in such circumstances, whether as the result of losing sight of a consciously transformative orientation or as the result of trying to integrate the two approaches into one. In neither instance are transformative objectives likely to be successfully achieved.

What can help mediators avoid this ultimate pitfall of the transformative approach? The best safeguard, perhaps the only one, is for mediators to have a profound understanding of the values underlying the transformative approach. It is not simply the *specifics* of empowerment and recognition, as detailed earlier, that constitute the alternative approach to mediation being proposed here. This approach includes the *overall orientation* on which these two concepts are based, and the critical element of that orientation is its conception that the purpose of mediation, as a method of responding to conflict, is not simply satisfying parties' needs but transforming parties as moral beings. Keeping the transformative orientation firmly in place, despite the visceral pulls described here, requires both great clarity about and deep commitment to this view of mediation's purpose.

The Importance of Purpose to Practice

The heart of the transformative approach, and the orientation on which it rests, is the goal of transformation: the realization by individuals of their highest potential as moral beings, and with this a changed and better world. It is the commitment to this goal or purpose that has attracted many to the transformative approach and to the Transformation Story of the mediation movement. Asking mediators to make the major shift from the problem-solving to the transformative approach means asking them also to see transformation as the most important goal or value of mediation and as superior to other important values, like the value of satisfaction that underlies the problem-solving approach and orientation.

In earlier chapters we stated that transformation should be considered the most important goal of mediation, indicating that a full explanation of the basis of this view would be offered at a later point. This is the time for that explanation. For unless mediators are convinced that transformation matters—that it is the highest purpose mediation serves—they will not be inspired to make the shift to a transformative approach. And unless mediators clearly understand this value and why it matters so much, they will find it difficult to maintain this approach when faced with the pulls and pressures of practice.

This was precisely the challenge posed by the questioner in the discussion of the bridesmaid case. In effect, he was asking someone to identify the value that would be served by empowerment and to explain why it was more important than the value of satisfaction (or avoidance of suffering) that he felt would be served by directive intervention in that case. What could be more important than avoiding suffering and securing satisfaction for people with problems? And if a more important value cannot be identified, then why should he and other mediators stick to empowerment and recognition rather than "stepping in" where necessary to solve those problems? Solid answers to these questions are necessary, both to persuade mediators to consider adopting the transformative approach and to help them maintain it and avoid its most serious pitfall.

The aim of the following chapter is to explain the view that, in mediation, transformation is the most important goal. We will show that the value of transformation is connected to a coherent worldview, which makes profound sense of our human world and which is gaining currency across the whole range of human knowledge and inquiry. For some, this explanation will confirm ideas and intuitions they already hold. For others, the ideas and concepts will be unfamiliar, even surprising. But the explanation is important for all, because it is the foundation on which the transformative approach ultimately rests. If this explanation makes sense, then so does transformative mediation. The question then is how to accomplish a shift to that approach within the present institutional context of the mediation movement.

Part Four

· ·

A Larger Context for Mediation

9

Underlying Values:
Why Transformation Matters

W hat makes the transformative approach to mediation important is the ultimate purpose it strives for and values. In the end, the case for the transformative approach rests on whether people believe in the value that drives it. In this chapter we explain why transformation matters, by clarifying this value and contrasting it with the value of satisfaction. We then show that the value of transformation does not stand alone but rather is linked to a coherent view of human nature and society, the Relational worldview. The transformative approach to mediation flows from and expresses this worldview. The central value of problem solving—satisfaction—is linked to a different view of human nature and society, the Individualist worldview. Thus the choice between approaches to mediation expresses a much deeper choice about how to look at the world as a whole.

We also describe how, beyond the borders of the dispute resolution field, there is a larger movement in the culture as a whole away from the Individualist worldview and toward the Relational worldview. This shift is emerging in many fields of knowledge and in current social and political events. While this shift may be only intuitive in some instances, in others it is beginning to be a matter of conscious choice. If people conclude that transformation matters and make a conscious effort to enact the Relational worldview in the mediation field, these actions have larger ramifications: the use of the transformative approach to mediation would support and further a progressive shift in human consciousness. Seen in this context, the choice to follow this approach is a decision to work concretely, in our field, toward the realization of this larger social development.

The Value of Transformation

In the preceding chapters, the value at the heart of the transformative approach to mediation has been identified as human moral growth in two specific dimensions *together:* strength of self *and* relation to other. Valuing moral growth in this sense ultimately means valuing a way of acting and behaving that is the object of the growth. It means valuing behavior that integrates strength of self and compassion for others, behavior that embodies compassionate strength. Such behavior is almost always the product of moral effort—growth and transformation—on the part of those who exhibit it. Achieving this kind of behavior, to any degree, is what is meant by moral growth or transformation within the transformative vision.

Exactly what is it that is being valued here, and why? Explaining this, with some concrete examples, will help clarify the meaning of the value of transformation. "Compassionate strength" integrates two forms of human behavior that are independently seen as highly estimable but which by themselves are actually incomplete and flawed. Thus, when a person facing adversity musters his or her resources and confronts the adverse circumstances, this strength of self is seen as admirable. Consider some examples: a person with disabilities who overcomes a physical limitation to pursue an important aim; an immigrant who fights against language and other cultural barriers to strive for success; a person of meager means who struggles with financial hardship to start a business; an artist or inventor who confronts the "common wisdom" and "blazes a path" to a new idea or invention. All of these situations involve the individual gathering strength and standing up for him- or herself "against all odds." This behavior is commonly seen as an intrinsically estimable form of human conduct—whether or not the individual's efforts result in success.

At the same time, when a person attends to others as much as or more than to themselves, serving those in need, this compassion for others is also seen as admirable. Again, consider some examples: a parent who sacrifices personal desires and ambitions to care for a child (or vice versa); a "saintly" person like Raoul Wallenberg who takes great personal risks to save people from religious persecution and genocide; a dedicated "public servant" like Martin Luther King who gives his energy and liberty, and ultimately his life, to the cause of civil rights; a philanthropist who gives away the bulk of an estate to support medical or scientific research. All these actions involve the individual looking beyond his or her own needs and attending to those of others, and this is also seen as intrinsically estimable conduct—whether or not the individual is successful in alleviating the other's needs.

Both of these modes of human conduct are commonly viewed as embodying something noble and good in themselves. Nevertheless, each mode of conduct, by itself, tends to be partial or even extreme. For example, the individual strength that stands up to adversity is admirable, but it loses that quality if it is not accompanied by a concern for something beyond self. The struggling inventor or entrepreneur becomes a contemptible rather than admirable figure if he tramples over others to succeed and then hoards everything for himself. Similarly, selfless devotion that involves not just the transcendence but the loss or degradation of self also loses its estimable quality. For example, the follower who abandons her own identity and judgment altogether, in "devotion" to a cult leader, likewise seems pathetic rather than admirable. These kinds of partial, one-dimensional modes of conduct are common, and they are far from embodying a quality regarded as admirable or good.

What most excites admiration and sustains it is conduct that expresses, but avoids the extremes of, each of these elements: in other words, conduct that combines and integrates them. When a person marshals his or her resources and strength, standing up to obstacles and difficulties, and at the same time uses that strength in a way that not only sustains the self but attends to the needs of others, we recognize something wholly and unqualifiedly admirable and good about that kind of conduct. For example, consider the tennis star Arthur Ashe, who by dint of his skill and effort attained great stature despite many obstacles, and then from his position of strength worked steadily, without glory or publicity, to remove similar obstacles from the paths of others. Then, in his confrontation with the fatal AIDS virus, he also balanced the desire to maintain his own and his family's privacy and dignity with consideration for the positive impact that disclosure of his condition might have for others suffering from the disease.

Ashe's conduct throughout his life was the kind of behavior that is universally recognized as admirable and fine. He is viewed as having lived an almost paradigmatically "good life." And the reason is that his conduct, and his life, exemplify the integration of both types of valued conduct: strength of self and compassion for others. Indeed, the same is true with the examples that were given earlier to illustrate separately the attributes of strength or compassion. Even though it was not emphasized there, what actually makes the conduct in each case seem admirable is not just the obvious presence of one attribute but an implicit assumption that the other is also present: the assumption is that King's and Wallenberg's compassion were founded on strength; the assumption is that the strength of the struggling immigrant, writer, and so on, ultimately were dedicated at least in part to serving family, community, or some larger cause outside of self. In all the examples, the integration of both strength and compassion, whether obvious or presumed, is what makes the conduct seem good and admirable.

However, the point is not that there is some value in integration per se. The reason for valuing compassionate strength (and movement or growth toward it) as a form of conduct is not that it embodies "integration" but that it embodies genuine goodness in human terms. The problem with strength and devotion by themselves is not that they are "un-integrated" but that they do not embody genuine goodness. Strength without compassion is selfishness; devotion without self-awareness is mindlessness. Selfish strength and mindless devotion are not expressions of goodness at all. Compassionate strength—devotion based on strength and free choice, strength dedicated to serving others—is. It is the embodiment in human conduct of genuine goodness, and that is the reason for valuing it.

This discussion explains the particular view taken here of moral growth. There are indeed other views of moral growth and the kind of conduct it aims for. Moral growth is viewed by some people as involving movement from dependent to autonomous conduct, and by others as involving movement from selfish to considerate conduct. But each of these views of moral growth seems one-dimensional and partial, focused on an end that by itself does not represent a form of conduct that is genuinely admirable or good. Growth along *both* dimensions, strength of self and relation to others, points to the end of compassionate strength, which embodies a genuine goodness and therefore what Carol Gilligan (1982, 1988) has called a "mature human morality." Of course, not only Ashe and other public figures but "ordinary people" faced with the constant pull between concern for self and other can aspire to and attain this form of truly "good" conduct, this mature morality.

One final and important point will clarify the reason for placing value on transformation and explain the use of the term itself. When compassionate strength is expressed, in whatever degree, it seems particularly valuable because the potential for a different and lesser form of conduct is always strongly present. If the expression of compassionate strength were natural or easy, in other words, its attainment would not seem so impressive, even though it would still embody goodness. Instead, it is almost always *not* natural but rather the product of individual effort to change and refine a natural reaction that tends toward either weakness or selfishness or both. Both the contrast with the lesser forms of conduct that it transcends, as well as the element of moral effort required to transcend them and attain it, reinforce the sense that the expression of compassionate strength has immense value. Indeed, the goodness it embodies seems clear precisely in the context of the transformation that is necessary to achieve it.

In sum, the value of transformation means the value of attaining a genuinely good form of human conduct, compassionate strength, by the required exercise of moral effort on an individual's part to transform him- or herself from a state of weakness and/or selfishness to one of strength and compassion. Transformation is so valuable, because of both the great goodness of the human conduct that results and the great moral effort that is required to produce it.

The Value of Satisfaction

In earlier chapters, the value identified as the heart of the problem-solving approach to mediation was the satisfaction of individuals' needs and desires. As with the value of transformation, we can ask, what is it that is really being valued here, and why? Though followers of the problem-solving approach have not always fully explained their value premises, it is important here to offer some fair account of what those premises mean, in order to pursue the contrast between the worldviews that flow from the two values in question. What follows is an attempt to provide such an account.

In the simplest sense, valuing satisfaction—not simply satisfaction of one's own desires, but satisfaction of human beings in general—means placing importance on having human beings get the most out of life and, conversely, having them avoid suffering. The reason this is valued is that life itself, the realm of experience open to human beings, is seen as something that is potentially precious and satisfying. The value of producing satisfaction is that doing so realizes the world's potential for bringing fulfillment rather than frustration to human beings. To put it another way, the value is in exploiting fully an inherently precious resource. Those who value satisfaction see it as important because the experience of life itself, with its potential for bringing enjoyment, seems a precious, priceless commodity that ought to be fully used and not squandered.

This idea of satisfaction as a value is commonly expressed in the ideal of "the good life," meaning a life filled with good and satisfying experiences. However, this does not imply that enjoyment comes only from simple or coarse experiences. Satisfaction can come equally from the most lofty and refined experiences, such as friendship or appreciation of beauty.

This last point suggests that another premise linked to the satisfaction value is the view that what is good and satisfying in life is not objectively definable at all. Rather, it is definable only by each individual for him- or herself. Therefore, attaining the value of satisfaction in general is only possible through attaining the satisfaction of individuals, each of whom defines his or her own good. This is precisely why satisfying individuals has importance. When each person attains some self-defined good, without preventing other individuals from doing the same—ideally, when all individuals can do this at once—it can be said that life's potential for bringing fulfillment has been realized, even though it has never been defined commonly. Indeed, placing value on satisfaction allows for the attainment of an indeterminate, undefinable good—a remarkable achievement in a subjective world. For those who view objective values as suspect, the conception of satisfaction as a value is thus very attractive and powerful.

Perhaps this point is why the model of the "marketplace" system has such attraction and power to many in our culture. The model promises that every individual can obtain what gives them satisfaction, without ever imposing any objective definition of good. In a perfect market, every individual gets what he or she thinks is good. And it is never necessary actually to define or give a common content to what is good, because everyone defines it for themselves, and no one's meaning is rejected if it can be accommodated without infringing someone else's. Marketplace exchange is classic "win-win." Indeed, it is noteworthy that the language of problem-solving mediation contains many of the same terms used to describe marketplace exchange: *optimization, joint gains, gains from exchange.* The reason for the similarity is that the driving value of both is satisfaction, as defined and explained here.

From Values to Worldviews

The values of transformation and satisfaction do not stand alone. Each of them is linked to an overall view of human nature and society. The contrast between the larger worldviews connected to the two values further explains why transformation matters.

Human beings need and construct organizing conceptual frameworks in order to make sense of the world. Such a framework, composed of a set of beliefs about the nature of the world—including the nature of human beings and their social processes and structures—provides the organized viewpoint from which one interprets the surrounding world. And individuals' viewpoints reflect generalized frameworks that operate within a culture or society. It is such frameworks that we mean by *worldviews.*

It is often assumed that a worldview starts from and rests on a particular conception of human nature, with different conceptions leading to different frameworks. However, human nature is complex and ambiguous, and our view of it depends very much on what we look for in the first place. Therefore any worldview, including its view of human nature, starts from some intuition of value or purpose. What is seen as important defines what is seen as central in human nature and social structure. Underlying everything is the assumption made at the outset about the nature of the good, about what matters and is important. Based on that assumption, the viewer perceives and stresses that aspect of human nature and social institutions that is capable of bringing it about. In the language of contemporary thought, this is a *social constructionist view* of human nature and society.

Therefore, starting with the value of transformation leads to the construction of one worldview, with a particular view of human nature, society, and social institutions, called the *Relational worldview*. Starting with the value of satisfaction, on the other hand, leads to a different framework with different views of human nature and society, called the *Individualist worldview*. Describing each of these worldviews shows how the choice to stress one value or the other is not merely a free-standing value preference but a choice linked to and embedded in an entire worldview. This analysis helps explain further the significance of the values themselves, by clarifying what each value leads to. More important, it shows that the two different approaches to mediation are tied not only to different values but to these two larger and very different worldviews.

Though our ultimate aim is to explain the significance of the value of transformation, it helps to start with what is more familiar. The worldview connected to the satisfaction value is more familiar and commonly held than the Relational worldview, at least at present. So we begin with the Individualist worldview. We also describe briefly a third framework, the Organic worldview, in order to lay a better foundation for understanding the Relational framework itself. Each of these worldviews has been identified and explained, with greater or lesser clarity, in either contemporary or past schools of thought. Later in the chapter we focus specifically on those schools of thought themselves. Here the point is simply to present and contrast the different worldviews.

The Individualist Worldview

This framework starts from the position that satisfaction is a supremely important value, because it means realizing life's potential for bringing fulfillment. Although it is impossible to define the goodness of life objectively, when all individuals are allowed and helped to seek and attain the good as they see it, life's potential for bringing fulfillment is fully utilized. Despite the fact that there is no common definition of the good, achieving satisfaction thus achieves something of undisputed value. From the starting point of this value, a certain view of the nature of the individual follows.

If the ultimate value is satisfaction—the experience of enjoyment of life, in subjectively defined terms—then the qualities of the human being that seem central are the ones that are necessary to achieve this purpose. These include the human capacities for self-knowledge, self-determination, and self-assertion. Focusing on these qualities as central leads to a view of the individual as unique, separate, and autonomous, as well as self-aware and deliberate. Each human being is a unique entity capable of appreciating life on his or her own terms, finding in it a value that only he or she can see and acting to secure this. Indeed, individuality—the capacity of each individual to define and experience the goodness of life in his or her own terms—is what makes it possible for life's potential to be fully utilized.

Focusing on these features also leads to a view of the individual as preoccupied with self and self-satisfaction. Others are viewed as instruments for self-satisfaction, either directly or indirectly. Of course, as noted earlier, self-satisfaction may mean something lofty like friendship or appreciation of beauty. It is still self-satisfaction, because its value rests entirely on the fact that it satisfies an individual's self-defined notion of what is good and valuable, not on any objective basis. In sum, starting from the value of satisfaction leads to a view of human nature that emphasizes separateness, autonomy, individuality, and self-interestedness.

A corresponding view of society and social institutions follows from this. Society has to be a kind of referee or intermediary between the multiplicity of separate and unique persons pursuing their own ideas of what is good and satisfying. It has to protect persons from each other's trespasses, intentional or otherwise; but it also has to support everyone's efforts to do everything they can, short of trespassing on others, to pursue their own subjectively defined satisfaction. In short, it has to be both protective and facilitative, but not directive. It has to help people do what they want, prevent them from stepping on each other's toes, but not tell them what they ought to do or want. For this reason, the kind of society this worldview demands must enshrine and balance the political values of freedom and equality, both of which find expression in the idea of rights.

This is the philosophy or worldview familiar to most of us as liberal individualism. It is deeply entrenched in our culture. The Individualist worldview starts with valuing individual satisfaction (for all individuals equally) as the greatest good, really the only workable idea of the good. Such a view of the good leads to this view of the person and society. It all holds together as a coherent view of what the human world is, beginning from this value position. However, starting from a different value leads to a different view of the human world.

Before considering the worldview linked to the transformation value, it is helpful to take note of a worldview based on a third value position, distinct from both satisfaction and transformation. Although some people see this third value as significant in the mediation movement today, we do not, and therefore we have not discussed it earlier. Nevertheless, discussing it here helps lay the foundation for explaining the worldview connected to the transformation value.

The Harmony Value and the Organic Worldview

Some have suggested, usually ironically, that the value underlying the mediation movement is neither satisfaction nor transformation but harmony. Proponents of this view do not really think highly of the kind of "harmony" they have in mind. For example, anthropologists like Laura Nader (1990) note that restoring harmony to a closely knit community is an important value often served by mediation in traditional societies. But in a modern society like ours, she suggests, "harmony" really means suppression of conflict for the sake of continued oppression of certain groups. It means sacrificing justice for peace. Nader and others who subscribe to the Oppression

Story of the movement are afraid that the mediation movement does just this (Abel, 1982; Fiss, 1984; Nader, 1992). However, this critique is not the point here. Rather, the point is to examine the value position pointed to by Nader and others, as a distinct alternative to both the satisfaction and transformation values.

Understood most simply, the valued end in this view is the survival and welfare of some collective entity—a family, tribe, community, society. Harmony is a way of describing the necessary condition for community well-being, because conflict can rip the entity apart. The value itself is really not harmony but community survival or welfare, to which harmony is instrumental. The good is understood as whatever the collective entity values and desires, and especially its own survival and welfare. As with the values of satisfaction and transformation, starting with the value of harmony leads to a coherent view of human nature and society.

If the ultimate value is collective welfare, the qualities of the human being that seem central are the ones that are necessary to achieve this purpose. These include the capacity to be aware of participating in something larger than self, to feel connected to others and to a common entity, and furthermore the capacity for subjugating the needs of self to the needs of the whole, for self-sacrifice and service. The person is seen as having an inherent consciousness of and responsiveness to something outside self. Focusing on these characteristics leads to a view of the human being as an entity dedicated to something outside the self, to a larger and central existence that the self simply exists to serve. Instead of other being instrumental to self, self is instrumental to other. Starting from the value of harmony, the view of human nature is one that emphasizes connectedness, devotion, commonality, and selflessness.

A view of society follows from this view of human nature. Society is the collective entity whose existence is primary, an organism with a life of its own apart from and superior to that of the individuals who make up its parts. It possesses a collective will, and whatever that will desires is the only definition of good. Satisfying the collective will is the general meaning of good. The function of social institutions, in this view, is both to provide some means for the articulation of the collective will and to channel and guide individuals into their proper places, where they can do their assigned part to serve the whole. Such a society enshrines political values such as hierarchy, loyalty, and service, which find expression in the idea of duties.

Though familiar in some degree to many of us from "intimate" social spheres like family, religious, or ethnic associations, this Organic worldview is not widely seen as relevant to the larger political culture in which we live. It is more identified with other cultures, including premodern Western societies and contemporary non-Western societies. Starting from a very different value, it offers a coherent view of human nature and society that is the very converse of the Individualist framework.

What is important to note about the Individualist and Organic worldviews, before going further, is that *both* are grounded in reality. Human nature contains the features stressed in the Individualist worldview as well as those stressed in the Organic view. Human beings have both capacities, for self-interestedness and for selfless devotion to other, and the various other qualities that relate to each. Which of the two sets of qualities is noticed and emphasized depends on the sense of purpose driving the inquiry. A view driven by one value sees one aspect of human nature; a different view based on a different value sees the other. Also, behavior is shaped and conditioned, and social institutions formed, in accordance with the aspect focused on. Social institutions can be either purely facilitative or constitutive, depending on the sense of purpose behind them. So the worldviews here are, in an important sense, like the stories of the mediation movement in Chapter One. The way each worldview describes human nature is accurate to some degree, because the phenomenon under observation—human nature—is genuinely complex and ambiguous. But each view focuses on a different aspect of human nature, because each starts out with a different sense of what matters most.

The Relational Worldview

Against this background of the Individualist and Organic worldviews, as driven by the values of individual satisfaction and collective welfare, we now consider the Relational worldview. This
framework starts from the position that the most important value
is transformation, the achievement of human conduct that integrates strength of self and compassion toward others—both because
of the great goodness of the human conduct that results and because
of the great moral effort that is required to produce it. From the
starting point of this value, a certain view of the nature of the individual follows.

If the ultimate value is transformation, the qualities of the
human being that seem central are the ones necessary to achieve
this end, to act with compassionate strength. These qualities
include *all* the features seen as central by *both* of the other two
worldviews just described—plus the ability to integrate them into
a balanced whole. If compassionate strength is possible in human
conduct, as the transformation value assumes, human beings must
be seen as capable of both strength of self and concern for others.
Therefore, starting from the value of transformation leads to the
view that human nature includes *both* the capacity for self-interestedness *and* the capacity for responsiveness to others. Individuals are
seen as both separate and connected, both individuated and similar.
They are viewed as being to some degree autonomous, self-aware,
and self-interested but also to some degree connected, sensitive, and
responsive to others. In short, from the starting point of this value,
the view of human nature takes on a fullness and complexity that
is largely missing in the other worldviews. Although all these features are present in human nature, the Individualist and the
Organic outlook each perceives only certain ones. Because its focus
is directed by the transformation value, the Relational worldview
sees them all.

At the same time, starting from the value of transformation leads
to the perception of a quality in human nature seen by *neither* of the

other worldviews. That is the capacity for balancing and relating, and thereby integrating, the individual's diverse aspects, so that neither wholly dominates and results in morally inferior forms of conduct. Indeed, the central feature of human nature, when perceived from the starting place of the transformation value, is neither individuality nor connectedness (and their associated qualities) but the element that relates the two in an integrated, whole human consciousness—the relational capacity. Human beings are thus simultaneously separate and connected, autonomous and linked, self-interested and self-transcending. Furthermore, they are capable of relating these dualities in an integrated wholeness that makes them capable of genuine goodness of conduct.

This relational capacity is seen as functioning both internally and externally. Internally, human beings can relate and integrate the dual aspects of self-interestedness and other-awareness within the individual's own consciousness. Externally, human beings can relate to others noninstrumentally, with an awareness of their common humanity. They can relate the needs of self and those of others, including both and not focusing exclusively on either alone. The development and use of the relational capacity leads to an integrated human consciousness that acts with both strength and compassion, the good as encompassed in the value of transformation.

However, the view of the individual here is that, while human nature includes both aspects of the self and the capacity to relate them, it also includes the ability to fail in all respects. That is, rather than being strong in themselves and compassionate toward others, human beings can be weak, or selfish, or both. Human nature is thus seen as possessing lower and higher potentials, and indeed part of what gives transformation such value, as noted earlier, is that it involves overcoming the lower and reaching the higher. Therefore, human nature includes the potential for strength, compassion, and integration; the potential for weakness, selfishness, and duality; and the capacity for achieving the higher rather than the lower—for transformation.

The view of society and social institutions that follows from the transformation value and the resultant view of human nature likewise differs from that of both other worldviews. Society is seen neither as a mere referee between separate and sovereign individuals nor as an organic entity in which individuals must serve their proper part. Rather, society is seen as a medium in which human beings can relate to one another and, in doing so, integrate the duality of human consciousness and achieve the kind of ideal human conduct that integrates strength and compassion. Society is a medium for the process of human relations and interaction, in which all the capacities of human nature, and especially the relational capacity, are enacted and the full potential of human decency is realized.

Social institutions therefore must do more than be facilitative and protective, according to this view. They must certainly be facilitative, providing opportunities for strengthening self and relating to others. And some of them must be protective, because of the potential in human nature for both weakness and selfishness. But their role extends beyond this in the Relational worldview. They also play what could be called a supportive and educative role. That is, social institutions must operate not just to allow but to *help* individuals strengthen themselves and show concern for each other— to enact and integrate their highest capacities rather than their lowest. Their function is not simply minimalist and limitative, as in the Individualist worldview, but positive and constructive. They serve not only to protect us from the worst in each other but also to help us find and enact the best in ourselves.

Unlike the two worldviews described before, the Relational worldview cannot be linked to a familiar philosophy. Because it represents an outlook that is just emerging, it has no widely recognized character or "name" as yet. Similarly, it is hard to point to social institutions, present or past, like the modern marketplace or the premodern caste system, that exemplify what relational social institutions look like. However, the mediation movement, insofar as it follows the transformative approach, could be one such social institution.

The Contrasts Between the Outlooks

It is helpful to summarize some of the important contrasts between the worldviews that emerge from the different values. The contrasts pointed to here are ways in which the Relational outlook differs from *both* of the others.

Both the Individualist and Organic outlooks focus on one aspect of human nature as central—either separateness/autonomy or connectedness/interdependence. The Relational outlook sees both together as constituting human nature. To put it differently, the Individualist and Organic outlooks both see human beings as torn by a duality in their consciousness. Furthermore, both outlooks suggest that the only way to deal with this duality is to exalt one form of awareness over the other. As a result, each casts the other's "strength" as a weakness to be overcome or eliminated, and each is thus exclusive of the other in this sense. For the Individualist view, autonomy is good because it expresses individual strength, while connection and convention are bad because they show weakness and dependency. For the Organic view, connection and devotion are good because they express selflessness and dedication, while autonomy is bad because it manifests selfishness. The strength or good of each is the weakness of the other; neither sees good in the value of the other.

By contrast, the Relational outlook, while it sees the different aspects of human awareness, does not view them as irreconcilably opposed. Rather, it sees them as capable of integration into a unity that forms a whole human consciousness, and sees this integrating capacity itself as a key element of human nature. Moreover, because it envisions the possibility of integration, the Relational outlook is not exclusive in its view of either aspect of human nature. It sees both aspects as potentially good or bad, strength or weakness, depending on whether they are integrated with one another. In the Relational outlook, both autonomy and caring are good when they are integrated with one another, because they then constitute compassionate strength, the highest form of human conduct. But both autonomy and caring are bad when they stand alone, because each alone represents or produces an extreme and truncated form of human conduct, whether selfishness or self-degradation. The Relational view of human nature is thus inclusive rather than exclusive, integrative rather than oppositional. In sum, the Relational outlook transcends the oppositions between the other two, and the partiality of each, in terms of the view that is offered of human nature.

As a consequence, what the other outlooks see as the highest potentials in human nature are, from the vantage of the Relational worldview, only different aspects of the *lower nature* of human beings—self-interestedness alone, which is a strength that expresses selfishness, or devotedness alone, which is a caring that expresses self-abandonment and submergence. The Relational outlook, by comprehending the possibility of integration, sees that both aspects together present the view of a *higher nature* of human beings, which integrates self-interestedness and concern for others, strength and compassion. The Relational outlook thus sees a potential good in human beings that neither of the other worldviews even imagines. In addition, it suggests the possibility that human life can be experienced with a different sense of both self and other—having a sense of connection to others that is not self-submergence and a sense of individuality that is not isolation. The possibility is one of a constant and balanced experience of self in relation to others and of a shared human existence in which this interrelationship unfolds.

Finally, there is another level on which the Relational outlook both integrates and transcends opposing elements of the other two worldviews. It might seem that in placing ultimate value on transformation, the Relational worldview disregards the values of the Individualist and Organic outlooks, which themselves seem irreconcilable with one another. In fact, this turns out not to be so. Valuing transformation does not mean that either satisfaction or organic welfare is simply sacrificed and lost. It does mean that neither is viewed as the prime aim of human effort, and transformation is.

However, when transformation is made the focus of human effort, its achievement makes it likely that, as a consequence, satisfaction and organic welfare will both be achieved as well. When human beings strive to live with both strength and compassion, success in doing so will mean that they will be appreciating life themselves and affording others the opportunity to do so, so that life's potential for enjoyment will be maximized. It will also mean that they will experience a sense of common humanity and shared human existence, so that society as a whole will be strengthened. Even though the Relational outlook values and pursues a conception of the good that is defined in terms of quality and refinement of human conduct, apart from its consequences in producing satisfaction or collective welfare, those consequences will follow as by-products of achievement of the ultimate goal of transformation. In sum, pursuing the goal of transformation within the Relational outlook will have the effect of including the goals of the other worldviews and transcending the opposition between them.

It should be clear now that the different values behind the different approaches to mediation do not stand alone but entail whole worldviews. Also, the contrasts between the Relational worldview and the other two explain why many see the Relational outlook as sounder and more reflective of the full character of human existence than either of the others. This distinction in turn helps answer the question at the heart of this chapter: why transformation matters. The value of transformation seems superior to the value of satisfaction (or collective welfare) not only because of the comparison between the values themselves but also because the Relational worldview that flows from the transformation value presents a more integrated, convincing picture of the world than the other outlooks.

The decision to adopt the transformative approach to mediation ultimately rests on making a firm commitment to the value of transformation. By fully explaining what that value means and how it entails a very powerful and appealing worldview, our intent is to show those involved in the mediation field that this commitment is one that makes profound sense. It is also a commitment with profoundly important consequences.

As noted earlier, all these outlooks are ultimately based on choice—which value we start with and which overall outlook seems soundest to us is a matter of choice and decision. Nevertheless, these choices have real consequences and, once made, powerful determinative effects on shaping social reality. Choices made in the past in favor of the values of collective welfare and individual satisfaction have produced individual behavior and social structures that many have found a profound disappointment. But the "reality" created by these choices has become so strongly established that it is difficult for many to see that it can be changed, and a very different reality created, on the basis of a different value position. Going back to the beginning point of values shows that social reality is constructed and can be *reconstructed*. One concrete way to reconstruct reality in relational rather than individualist form is by practicing transformative mediation. The choice of which approach to follow in mediation practice has immense stakes, because it involves not just the techniques of dispute resolution but the construction and constitution of human nature and society themselves.

The Transformative and Problem-Solving Approaches: Relational or Individualist Mediation

The process of mediation as used within the contemporary mediation movement, like any organized and regularized process for responding to conflict, is a social institution. The key question is: What kind of social institution do we want it to be? This question describes the crossroads at which the movement presently stands. There are two possible answers, two paths the movement may take. When those involved in mediation choose one approach rather than the other, they are deciding whether mediation will be an essentially Individualist institution or a Relational one.

The two distinct worldviews called the Individualist and Relational outlooks, flowing from the distinct values of satisfaction and transformation, respectively, are the underlying bases of the two orientations to conflict and approaches to mediation discussed in this book. Conversely, these two orientations and approaches are expressions of the worldviews and values they rest on. The relationship is clear if the definitions and descriptions in Chapters Three and Four are reviewed and read against the larger context described in this chapter.

The transformative orientation sees conflicts themselves (like other social situations such as work, friendship, commerce, or illness) as opportunities, for individuals who are by nature both self-interested and responsive to others, to develop and integrate their capacities for both strength of self and concern for others. Conflict is an opportunity to transform human consciousness and conduct to the highest level of compassionate strength. The view of the individual taken here is clearly relational, seeing both "sides" of human nature as well as the potential for growth or transformation that can integrate the two sides and also relate self and other. Going further, the transformative orientation sees the ideal response to conflict as helping parties take advantage of the opportunities presented, so as actually to achieve transformation (compassionate strength) in some degree. The view of conflict resolution as social institution here is also relational, seeing it as not simply protective or facilitative but as educative, encouraging and helping individuals to integrate and enact their highest potential as human beings.

The transformative approach to mediation that grows out of this orientation focuses on empowerment and recognition, both as objectives and as methods of mediation, in order to help parties achieve increased strength of self and responsiveness to one another, however the immediate "problem" is solved. This summary statement of the transformative approach matches perfectly the description of conflict resolution as a relational social institution, aimed at helping individuals enact the highest human potential of compassionate strength. In short, transformative mediation is relational mediation, a concrete enactment of the Relational worldview in one important area of social life.

By contrast, the problem-solving orientation sees conflicts as obstructions to the satisfaction of individuals' self-defined desires, faced by self-interested individuals who are capable of knowing what will bring them fulfillment and acting to secure it for themselves. These obstructions to satisfaction are caused by other individuals' separate pursuit of their own desires. The view of the person here is individualist, focusing on the features of human nature that manifest autonomy and self-interest, and regarding individuals as preoccupied with satisfaction of their self-defined desires or needs. Further, the problem-solving orientation sees the ideal response to conflict as clearing away the obstructions to satisfaction by finding ways to meet both parties' needs or desires to the greatest degree possible. This view of conflict resolution as social institution is also individualist, seeing it as facilitative and protective, helping individuals to find ways of satisfying themselves while keeping them from doing so at the expense of others.

The problem-solving approach to mediation that grows out of this orientation focuses on reframing conflicts into solvable problems and directing parties toward settlements that mediators see as good-quality solutions, in order to help parties achieve mutual needs satisfaction or "maximum joint gains." This summary statement closely matches the description of conflict resolution as an individualist social institution, aimed at helping individuals satisfy their self-defined visions of good without infringing on each other. Problem-solving mediation is individualist mediation. It is an enactment of the Individualist worldview, as are most current conflict resolution and other social institutions.

Is this characterization really fair to the problem-solving approach? Some may argue that problem-solving mediation is indeed relational, precisely because it does include transformative elements. Indeed, some people claim that there are transformative elements within problem-solving mediation practice: empowerment is practiced to help define problems and identify solutions, and recognition is implicit in every win-win solution that accommodates both sides' needs. It is not simply an individualist exercise in pursuit of self-interest by both sides.

The answer to this claim is that, if in fact it worked this way, problem-solving mediation might be seen as relational, even if not as clearly or intentionally relational as the transformative approach. However, as explained in earlier chapters, problem-solving mediation does *not* work this way in actual practice, and *cannot* as long as it is driven by the problem-solving orientation. In practice, problem-solving mediation remains strongly individualist.

Therefore, the connection can be traced in parallel lines from foundational value to worldview, to orientation to conflict, to approach to mediation. Figure 9.1 clarifies this relationship. One line leads from the satisfaction value to the Individualist worldview, and then to the problem-solving orientation and approach. The other leads from the transformation value to the Relational worldview, and then to the transformative orientation and approach. Problem-solving mediation is an individualist institution, transformative mediation a relational one. When mediators choose their approach to practice, therefore, they are doing more than that. They are also choosing which worldview they want to enact and what kind of world they want to construct and inhabit.

The larger context of the mediation movement, composed of the underlying values and worldviews discussed here, defines the larger stakes of the choice between approaches to mediation. The case for the transformative approach to mediation is the case for the Relational worldview itself and for a human reality constructed on that basis rather than on the basis of the Individualist outlook. The reason for shifting to a transformative approach to mediation is that it is one important step toward constructing a different type of social reality, preferable by far to the one that now exists.

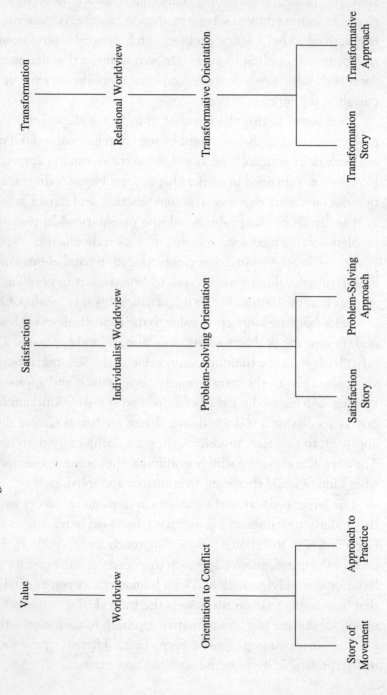

Figure 9.1. The Links Between Worldviews and Practices.

Transformative Mediation and the Shift to a New, Relational, Paradigm

One reason that the larger dimensions explored in this chapter are rarely discussed by those involved with mediation seems to be a concern that anyone referring to these dimensions will quickly be seen as unrealistic, idealistic, utopian, or just plain foolish. The best way to address such concerns is to make clear how much interest there is today, across all fields of knowledge, in the theme of transformation and in the Relational worldview as a whole. Indeed, the Relational worldview seems to be gradually emerging as a new paradigm. Our hopes for mediation do not represent an idiosyncratic impulse to create some small utopian enterprise; rather, they express shared values being explored by thinkers in widely different contexts, aimed at changing the way our culture sees and thinks about the human world as a whole. Understanding this larger context helps clarify further the significance of choosing the transformative approach to mediation.

The Shift to the Individualist Paradigm

As acknowledged earlier, the Individualist, Organic, and Relational worldviews have been recognized and discussed by people well beyond the bounds of the dispute resolution field. In the case of the first two views, we drew our presentation from well-known bodies of thought, contemporary or historical. The Organic worldview was articulated by many thinkers, from the classic Greek philosophers to the church scholars of the middle ages. The Individualist worldview—or some version of it—has been articulated by many others, from Thomas Hobbes and John Locke to present-day philosophers like John Rawls (1971), Robert Nozick (1974), and Ronald Dworkin (1977), among others. (Even though these thinkers differ greatly from one another in their views, they can all be seen as holding and helping to articulate a broadly Individualist worldview.)

These references themselves suggest that each of these worldviews is associated with a particular historical period, at least in

Western society, during which that worldview dominated. Indeed, the common view today is that each of these worldviews has served in a different period as the dominant worldview, or paradigm, in Western thought and society. The Organic worldview is identified as the "classical" paradigm, which held sway from the period identified with the beginnings of Western society, the era of the Greek and Roman cultures, through the feudal order of the early Middle Ages. The Individualist worldview is identified as the "modern" paradigm, which displaced its predecessor roughly three centuries ago, beginning in the Renaissance and Enlightenment eras (Sherry, 1986).

In its period of domination, each paradigm not only dominated thought but powerfully shaped social and political institutions. The classical paradigm supported organic social orders from the Greek polis to the hierarchical structures of imperial, church, and feudal societies. The modern paradigm, in its turn, has supported individualist social institutions from marketplace economic structures, to political democracy, to civil and human rights guarantees.

When the Individualist worldview displaced the Organic worldview as the dominant framework, there was a "paradigm shift," a shift from the classical to the modern paradigm that reached across the entire world of human thought and institutions. Of course, this move occurred gradually, with the Individualist outlook emerging and gaining force over time. But at some point it became identifiable that the entire set of assumptions by which human beings understood the world—including their own natures—was shifting. And at some further point that shift progressed to the point where the Individualist outlook gained dominance. As a result of the paradigm shift, it became a given that human beings are not essentially parts of an organic whole but separate and autonomous individuals (MacIntyre, 1981; West, 1988). Changes in the shape of social institutions not only reflected this paradigm shift but also supported it and gave it momentum. The relevance of this history to the present day is not hard to see, once a final set of references is added, which locates the sources of our description of the Relational worldview.

The Shift to the Relational Paradigm

It is hard to identify the Relational outlook with a familiar philosophy, as is possible with the other two worldviews. It has no definitive articulation through an established line of thinkers related in a clear way with one another. Nevertheless, we can identify works in many different fields of inquiry today that not only reflect aspects of this worldview but are coming together to constitute it. The account we presented earlier was based on a number of these sources, though it is our own construction.

For example, Carol Gilligan's (1982, 1988) work on moral theory and development stresses the equal importance of both individuality and connectedness in human consciousness and the resulting capacity for integrating strength of self with concern for other. Her definition of moral maturity in these terms was the basis for our description of the value of transformation as movement toward conduct embodying compassionate strength, as we noted. In another field, Michael Sandel's (1982) formulation of political philosophy also stresses the importance of integrating individuality and connectedness. Sandel and other "communitarian" or "dialogist" thinkers, like Richard Bernstein (1983) and Alasdair MacIntyre (1981), argue that human nature finds expression through interpersonal relations of "authentic mutual recognition among individuals (Handler, 1988, p. 1067)," which can occur only in small-scale dialogic encounters—as in our picture of what can happen in transformative mediation.

In other fields, sociologists like Robert Bellah and his colleagues (1985) and Amitai Etzioni (1993) focus on the need to pay more attention to structures of relationship and community in social institutions of all kinds. Feminist legal scholars like Robin West (1988), Lynn Henderson (1987), Martha Minow (1987), and others argue, based on some of the previously cited work, for a greater emphasis on principles of care, connection, and empathy in legal rules and institutions, in different contexts. Other legal scholars like Ian Macneill (1984) call for legal structures that can integrate individual and collective interests, rights, and responsibilities. In the sciences, medical researchers like James Lynch (1986) suggest that the physiological functioning of the individual cannot properly be understood except by reference to the relation between self and other.

In the work of contemporary thinkers such as these in many different fields (and others could be added), the shape of the Relational worldview is emerging. Moreover, most of these thinkers are quite explicit about the fact that their ideas are meant to express a new worldview that contrasts with the Individualist outlook. Indeed, almost all of these "relational" writers explicitly criticize the Individualist worldview, usually in quite similar terms. The fact that elements of this worldview are being expressed similarly, across such a range of fields, signals the beginning of another paradigm shift, from the Individualist to the Relational worldview.

Of course, we are not suggesting that this paradigm shift has taken place and that the Individualist view no longer has any vitality. This is obviously not the case. But more and more evidence indicates that a potential paradigm shift is beginning. The increasing commonness of works evincing a similar critique of the Individualist outlook and a similar, relational alternative can fairly be seen as the sign of such a shift. How far it will go, whether the new paradigm will succeed, and what form it will ultimately take are all questions that cannot be answered yet. Nevertheless, even at this stage, the fact that the Relational worldview has begun to take root, on such a widespread basis, has some important implications and consequences for those who are interested in transformative mediation.

Choosing the Transformative Approach: The Largest Context

The first implication is that, when relational and transformative values are held out as important today in a field like mediation, this viewpoint cannot be discounted as isolated or marginal. The widespread attention these values are receiving across many fields makes it clear that they deserve serious consideration. This is not to say that transformation should be considered important simply because many people say so. The case for this or any value, or world-view, must be based on justification, not popularity or acceptance. For this reason, the main aim of this chapter has been to offer a jus-tification for considering transformation the most important goal of mediation. Nevertheless, the fact that there is such widespread interest in the Relational worldview offers some assurance, to those who want to pursue transformative values and aims, that doing so cannot simply be dismissed as naive and utopian. In the mediation field, those interested in the transformative approach can point to this larger context, not as a substitute for explaining and justifying their views but as a means of preventing others from simply dis-missing these views without serious discussion. Awareness of the larger context should thus encourage people interested in transfor-mation to speak up, with less concern that their views might be labeled unrealistic.

A second consequence of the fact that relational values are being explored in many fields is that the work done there can help those interested in transformative mediation better understand and articulate the underlying concepts and values of the approach. One of the real difficulties in pursuing the transformative approach, and justifying it to others, has been a lack of clarity about what it entails, in both practice and theory. Work on relational values and struc-tures in other fields offers a rich body of knowledge that can be drawn on to help build the theory and practice of transformative mediation. Indeed, many of the key constructs presented in this book were based on or inspired by ideas gleaned from the work of "relational" writers in other fields. Again, the larger context can offer support to those interested in choosing the transformative approach to mediation.

There is one more implication that the larger context carries for those interested in transformative mediation, and it is the most important of all. From the response that has greeted the work of many of the "relational" thinkers just mentioned, it is clear that just as there are those who welcome and support a shift to a Relational paradigm, many others will oppose it and argue for retaining the Individualist worldview (see Card, 1988; McClain, 1992). By being conscious of what is at stake in this larger context, those of us in the mediation field can make choices about our work with a full understanding of the possible impact of those choices. In other words, the future of the Relational worldview is by no means assured. If we believe, based on reasons like those presented earlier in this chapter, that this vision offers a richer, sounder basis for constructing social reality, then we can help establish it as a paradigm by the concrete choices we make about how to practice mediation. Just as the larger context can support the choice of transformative mediation, that concrete choice can support the larger shift to the Relational vision as a whole.

In a paradigm shift, social institutions not only reflect the shift, they also provide momentum to carry it forward. As the shift begins, new social forms and structures are inspired and legitimized. At the same time, these structures themselves give expression and strength to the new outlook. In short, there is an interplay between the worldview and the social reality it helps to construct. This is the case as the Relational worldview emerges today. On the one hand, the development of relational social institutions is a consequence of the new outlook embodied in the Relational worldview. Even if the connection is not articulated, such institutions intuitively express different assumptions about human nature and society from the Individualist framework. Indeed, it is a further sign of the emergent paradigm shift that relational social forms are more and more visible across the culture. One major point of our Transformation Story of the mediation movement is that the broad interest in mediation as a form of conflict resolution is one such phenomenon. The intuition that this is a potentially relational social institution is a large part of what makes people interested in the mediation process, whether as parties or as mediators. From this viewpoint, the emerging paradigm is shaping the social reality, at an intuitive level.

But the reverse can also occur, through choice at the conscious level. The conscious choice to employ certain social processes can itself help enact and reinforce an emerging paradigm. Because transformative mediation is a relational institution, choosing the transformative approach and practicing it supports and reinforces the emergence of the Relational outlook in a very concrete way. And it does so at a critical historical juncture, the point of its possible emergence as a new paradigm. Conscious adoption of a transformative approach to mediation is thus a way of strengthening the movement toward the new paradigm, by enacting it in concrete form. Certainly, other relational institutions may eventually be constructed, within the dispute resolution and other fields. However, because of its transformative potential, the mediation process offers a very good place to start.

In effect, by their choice between the problem-solving and transformative approaches, people in the mediation movement are deciding whether mediation will remain one more institution in an individualist society or become a foundational part of a different, relational society that is not a utopian dream but a gradually emerging reality. Given the possibility of a paradigm shift to the Relational worldview, the stakes of the choice between the two approaches take on even more importance. Not just the mediation movement but the entire society stands at a crossroads, choosing which path to take. The path toward the transformative approach to mediation is also the path toward a social reality founded on a new, relational vision of human life, a vision that offers a way of transcending old dichotomies and opening new possibilities for human consciousness and interaction. The future of mediation is a matter of utmost importance, not just for its own sake but for the sake of the much larger choice involved.

10

. . . .

Implementing the
Transformative Approach:
Inroads and Obstacles

Throughout this book, we have tried to show that a transformative approach to mediation is desirable and possible. This approach already appeals to many practitioners who aspire to its objectives and attempt to foster empowerment and recognition in their practice. They have an intuitive sense of what transformative practice is, and they are aware of its potential accomplishments and their value. However, if this awareness remains only a vague appreciation, transformative practice will remain a secondary story of the mediation movement.

Conducting transformative practice requires that individual mediators adopt a proactive stance and make a deep commitment to enacting the objectives of this vision. In concrete terms, making this commitment means accepting the need to adopt a new mind-set and thus to carry the transformative vision, as a whole, into every case. It also means adopting a vigilant stance throughout practice, a stance that guards against the strong reactions and hidden investments that pull mediators away from transformative objectives.

However, even a firm commitment to the transformative vision cannot be fulfilled unless mediators have adequate practical tools and a supportive environment to help them put transformative practice into place. This means coming to grips with the concrete requirements of practice and with the range of institutional constraints and opportunities that can inhibit or support transformative practice. Beyond the specific tools discussed in earlier chapters, effecting a shift to the transformative approach will require the development of new *training materials and methods* that provide mediators with the skills needed to foster empowerment and recognition. It will also require a shift in perceptions about the "demand side" of mediation—the *institutional context* that generates expectations about what mediation can and should accomplish. In this chapter, we will discuss specific changes and developments that are needed in both of these areas to advance a transformative vision of practice.

Approaches to Training

Many models of mediation training endorse empowerment or recognition as important elements of practice, although none have linked the two goals together in a single vision or discussed the deeper view of dispute resolution they carry. Rather, when empowerment or recognition are mentioned in the training literature, they are typically treated in one of two ways. At times they are discussed as tools for improving problem solving—they are cast essentially in the service of constructing settlements. In other instances, empowerment and recognition are marked as important goals of the process, but they are left at an abstract level. Their importance is discussed in goes-without-saying terms and they remain detached from the how-to of training. As a result, mediators are not shown what fostering empowerment or recognition means in any practical sense. There is little or no instruction on the move-by-move decisions that mediators must make as they walk through a case.

In order to translate the transformative vision into practice, new approaches to training need to be developed that provide concrete instruction in this approach. Specifically, training materials and programs need to do three things: teach mediators the transformative *model* of mediation, identify *standard procedures* that can be built into the process to keep mediation on a transformative track, and provide *skills* that are the basis for practicing empowerment and recognition. In the suggestions that follow, our goal is not to detail a comprehensive training package but to sketch an approach to training that is aligned with transformative objectives and to spark ideas in others who might use such an approach.

Teaching the Transformative Model

The first step in training for transformative mediation must be to make clear its purpose and goals and to provide an overview of how mediation unfolds in this approach. Early in the training, mediators should be introduced to the goals of empowerment and recognition, their linkage, and the broader vision of which they are a part. Mediators then need to see, in a general way, how mediation can enact these objectives. Discussing a map of the transformative process, like that depicted in Chapter Seven, can provide practitioners with an overview of the process. Mediators also need vivid illustrations of what moves they are likely to make as the process unfolds. Identifying signpost events that mark opportunities for empowerment and recognition, like those noted in Table 7.1, offers mediators a concrete sense of the type of moves that transformative mediators are called on to make. In general, the goal of this introductory phase of the training is to enable mediators to recognize opportunities for empowerment and recognition, understand their importance in reaching transformative ends, and learn how to respond to such opportunities when they arise.

Building in Standard Procedures

The standard procedures of mediation—the built-in features and ground rules that apply to every session—need to be rethought. New procedures need to be included in training as part of the "how-to" of transformative practice.

Currently, standard procedures include such things as the mediator's opening statement, ground rules the parties should follow (such as no interruptions), and guidelines for what should go in written agreements. Trainers need to determine which of these procedural formats serve transformative practice and which do not. And they need to create new standard procedures that are specifically aimed at fostering empowerment and recognition. To illustrate the way standard procedures might change in a transformative approach to practice, we offer the following recommendations.

• *Change mediators' opening statements to reflect transformative objectives.* This means emphasizing that all decision-making power is left in the parties' hands, as well as noting that the process offers an opportunity for people to achieve greater understanding of both their own options and each other. The opening statement should indicate that if the parties agree to take steps to deal with their situation, these steps can be written into a final agreement. The opening should also suggest, however, that other accomplishments of the session can also be written up, even if a specific solution to the parties' situation cannot be found. These other accomplishments might include, for example, understandings reached, new information that was exchanged during the session, and descriptions, in the parties own words, of new ways of communicating that were followed in the mediation—new ways that might help them in their discussions after the session.

• *Shift expectations for what parties do as they listen to each other's opening statements.* Most ground rules for mediation ask disputants not to interrupt while the other party gives his or her opening account of what the dispute is about. If listening parties disagree or object to what is being said, they are asked to write their concerns down so they do not forget them and are told that they will be given a chance to raise their points after the other party finishes speaking. In a transformative process, not interrupting remains an important ground rule; but this, in itself, may not be all that the listening party should do. A more pointed shift in the listening party's point of view might direct interaction toward transformative objectives.

In our practice, for example, we have sometimes asked listening parties to take a more proactive stance. As one party gives an opening statement, we have asked the listener to write down any "news" they hear as the other party speaks—to mark down points of information they did not know, things they did not realize about the other party but that are now evident from hearing the other's opening statement. After the other party finishes speaking, we turn to the listener and ask what he or she heard in the other party's statement.

This "listen for news" approach accomplishes several things. First, it sets an expectation right from the start that part of what might happen in mediation is that parties will learn things from each other. It marks achieving understanding and seeing the other's point of view as important goals of the process. Second, it opens up possible opportunities for recognition in the case at hand. The parties themselves begin to identify places where they might consider a different perspective, gain an appreciation of the other's point of view, or consider an alternative understanding of past events. In short, from the outset of a session, this approach involves the parties in the process of fostering recognition.

• *Specify a period of time after the parties' opening statements when the disputants are encouraged to ask questions that arise from their genuine curiosity about the other party, past events, or future possibilities.* At the beginning of many mediations, disputants are ready to attack each other and defend themselves. Accommodating these behaviors is often necessary and useful. Mediators often need to let the parties vent, speak openly, and register the depth of their feelings about the issues. But this type of interaction alone does nothing to encourage more productive forms of dialogue during the session. Surprisingly, there are very few procedural ground rules in any models of mediation that build in expectations for more productive forms of communication in the early stages of a session.

Several public dialogue projects that bring together people with strong ideological differences (over abortion, gun control, and so forth) specify periods of time in the process when people seek answers to questions that stem from true curiosity, from things they have honestly wondered about or did not know about the other "side." For example, The Public Conversations Project of Cambridge, Massachusetts, centers their process in part around the notion of reducing uncertainty. Some discussions are designed to encourage parties to pursue their curiosities about people who think very differently than they do. The goal is to break down barriers that stem from misunderstandings, false assumptions, and stereotypical thinking.

Using proactive procedural formats like this one in mediation can go quite far in surfacing opportunities for recognition. Even if the question period is unsuccessful—if, for example, the parties resist or cannot let go of their defensive posture to ask questions—the mere suggestion that time should be taken for questioning about their own curiosities sends a message that recognition is a central goal of the process. It is a procedural expectation that is clearly in line with the goals of transformative practice.

• *Identify a point in the process in which each party indicates what they think the other does not understand about them.* After opening statements are made and the parties discuss their views of the situation, they may still feel as if they are not completely understood. Setting aside a time when parties can say what they think the other party does not understand about them furthers discussion about differences and misunderstandings. This procedure serves the same general purpose as "listening for news" and asking curiosity questions. It encourages interaction among the parties that fosters opportunities for recognition.

• *Expand what can be included in the written agreements—the "official" outcomes of mediation.* The transformative vision of practice changes what might be written up as possible outcomes of the process. It shifts agreements away from a narrow conception of "settlement" terms as only the set of commitments parties make to solve the problem. This narrow sense of settlement can be replaced with a much broader conception of mediation outcomes. Every session might conclude with a memorandum of understanding that provides a synopsis, perhaps in the parties' own words, of what occurred. This would include points of agreement—commitments the parties make—about what to do about the situation or problem. But it would also include a record of such things as the clarity that individual parties achieved about their own choices and options, misunderstandings between parties that were cleared up, and summaries of new ways that the parties found, through their participation in mediation, for communicating with each other.

Written agreements might also include succinct descriptions of the points on which the parties could not agree—their impasses. Although descriptions of impasses may seem like unlikely candidates for outcomes of the process, they may have more value than we might first think. A director of a farmer-creditor mediation program in the Midwest said recently that parties' impasses often represent important steps toward settlement that are worthy of writing up in a final agreement. In informal follow-up he has done, he has been surprised at the number of cases in which clarity on impasse was an important first step in allowing the parties to reach a settlement after the mediation ended. Such clarity gives parties a sense of what issues are in front of them and, in identifying points of disagreement, encourages parties to keep talking after the mediation session ends.

This view of impasse as a "step along the way" is consistent with phase theories of conflict, which suggest that a period of differentiation—articulating clear differences—is necessary before parties can reach greater integration (see, for example, Folger, Poole, and Stutman, 1993). From a transformative perspective, writing up parties' impasses is consistent with a view of mediation as being only part of an ongoing conflict interaction, a stream that starts before the session begins and will, in many instances, continue after it is over, whether or not a specific "settlement" is achieved in the session.

Providing Transformative Skills

Besides teaching a general model of transformative mediation and building new standard procedures into the process, training programs

need to provide mediators with specific skills that advance transformative objectives. Mediators need to sharpen their abilities to
identify and work with opportunities for empowerment and recognition. They need to develop a range of skills to conduct transformative mediation. Many of these skills are captured in the
transformative moves we analyzed in Chapters Five and Six. They
include the ability to

- Offer summaries of parties' views and positions without
  substantively reshaping what parties have said.

- Translate one party's statements so the other is more
  likely to hear them accurately or consider them
  sympathetically.

- Offer possible reinterpretations of parties' actions or
  motives without trying to convince disputants that any
  one interpretation is necessarily correct or better.

- Use caucuses in ways that help parties understand their
  own choices and consider the other party's perspective.

- Encourage and help parties to evaluate options and
  make choices without leading them in a preferred
  direction.

- Ask questions that reveal how each party wants to be
  seen by the other.

- Write agreements that reflect the transformative
  accomplishments of the session.

These abilities, among others, should be the measurable objectives
of skills training. Specific exercises and materials can enhance mediators' performance in each of these areas. We will briefly discuss
three of these skills areas to illustrate what is entailed in designing
transformative skills training.

Offering Nonimpositional Summaries. Mediators need to be able to provide accurate, useful summaries of parties' comments and positions. Summaries help parties understand and make decisions about their own situations and options, and they provide structure for the discussions. In transformative mediation, it is essential that mediators provide summaries without imposing their own perspectives or attitudes.

Specific training exercises can help mediators learn to avoid letting their own assumptions and perspectives influence the summaries they construct. Some training programs we have seen include such exercises in an effort to raise mediators' consciousness about the tendency to become overly directive. For example, one program developed by Ellen Raider and Susan Coleman (1992) of the International Center for Cooperation and Conflict Resolution includes an exercise in which mediators practice how to step away from their own assumptions as they construct summaries of parties' discussions. Mediators first listen to a set of statements by a speaker and offer a summary of what they heard. They then listen to their summaries and examine with the trainer how their own assumptions and perspectives influenced and distorted their summaries. They conclude by offering alternative summaries, consciously stepping away from their assumptions and remaining true to the speaker's statements.

Reinterpreting Actions/Motives. Offering possible reinterpretations of parties' actions or motives is an important skill that transformative mediators use to foster recognition. Training programs can include exercises that teach mediators how to recognize where opportunities to reinterpret arise and how to frame and offer reinterpretations. This can be done by role-playing segments of a session in which one party asserts a negative interpretation of the other party's behavior or past actions. Trainers then ask mediators to think of four or five other possible explanations for the behavior that are less negative, explanations that do not automatically assume the worst about the person. Mediators then practice offering these alternative interpretations to the accusing party in ways that encourage him or her to consider whether such alternative, less damaging, interpretations and attributions might be possible. The goal is not to convince the accusing party that they are wrong, but simply to open up their thinking by asking them to entertain the possibility that they may be making unnecessary assumptions.

The skills involved in offering reinterpretations include both learning how to construct them realistically and quickly and learning how to phrase them provisionally—suggesting that alternative interpretations are possible without pressuring parties to move from their views.

Using Caucuses Transformatively. Learning how and when to use caucuses is a staple of most mediation training programs. Caucuses are often used to find out what parties are *not* saying in joint session and to "test the waters"—to determine what parties might be willing to agree to in a settlement. From this perspective, it is easy to think that caucuses are necessarily inconsistent with transformative objectives. If mediators are determined to reach settlements, caucuses offer mediators a chance, under cover, to persuade parties of certain choices. And, because parties do not talk directly to one another, caucuses can easily remove possibilities for recognition.

If mediators see caucuses as convenient times to control outcomes and to prevent parties from offering recognition to each other, then caucuses may, indeed, undercut transformative objectives. However, a skillful transformative mediator can use caucuses in a manner that not only avoids the problem-solving pitfalls but actually builds transformative momentum over the course of a session.

The Landlord-Tenant case in Chapter Six illustrates how caucusing early in a session, especially when parties are unclear about how they view the situation and what their options are, can give parties a sense of personal control. Caucuses can, in other words, empower parties to see what they want and what their options are. Moreover, once parties are empowered by clarifying their positions, important grounds for recognition have been laid. The strength achieved when parties clarify issues and positions in caucus allows them to risk looking at threatening issues from the other's perspective. Parties may be more likely to give recognition, because they have achieved a certain amount of confidence about what is important to them.

In addition, these early caucuses also inform the mediator about what recognition the parties may want from each other. Disputants often state or imply, in caucus, how the other party has threatened or ignored important images they hold of themselves. Mediators can work with these revelations, as opportunities for recognition, when the parties discuss later how they see each other and why these views are important to the dispute.

Although the Landlord-Tenant case illustrates how caucusing early in a session can foster transformative objectives, caucusing may be unnecessary, or even counterproductive, in the early stages of other sessions. Caucusing was not necessary in the Sensitive Bully case discussed in the Introduction, for example, because the parties offered important recognition to each other in the face-to-face discussion they had at the beginning of the session. If the mediators had decided to break into caucus immediately following the parties' opening statements, the transformative momentum might well have been lost.

The point is that mediators need to be skilled in deciding when a caucus is needed to further empowerment and recognition, and intervening in ways that take advantage of the unique opportunities for empowerment and recognition that arise in these one-on-one sessions. Thoughtful training can provide these skills through role-plays, critiques of case studies, and focused discussions on the role that caucuses play in transformative mediation.

Addressing the Current Institutional Context

The recommendations for developing training models deal with what could be called the "supply side" of a shift to the transformative approach. They illustrate the kinds of concrete steps that must be taken by the suppliers of mediation—mediators, mediation administrators, and trainers—to put the transformative approach into place. However, suppliers will be very hesitant to take these steps, unless they feel confident that *users* of the process will be interested in transformative mediation. The current or potential users of the process, public and private, institutional and individual, make up what could be called the "demand side" of the potential shift to the transformative approach. The demand side is often referred to as the "institutional context" of mediation—including the courts, the legal profession, the business sector, government agencies, and private disputants. If the demand side is viewed as hostile or indifferent to the transformative approach, a supply side shift will be seen as pointless by mediation providers, and they simply will not take the kinds of steps called for to develop transformative practice.

In fact, based on responses to our presentation of the transformative approach on many occasions, it seems there is a widespread assumption that the institutional context would indeed be hostile or indifferent to transformative mediation, for a variety of reasons. However, that assumption is unwarranted. There is already substantial interest in transformative mediation on the demand side, and there are many good ways to enhance such interest. Therefore, supporters of the transformative approach must go beyond simply taking for themselves the steps outlined earlier to implement transformative practice. In addition, they must become advocates, engaging in a persuasive campaign aimed at changing attitudes—in both the mediation field and the various institutional contexts it serves—about what mediation can and should accomplish.

The best tools for engaging in this kind of campaign are (1) advance knowledge of the main questions raised about the acceptability of a transformative approach to mediation in the current institutional context, and (2) some clear and persuasive points that can be offered in response to these questions. We present here the major questions that are regularly raised about the viability of the transformative approach, together with suggestions as to how these questions can be answered. This information can provide some beginning tools for showing that the institutional context need not be averse to the transformative approach.

• • • • • • • •

Question 1: If mediators employ a transformative approach stressing empowerment and recognition, won't this necessarily result in both lower settlement rates and more time expended per case, by comparison to problem-solving mediation? If so, how can this be as attractive to users—including courts, businesses, lawyers, and private individuals—who place great value on settlement and efficiency?

Since transformative mediation has not been widely practiced or studied, there is actually no evidence showing that settlement rates are lower and time per case higher using this approach. Instead of simply assuming this, the more sensible course would be to try the approach and study the results to see if the assumption is correct.

Even if this assumption is correct, a higher settlement rate for problem-solving mediation does not by itself mean that users will prefer it to the transformative approach. The settlements produced by problem solving will, predictably, often be either illusory or unjust, because of mediator directiveness, whereas those produced by transformative mediation will be genuine and fair, because of empowerment and recognition.

Therefore, even if it produces fewer settlements, transformative mediation can be expected to produce settlements of better quality, in terms of parties' mutual satisfaction. Indeed, the settlements "lost" by using a transformative approach may themselves be considered a gain, because they would have been the product of mediator directiveness rather than party choice. In short, unless users care only about the superficial numbers of "settlements" and not about their quality and the satisfaction they represent, lower settlement rates in transformative mediation do not necessarily make it less attractive. Rather, the higher quality of settlements produced by this approach should make it more attractive to those concerned with settlement as a goal.

In fact, mediation users themselves are increasingly aware of and receptive to this point. For example, we have spoken to several mediation administrators who are exploring advanced training for mediators in how *not* to be directive—that is, training in empowerment—after concluding that the "settlements" produced by overly directive mediation were more illusory than real. We pointed out to the administrators that nondirectiveness in practice might mean some reduction in settlement rates and increased time per case. Their response was that they had learned that quality of settlements had to be considered primary if the whole enterprise was to be meaningful. They also explained that the courts they were associated with were no longer so concerned with raw settlement rates or time/cost figures and more interested in knowing that the mediation program was providing a valuable "community service." These kinds of attitudes in the institutional context are certainly not hostile or indifferent to the transformative approach; on the contrary, they bespeak real receptiveness to it—once people understand the contrast between the problem solving and transformative approaches.

Even in cases in which no settlement occurs, transformative mediation may serve users in other ways that are valued. For example, the empowerment and recognition achieved in mediation may make the future course of a nonsettled case smoother, whether in court, ongoing negotiations, or otherwise. The parties' greater understanding of their own needs and options, and of the other party, make this likely.

Of course, if transformative mediation is advocated on grounds such as these, new research models and evaluation measures must be developed to test its claims. Research needs to look beyond numerical settlement rates, develop more reliable and focused indicators of party satisfaction, and track the subsequent history of both settled and nonsettled cases. The current lack of such data is only a temporary problem. If users are interested in this information, it is likely that researchers will find ways of obtaining it.

· · · · · · · ·

Question 2: *If mediators employ a transformative approach and refrain from evaluating and monitoring the quality of settlements, won't this necessarily result in more unfair settlements, by comparison to problem-solving mediation, as weaker parties are more often pressured and outmaneuvered by stronger opponents into accepting one-sided deals?*

As in question 1, this question is based on an assumption about the impact of transformative mediation on fairness, and no evidence exists to support it. Moreover, there is no evidence documenting the "fairness" of settlements obtained in problem-solving mediation. Indeed, some have claimed that outcomes of problem-solving mediation typically disfavor weaker parties, and some preliminary research suggests this may be true (Hermann and others, 1993).

More important, once the nature of transformative mediation is understood, including the meaning and central place of empowerment in this approach, the concern for fairness is directly addressed. When the mediator's role and skills are dedicated to helping parties make their own decisions on all points and *not* to producing solutions per se, "weaker parties" are helped to *resist* pressures to accept deals they consider unacceptable and to exercise the option of nonagreement and removal to another forum more advantageous to them than mediation, if one exists. The real opportunity to reject a settlement and go elsewhere is what guarantees fairness in mediation, and empowerment ensures that this opportunity is real.

Since the question poses a comparison with problem-solving mediation, it invites the further response that the problem-solving approach itself, with its tendency to directiveness, is much more likely to engender unfair settlements than the transformative approach. This is because the mediator's tendency to push for some sort of settlement will dilute the ability of weaker parties to reject settlement entirely and go elsewhere—which is their real protection against unfairness. In addition, a directive mediator's own biases may lead him or her to push for specific terms of settlement that disfavor a weaker party. Thus, the directiveness inherent in it makes problem solving more of a threat to fairness than a guarantee against unfairness. The empowerment inherent in transformative mediation has just the opposite impact.

• • • • • • •

Question 3: Even if transformative mediation can match or better the performance of problem-solving mediation in terms of producing quality settlements (including fairness), isn't the focus on transformation itself simply foreign to what parties want from dispute resolution? Therefore, even if problem solving usually involves mediator directiveness, with some likelihood of dissatisfaction or unfairness, aren't parties really just interested in having someone guide them to a solution that ends the dispute, rather than in transforming themselves through empowerment and recognition (and thereby coming to a solution)?

There is no evidence that what disputing parties most want is a strong hand to guide them out of their conflicts, rather than an opportunity to handle their conflicts for themselves with dignity, self-respect, and consideration for the other side. This assumption underlies the question and may be persuasive to some, but it is simply an assumption.

If it turns out that this assumption does reflect current attitudes of disputants, these attitudes are still open to change, in response to new options presented. Given a choice between lengthy, formal litigation and directive mediation, users may prefer the latter. But this does not mean that the possibility of self-determination and consideration, in transformative mediation, would not be considered an even better choice once it became known and understood. In fact, this is one way to describe what happened with problem-solving mediation itself. When it was first introduced, most parties preferred vindication in court to any alternative. Compromise in any form connoted weakness and lack of resolve. The advocates of problem solving then showed potential users something new, a win-win instead of win-lose option, and over time persuaded them of its value. The same can occur with transformative mediation today.

The most important response here is that the assumption of the question very likely does *not* reflect current attitudes of mediation users. That is, even without efforts to change attitudes, there are many indications today that potential users already value exactly what transformative mediation offers—the opportunity for empowerment and recognition, for both strengthening self and relating compassionately to others. The rapid growth of the human potential and self-help movements, the demand for participatory management in both the private and public sectors, the focus in education on teaching decision making and responsibility rather than simple information acquisition—all these trends indicate the value people place on empowerment today.

As for recognition, the widespread interest today in interpersonal communication skills, intercultural awareness and sensitivity, awareness of the impact of gender on human behavior and interaction, and "relationship enhancement" within and beyond the family context—these focal points of public interest all indicate the value people place on finding ways to recognize and relate to others, not only as a matter of self-interest but out of genuine concern for something beyond self.

Given these indications, it seems unlikely that, if presented with the opportunity to handle conflict in a way that both strengthens the self and expresses concern for the other party, potential users of mediation would reject it. It makes more sense to assume that, just as people are interested today in social tools that help them grow in the dimensions of empowerment and recognition in other aspects of their lives, they will be similarly interested in conflict resolution tools that do the same thing.

If people want to act with greater strength and compassion in their lives generally (and there are widespread indications of this today), they are likely to be interested in an approach to mediation that lets them behave similarly when involved in conflict, instead of one that ignores the transformative dimension and enacts a more defensive, self-interested form of behavior. If transformative mediation is properly presented and explained, we have good reason to believe that potential users of mediation will be quite interested in it rather than indifferent or hostile.

In fact, just as they have come to understand the importance of the quality of settlement, many mediators and program administrators have already realized that mediation's transformative dimensions are attractive to disputing parties. In conversations with several administrators, we asked them to describe what they saw as examples of real success in mediations they had seen or conducted. Invariably, they pointed not to settlement rates or specific settlement outcomes but to cases in which empowerment and recognition occurred and the parties themselves were changed by what happened. They saw that the parties themselves valued this experience far more than the mere production of a settlement that ended the dispute. They were troubled by the inability to measure, evaluate, and thereby demonstrate this achievement, but they did not hesitate to point to it as the true measure of success. The need for evaluation measures will be filled once researchers know that these dimensions are what users are most interested in.

. . . .

Question 4: *If it is true that people value both solutions and transformation, why can mediation practice not strive for both, by simply integrating the two approaches?*

Despite the appeal of the idea of integrating the approaches, at the practical level they are difficult if not impossible to meld into one. First of all, the core practices of each approach are mutually inconsistent. For example, macrofocusing on the parties' *situation*, in order to identify the problem and possible solutions, works against microfocusing on the parties' *interaction* in order to spot opportunities for empowerment and recognition. The reverse is also true. Similarly, steering away from the past and emphasizing the future, in order to work towards a concrete settlement, works against exploring parties' perceptions of past conduct in order to surface opportunities for recognition. Both examples demonstrate that taking one approach means doing the opposite of what is called for in the other. Integrating the practices associated with both approaches is a practical impossibility.

At a more general level, the very different objectives of the two approaches make it extremely unlikely that mediators will be able to integrate them in practice. For mediators, focusing on finding solutions makes transformative moves unlikely, and focusing on transformation requires avoidance of moves that directly seek settlement. In practice, attempting to integrate the two approaches winds up leading to the pursuit of problem solving at the expense of transformation. Both empowerment and recognition are ignored whenever achieving a settlement requires a more directive, instrumental approach.

Finally, not only is integration of the approaches impossible, it is also unnecessary. Since empowerment and recognition will probably produce desired settlements wherever they are really possible, mediation practice *can* attain both solutions and transformation—*not* by striving directly for both but by following the transformative approach alone. Practicing transformative mediation is the best way to meet both goals, because it will lead not only to transformation but to settlement as well, whenever a settlement is genuinely acceptable to both sides.

* * * * * * *

Question 5: Even if a transformative approach stressing empowerment and recognition is useful and preferable in certain types of cases—like community and family conflicts— isn't its preferability limited to those contexts?

The argument for the transformative approach applies equally in all kinds of cases. Directiveness in mediation is just as problematic in business and legal disputes as in interpersonal cases, if not more so. When mediators suggest "settlement values" or "ranges" to parties, which is one common form that directiveness takes in such cases, they effectively decide the limits within which settlement will occur. They decide what is "on the table," just as interpersonal mediators often decide which issues get discussed. All these decisions are secret and nonreviewable, and though everyone is free to leave, the pressure to stay and settle is difficult to resist.

One business lawyer familiar with current, problem-solving mediation practice commented that he sees mediation of this kind as dangerous and counterproductive for his clients, since it is like "court without the guarantees and safeguards." If a third party is effectively making decisions on how to resolve the matter, he tells clients, it is better that the third party be a judge bound by rules and procedures. Significantly, this is the very same argument made by those who criticize the use of problem-solving mediation in interpersonal and family disputes. The critique is the same because the problem-solving approach affects all kinds of disputes in similar fashion. It is a highly risky and unpredictable process, likely to produce settlements that satisfy no one. There simply are no types of cases in which people would not be concerned about these limits of the problem-solving approach, if made aware of them.

From the other side, the values of empowerment and recognition are just as real, regardless of the type of dispute in question. All conflicts, not just community and family conflicts, embody opportunities for empowerment and recognition, and hence moral transformation. No matter what the context, conflicts make parties feel

vulnerable and defensive—even businesspeople and professionals—
and thus open up opportunities for developing strength and compassion in the place of weakness and self-centeredness. Not only
neighbors in interpersonal disputes and divorcing spouses but businesspeople, consumers, doctors and other professionals, and even
representatives of large institutions and public agencies, are all
human beings who may be interested in growing in the dimensions
of empowerment and recognition, in behaving with greater strength
and compassion in their lives generally, whenever possible. As noted
earlier, there are many indications in the popular culture that individuals in all these contexts place increasing value on this type of
human growth. If it is possible to handle conflicts in a way that fosters such growth and behavior *and* helps achieve settlements when
they are genuinely acceptable, parties across all these contexts
would probably *prefer* this approach to one that ignores such growth
and pushes them into settlements that are often illusory.

For example, the same business lawyer mentioned earlier commented that he sees current mediation practice as "aiming way too
low." He explained that by focusing entirely on settlement production, mediation is missing the chance to give his clients something
he thinks they would find much more valuable—a way to handle
conflict that corresponds to their higher aspirations in doing business generally. The businessperson's ethic is a combination of entre-
preneurialism and service, strength and consideration for others.
Mediation can allow businesspeople to realize this ethic not only in
doing business but in dealing with conflict, if the approach is transformative rather than problem solving. The same kind of argument
applies to parties in many different contexts.

The question nevertheless implies that in most contexts, even
if growth and transformation matter to parties, it is still the "bottom line" that matters most—getting the dispute settled and the
problem solved. Two brief points can be made in response. First, not
only settlement but quality of settlement counts, and the transformative approach promises to improve the quality of settlements by

comparison to those now produced in mediation. Second, even if the transformative approach may more often leave disputes unresolved, it will not exist in a vacuum. There will continue to be other processes to which parties can turn for settlement per se. Allowing those processes to concentrate on settlement alone will allow mediation to "aim higher" and achieve something that those other processes cannot—transformation.

• • • • • • •

> **Question 6:** *If a transformative approach to mediation, derived from the Relational view of human nature and society, is used in all kinds of disputes, won't parties often reject opportunities for empowerment and recognition and continue to behave in self-interested, Individualist fashion? If so, isn't the approach futile—or even foolish and dangerous—because the failure to "transform" parties will either leave disputes unresolved altogether or else allow the "selfish" to take advantage of the "compassionate"?*

The first part of the question must certainly be answered in the affirmative. Even those who favor the Relational worldview must acknowledge that, at best, our society is just beginning to shift toward that outlook. The Individualist outlook is still alive and well, and dominant. Therefore transformative mediation will often produce only small increments of empowerment and recognition. However, the conclusion implied in the second part of the question—that transformative mediation is futile or dangerous—does not follow. The transformative process of empowerment and recognition, even when it is only partial and incremental, will often produce settlements, and ones of better quality than a directive process like problem solving. This is no futile endeavor.

It is also not a foolish or dangerous endeavor, unless we accept what seems to be the assumption of the second part of the question: that adopting the transformative approach to mediation, making it a relational conflict resolution institution, means doing away with all other, individualist conflict resolution institutions. This assumption, however, is not part of the case for transformative mediation. On the contrary, making mediation practice transformative makes accessibility to arbitration, adjudication, and other more protective and authoritative processes all the more important. If transformative mediation ends in impasse, whether because of rejected opportunities for empowerment and recognition or because of real external limitations on parties, the parties must indeed have some place to turn for the "bottom line"—a decision on how to put an end to their dispute.

The point is that mediation need not and should not be the place parties turn for this bottom line, because other institutions with more formal protective features are better equipped to make such decisions. When imposed judgment is required, it is often because one or both parties are functioning, in relational terms, at the lower level of human nature rather than the higher; and when this is so, the institution dealing with the conflict must be protective in character, like courts. Mediation is a poor substitute for adjudication. Adopting transformative mediation would put responsibility for judgment back on judges, where critics of mediation have long claimed it belongs.

"Aiming Higher": Allowing Mediation to Be a True Alternative

Although being able to answer any of these specific questions is important in advancing the transformative approach, there is a larger message—a pivotal argument—that lies at the heart of many of these responses. This message is one that people in the field will find convincing if they look inward and make an honest appraisal of whether mediation, as currently practiced, actually constitutes an *alternative* dispute resolution process (see Kolb, 1989; Menkel-Meadow, 1991; McEwen, 1991). The problem-solving approach to mediation does not offer a meaningful alternative to adjudicative forums. Reaching settlements through mediation as currently practiced is, in a fundamental sense, not that different from settling disputes through arbitration. In both methods, disputes are settled and problems get solved primarily through third-party influence. Both forums seek the same individualistic aspirations for the resolution of social conflict. Transformative mediation, on the other hand, starts from a very different place—it holds different assumptions about what people are capable of and what conflict interaction might achieve. It sets much higher stakes. And, although it does not ensure success in each case, it provides an opportunity for approaching disputes in ways that no other formal dispute resolution process affords. It creates the possibility for disputants to integrate strength of self and compassion toward others—a goal that neither problem-solving mediation as currently practiced nor other institutionalized forms of dispute resolution even seeks.

Mediation can and should be a true alternative to other processes. Mediation should *not* be the place parties turn for the bottom line of settlement, precisely because it can "aim higher." Given the transitional state of our society between Individualist and Relational worldviews, protective individualist institutions are necessary, especially in the arena of conflict resolution. However, this does not mean that *all* institutions must be individualist. On the contrary, some institutions can be educative and encourage the emergent impulse across society to develop our highest natures and deal with one another in relational terms. Indeed, some institutions *must* allow for and explore the development of the Relational vision, if it is ever to become a reality.

Mediation can be one such institution, but only if it follows the transformative approach. Only then will it fulfill its unique promise. And since it will not exist in a vacuum, but rather in a context in which individualist dispute resolution institutions continue to function and even dominate, it can be permitted to flourish on its own terms. Thus, allowing mediation to enact the Relational vision will be neither foolish nor unduly risky. As many have begun to see, it might even be wise.

References

Abel, R., "The Contradictions of Informal Justice." In R. Abel (ed.), *The Politics of Informal Justice*. New York: Academic Press, 1982.

Alfini, J. J. "Trashing, Bashing, and Hashing It Out: Is This the End of 'Good Mediation'?" *Florida State University Law Review*, 1991, *19* (1), 47–75.

Bellah, R. N., and others. *Habits of the Heart: Individualism and Commitment in American Life*. Berkeley: University of California Press, 1985.

Bellah, R. N., and others. *The Good Society*. New York: Knopf, 1991.

Bernard, S., Folger, J. P., Weingarten, H., and Zumeta, Z. "The Neutral Mediator: Value Dilemmas in Divorce Mediation." *Mediation Quarterly*, 1984, *4*, 61–74.

Bernstein, R. *Beyond Objectivism and Relativism: Science, Hermeneutics and Praxis*. Philadelphia: University of Pennsylvania Press, 1983.

Blake, R. R., and Mouton, J. S. *The Managerial Grid*. Houston: Gulf, 1964.

Borisoff, D., and Victor, D. A. *Conflict Management: A Communication Skills Approach*. Englewood Cliffs, N.J.: Prentice-Hall, 1989.

Boszormenyi-Nagy, I., and Krasner, B. R. *Between Give and Take: A Clinical Guide to Contextual Therapy*. New York: Brunner/Mazel, 1986.

Bouman, A. "Liberating Literacy: Writing on the Margins of American Society." *Educator*, 1991, *5*(2), 48–51.

Bryan, P. E. "Killing Us Softly: Divorce Mediation and the Politics of Power." *Buffalo Law Review*, 1992, *40*(2), 441–523.

Burger, W. "Isn't There a Better Way?" *American Bar Association Journal*, 1982, *68*, 274–277.

Bush, R.A.B. "Efficiency and Protection, or Empowerment and Recognition? The Mediator's Role and Ethical Standards in Mediation." *Florida Law Review*, 1989, *41*(2), 253–286.

Bush, R.A.B. "Mediation and Adjudication, Dispute Resolution and Ideology: An Imaginary Conversation." *Journal of Contemporary Legal Issues*, 1989–1990, *3*, 1–35.

Bush, R.A.B. *The Dilemmas of Mediation Practice: A Study of Ethical Dilemmas and Policy Implications*. Washington, D.C.: National Institute for Dispute Resolution, 1992.

Card, C. "Women's Voices and Ethical Ideals: Must We Mean What We Say?" *Ethics*, 1988, 99, 125–135.

Carnevale, P. J., Conlon, D. E., Hanisch, K. A., and Harris, K. L. "Experimental Research on the Strategic Choice Model of Mediation." In K. Kressel and D. G. Pruitt (eds.), *Mediation Research: The Process and Effectiveness of Third-Party Intervention*. San Francisco: Jossey-Bass, 1989.

Cobb, S. "Einsteinian Practice and Newtonian Discourse: Ethical Crisis in Mediation." *Negotiation Journal*, 1991, 7(1), 87–102.

Danzig, R., and Lowy, M. J. "Everyday Disputes and Mediation in the United States: A Reply to Professor Felstiner." *Law and Society Review*, 1975, 9, 675–694.

Davis, A. "The Logic Behind the Magic of Mediation." *Negotiation Journal*, 1989, 5(1), 17–24.

Davis, A., and Porter, K. "Dispute Resolution: the Fourth 'R'." *Journal of Dispute Resolution*, 1985, pp. 121–139.

Delgado, R., and others. "Fairness and Formality: Minimizing the Risk of Prejudice in Alternative Dispute Resolution." *Wisconsin Law Review*, 1985, 6, 1359–1404.

Deutsch, M. "Conflict Resolution and Cooperative in an Alternative High School." *Cooperative Learning*, 1993, 13(4), 2–5.

Dingwall, R. "Empowerment or Enforcement? Some Questions About Power and Control in Divorce Mediation." In R. Dingwall and J. M. Eekelaar (eds.), *Divorce Mediation and the Legal Process: British Practice and International Experience*. Oxford: Oxford University Press, 1988.

Donohue, W. *Communication, Marital Dispute and Divorce Mediation*. Hillsdale, N.J.: Erlbaum, 1991.

Dukes, F. "Public Conflict Resolution: A Transformative Approach." *Negotiation Journal*, 1993, 9(1), 45–57.

Dworkin, R. *Taking Rights Seriously*. Cambridge, Mass.: Harvard University Press, 1977.

Etzioni, A. *The Spirit of Community: Rights, Responsibilities, and the Communitarian Agenda*. New York: Crown Publishing Group, 1993.

Felstiner, W., and Williams, L. "Mediation as an Alternative to Criminal Prosecution." *Law and Human Behavior*, 1978, 2(3), 223–244.

Filley, A. C. *Interpersonal Conflict Resolution*. Glenview, Ill.: Scott, Foresman, 1975.

Fineman, M. "Dominant Discourse, Professional Language and Legal Change in Child Custody Decisionmaking." *Harvard Law Review*, 1988, 101(4), 727–774.

Fisher, R., and Brown, S. *Getting Together*. New York: Viking Penguin, 1989.

Fisher, R., and Ury, W. *Getting to Yes: Negotiating Agreement Without Giving In.*
    Boston: Houghton Mifflin, 1981.
Fiss, O. M. "Against Settlement." *Yale Law Journal*, 1984, 93, 1073–1090.
Folberg, J., and Taylor, A. *Mediation: A Comprehensive Guide to Resolving Con-
    flicts Without Litigation.* San Francisco: Jossey-Bass, 1984.
Folger, J. P., and Bernard, S. "Divorce Mediation: When Mediators Challenge
    the Divorcing Parties." *Mediation Quarterly*, 1985, 10, 5–23.
Folger, J. P., and Bush, R. A. B. "Ideology, Orientations to Conflict and Media-
    tion Discourse." In J. P. Folger and T. S. Jones (eds.), *New Directions in
    Mediation: Communication Research and Perspectives.* Newbury Park, Calif.:
    Sage, 1994.
Folger, J. P., Poole, M. S., and Stutman, R. K. *Working Through Conflict: Strategies
    for Relationships, Groups and Organizations.* New York: HarperCollins,
    1993.
Forlenza, S. G. "Mediation and Psychotherapy: Parallel Processes." In K. G.
    Duffy, J. W. Grosch, and P. Olczak (eds.), *Community Mediation: A Hand-
    book for Practitioners and Researchers.* New York: Guilford, 1991.
Fuller, L. "Mediation—Its Forms and Functions." *Southern California Law
    Review*, 1971, 44, 305–339.
Galanter, M. ". . . A Settlement Judge, Not a Trial Judge: Judicial Mediation in
    the United States." *Journal of Law and Society*, 1985, 12, 1–18.
Gilligan, C. *In a Different Voice: Psychological Theory and Women's Development.*
    Cambridge, Mass.: Harvard University Press, 1982.
Gilligan, C. "Adolescent Development Reconsidered." In C. Gilligan, J. V.
    Ward, and J. McLean Taylor (eds.), *Mapping the Moral Domain.* Cam-
    bridge, Mass.: Harvard University Press, 1988.
Greatbatch, D., and Dingwall, R. "Selective Facilitation: Some Preliminary
    Observations on a Strategy Used by Divorce Mediators." *Law and Society
    Review*, 1989, 23, 613–641.
Greatbatch, D., and Dingwall, R. "The Interactive Construction of Interven-
    tions by Divorce Mediators." In J. P. Folger and T. S. Jones (eds.), *New
    Directions in Mediation: Communication Research and Perspectives.* Newbury
    Park, Calif.: Sage, 1994.
Grillo, T. "The Mediation Alternative: Process Dangers for Women." *Yale Law
    Journal*, 1991, 100, 1545–1610.
Haley, J. *Problem-Solving Therapy.* San Francisco: Jossey-Bass, 1987.
Handler, J. F. "Dependent People, the State, and the Modern/Postmodern
    Search for the Dialogic Community." *University of California Los Angeles
    Law Review*, 1988, 35(6), 999–1113.
Harrington, C. *Shadow Justice: The Ideology and Institutionalization of Alternatives
    to Court.* Westport, Conn.: Greenwood, 1985.
Harrington, C. B., and Merry, S. E. "Ideological Production: The Making of
    Community Mediation." *Law and Society Review*, 1988, 22(4), 709–735.

Haynes, J. M. "Mediation and Therapy: An Alternative View." *Mediation Quarterly*, 1992, 10(1), 21–33.

Henderson, L. "Legality and Empathy." *Michigan Law Review*, 1987, 85, 1574–1653.

Hermann, M., and others. "The MetroCourt Project Final Report: A Study of the Effects of Ethnicity and Gender in Mediated and Adjudicated Small Claims Cases." Albuquerque, New Mexico: Metro Court Project, 1993.

Herrman, M. S. "ADR in Context—Linking Our Past, Present and Possible Future." *Journal of Contemporary Legal Issues*, 1989–90, 3, 35–55.

Herrman, M. S. "On Balance: Promoting Integrity Under Conflicted Mandates." *Mediation Quarterly*, 1993, 11(2), 123–138.

Johnson, J. M. *Dispute Resolution Directory*. Washington, D.C.: American Bar Association, 1993.

Kepner, C. H., and Tregoe, B. B. *The Rational Manager*. New York: McGraw-Hill, 1965.

Kohn, A. *The Brighter Side of Human Nature: Altruism and Empathy in Everyday Life*. New York: Basic Books, 1990.

Kolb, D. *The Mediators*. Cambridge, Mass.: MIT Press, 1983.

Kolb, D. M. "How Existing Procedures Shape Alternatives: The Case of Grievance Mediation." *Journal of Dispute Resolution*, 1989, pp. 59–87.

Kressel, K., and Pruitt, D. "Conclusion: A Research Perspective on the Mediation of Social Conflict." In K. Kressel and D. Pruitt (eds.), *Mediation Research: The Process and Effectiveness of Third-Party Intervention*. San Francisco: Jossey-Bass, 1989.

Kressel, K., Pruitt, D., and Associates. *Mediation Research: The Process and Effectiveness of Third-Party Intervention*. San Francisco: Jossey-Bass, 1989.

Kressel, K., and others. "The Settlement-Orientation vs. the Problem-Solving Style in Custody Mediation." *Journal of Social Issues*, 1994, 50(1), 67–84.

Lam, J. A., Rifkin, J., and Townley, A. "Reframing Conflict: Implications for Fairness in Parent-Adolescent Mediation." *Mediation Quarterly*, 1989, 7(1), 15–31.

Lappé, F. M., and DuBois, P. *The Quickening of America: Rebuilding Our Nation, Remaking Our Lives*. San Francisco: Jossey-Bass, 1994.

Lax, D., and Sibenius, J. *The Manager as Negotiator: Bargaining for Cooperation and Competitive Gain*. New York: Free Press, 1987.

Likert, R., and Likert, J. G. *New Ways of Managing Conflict*. New York: McGraw-Hill, 1976.

Littlejohn, S., Shailor, J., and Pearce, W. B. "The Deep Structure of Reality in Mediation." In J. P. Folger and T. S. Jones (eds.), *New Directions in Mediation: Communication Research and Perspectives*. Newbury Park, Calif.: Sage, 1994.

Lynch, J. *The Language of the Heart: The Body's Response to Human Dialogue*. New York: Basic Books, 1986.

McClain, L. "'Atomistic Man' Revisited: Liberalism, Connection, and Feminist Jurisprudence." *Southern California Law Review*, 1992, 65 (3), 1171–1264.

McEwen, C. A. "Pursuing Problem-Solving or Predictive Settlement." *Florida State University Law Review*, 1991, 19(1), 77–88.

McEwen, C. A., and Maiman, R. J. "Mediation in a Small Claims Court: Achieving Compliance through Consent." *Law and Society Review*, 1984, 18(1), 11–49.

MacIntyre, A. *After Virtue: A Study in Moral Theory.* Notre Dame, Ind.: University of Notre Dame Press, 1981.

McKersie, R. B. "Avoiding Written Grievances by Problem-Solving: An Outside View." *Personnel Psychology*, 1964, 17, 367–379.

Macneill, I. "Bureaucracy, Liberalism and Community—American Style." *Northwestern University Law Review*, 1984, 79, 900–948.

Maier, N. R. F. "Assets and Liabilities in Group Problem-Solving: The Need for an Integrative Function." *Psychological Review*, 1967, 74, 239–249.

Maier, N.R.F., and Solem, A. F. "Improving Solutions by Turning Choice Situations into Problems." *Personnel Psychology*, 1962, 15(2), 151–157.

Mather, L., and Yngvesson, B. "Language, Audience and the Transformation of Disputes." *Law and Society Review*, 1980–81, 15(3–4), 775–821.

Menkel-Meadow, C. "Toward Another View of Legal Negotiation: The Structure of Problem-Solving." *UCLA Law Review*, 1984, 31, 754–842.

Menkel-Meadow, C. "Pursuing Settlement in an Adversary Culture: A Tale of Innovation Co-Opted or 'the Law of ADR'." *Florida State University Law Review*, 1991, 19(1), 1–46.

Merry, S. E. "Defining 'Success' in the Neighborhood Justice Movement." In R. Tomasic and M. M. Feeley (eds.), *Neighborhood Justice: Assessment of an Emerging Idea.* New York: Longman, 1982.

Minow, M. "Forward: Justice Engendered." *Harvard Law Review*, 1987, 101, 10–95.

Moore, C. M. "Why Do We Mediate?" In J. P. Folger and T. S. Jones (eds.), *New Directions in Mediation: Communication Research and Perspectives.* Newbury Park, Calif.: Sage, 1994.

Nader, L. "Disputing Without the Force of Law." *Yale Law Journal*, 1979, 88, 1019–1021.

Nader, L. *No Access to Law: Alternatives to the American Judicial System.* New York: Academic Press, 1980.

Nader, L. *Harmony Ideology: Justice and Control in a Zapotec Mountain Village.* Stanford, Calif: Stanford University Press, 1990.

Nader, L. "Trading Justice for Harmony." *Forum*, Winter 1992, pp. 12–14.

Nozick, R. *Anarchy, State and Utopia.* New York: Basic Books, 1974.

Osborne, D., and Gaebler, T. *Reinventing Government.* Redding, Mass: Addison-Wesley, 1992.

Pearson, H. "Racial Fear Played Out in Hall of Mirrors." *New York Newsday*, May 31, 1992, p. 27.

Pearson, J., and Thoennes, N. "Mediating and Litigating Custody Disputes: A Longitudinal Evaluation." *Family Law Quarterly*, 17, 497–524.

Pearson, J., and Thoennes, N. "Divorce Mediation: Reflections on a Decade of Research." In K. Kressel and D. G. Pruitt (eds.), *Mediation Research*. San Francisco: Jossey-Bass, 1989.

Pruitt, D. G. "Achieving Integrative Agreements." In M. Bazerman and R. J. Lewicki (eds.), *Negotiation in Organizations*. Newbury Park, Calif.: Sage, 1983.

Pruitt, D. G., and Lewis, S. "The Psychology of Integrative Bargaining." In D. Druckman (ed.), *Negotiations*. Beverly Hills: Sage, 1977.

Pruitt, D. G., McGilludy, B., Welton, G. L., and Fry, W. R. "Process of Mediation in Dispute Settlement Centers." In K. Kressel and D. G. Pruitt (eds.), *Mediation Research*. San Francisco: Jossey-Bass, 1989.

Pruitt, D. G., and Rubin, J. Z. *Social Conflict: Escalation, Stalemate and Settlement*. New York: Random House, 1986.

Putnam, L., and Poole, M. S. "Conflict and Negotiation." In F. Jablin, L. Putnam, K. Roberts, and L. Porter (eds.), *Handbook of Organizational Communication*. Beverly Hills: Sage, 1987.

Raider, E., and Coleman, S. *School Change by Agreement. Part 2: Mediation Skills*. New Paltz, N.Y.: Ellen Raider International, 1992.

Rawls, J. *A Theory of Justice*. Cambridge, Mass.: Harvard University Press, 1971.

Rifkin, J., Millen, J., and Cobb, S. "Toward a New Discourse for Mediation: A Critique of Neutrality." *Mediation Quarterly*, 1991, 9, 151–164.

Riskin, L. "Mediation and Lawyers." *Ohio State Law Journal*, 1982, 43, 29–60.

Riskin, L. "Toward New Standards for the Neutral Lawyer in Mediation." *Arizona Law Review*, 1984, 26, 329–362.

Riskin, L. L. "The Represented Client in a Settlement Conference: The Lessons of G. Heilman Brewing Co. v. Joseph Oat Corp." *Washington University Law Quarterly*, 1991, 69(4), 1059–1116.

Riskin, L. L. "Two Concepts of Mediation in the FHMA's Farmer-Lender Mediation Program." *Adminstrative Law Review*, 1993, 45(1), 21–64.

Roberts, M. "Systems or Selves? Some Ethical Issues in Family Mediation." *Mediation Quarterly*, 1992, 10(1), 3–19.

Rosen, R., and Berger, L. *The Healthy Company: Eight Strategies to Develop People, Productivity, and Profits*. Los Angeles: Tarcher, 1992.

Ruble, T. L., and Thomas, K. W. "Support for a Two-Dimensional Model of Conflict Behavior." *Organizational Behavior and Human Performance*, 1976, 16, 143–155.

Sandel, M. *Liberalism and the Limits of Justice*. Cambridge: Cambridge University Press, 1982.

Sarat, A. "The 'New Formalism' in Disputing and Dispute Processing." *Law and Society Review*, 1988, 21(3), 695–715.

Scheff, T. *Microsociology: Discourse, Emotion and Social Structure*. Chicago: University of Chicago Press, 1990.

Schmidt, W., and Tannenbaum, R. "The Management of Differences." *Harvard Business Review*, 1960, *38*, 107–115.

Shailor, J. *Empowerment in Dispute Mediation: A Critical Analysis of Communication*. Westport, Conn.: Praeger, 1994.

Shapiro, D., Drieghe, R., and Brett, J. "Mediator Behavior and the Outcome of Mediation." *Journal of Social Issues*, 1985, *41*(2), 101–114.

Sherry, S. "Civic Virtue and the Feminine Voice in Constitutional Adjudication." *Virginia Law Review*, 1986, *72*, 543–616.

Shonholtz, R. "Neighborhood Justice Systems: Work, Structure and Guiding Principles." *Mediation Quarterly*, 1984, *5*, 3–16.

Shonholtz, R. "The Citizens' Role in Justice: Building a Primary Justice and Prevention System at the Neighborhood Level." *The Annals of the American Academy of Political and Social Science*, 1987, *494*, 42–52.

Silbey, S. S., and Merry, S. "Mediator Settlement Strategies." *Law and Policy*, 1986, *8*, 7–32.

Sillars, A., and Weisberg, J. "Conflict as a Social Skill." In M. E. Roloff and G. R. Miller (eds.), *Interpersonal Processes: New Directions in Communication Research*. Newbury Park, Calif.: Sage, 1987.

Singer, L. R. *Settling Disputes: Conflict Resolution in Business, Families, and the Legal System*. San Francisco: Westview Press, 1990.

Spiegel, D. *Living Beyond Limits: A Scientific Mind-Body Approach to Facing Life-Threatening Illness*. New York: Random, 1993.

Stulberg, J. B. "A Civil Alternative to Criminal Prosecution." *Albany Law Review*, 1975, *39*, 359–376.

Stulberg, J. B. "The Theory and Practice of Mediation: A Reply to Professor Susskind." *Vermont Law Review*, 1981, *6*, 85–117.

Stulberg, J. B. *Taking Charge: Managing Conflict*. New York: Free Press, 1987.

Susskind, L., and Cruikshank, J. *Breaking the Impasse: Consensual Approaches to Resolving Public Disputes*. New York: Basic Books, 1987.

Tomasic, R. "Mediation as an Alternative to Adjudication: Rhetoric and Reality in the Neighborhood Justice Movement." In R. Tomasic and M. M. Feeley (eds.), *Neighborhood Justice: Assessment of an Emerging Idea*. New York: Longman, 1982.

Tyler, T. "The Psychology of Disputant Concerns in Mediation." *Negotiation Journal*, 1987, *3*, 367–374.

Wahrhaftig, P. "An Overview of Community-Oriented Citizen Dispute Resolution Programs in the United States." In R. Abel (ed.), *The Politics of Informal Justice*. Vol. 1: *The American Experience*. New York: Academic Press, 1982.

West, R. "Jurisprudence and Gender." *The University of Chicago Law Review*, 1988, *55*(1), 1–72.

Index